COOKING & TRAVELLING IN SOUTH-WEST FRANCE

STEPHANIE ALEXANDER

Photography by Simon Griffiths

LANTERN
an imprint of
PENGUIN BOOKS

Acknowledgements

I would like to thank the people and organisations who provided assistance while I was in south-west France: Wendely Harvey and Robert Cave-Rogers of La Combe en Périgord; Simply Périgord (Le Bugue); Ingrid de Monte at Le Carnichette (Saint-Cyprien), for antiques for use in photographs; Roger Haigh at L'École Hôtelière in Périgueux; Jean Lagarde of the Bureau Interprofessionel du Pruneau; and Henriette and André Deroeux. My sincere thanks go to the cooks and chefs who shared their recipes with me, and to Philippe Jacques, the photographer who worked with me during my visit in winter 1999 and who was at all times enthusiastic about the project.

Many thanks to my travelling companions, Anna Dollard, Maggie and Colin Beer, Duffy and Angie Clemens, Will and Bonnie Studd, Julie Gibbs and Simon Griffiths. What a marvellous time we had! A very special thank-you goes to my personal assistant, Anna Dollard, who not only organised a million essential details but constantly surprised us by transforming the necessary into an adventure.

My thanks also go to John Tinney, friend and authority on the French language; Phillippa Grogan of Phillippa's in Armadale (Melbourne); author Paula Wolfert; and Hélène Rossi, formerly Attachée Commerciale, Vins et Agroalimentaire, at the French Trade Commission in Australia.

Once again I have been fortunate to work with a great team of people to produce this book: publisher Julie Gibbs, photographer Simon Griffiths, designer Danie Pout, editor Katie Purvis and production controller Leah Maarse.

And last, but not least, thank you to all the food-lovers of the south-west whom I met in shops, markets, cafés and small factories, who offered information in an unfailingly generous and warm-hearted manner.

LANTERN
Published by the Penguin Group
Penguin Group (Australia)
250 Camberwell Road, Camberwell, Victoria 3124, Australia
(a division of Pearson Australia Group Pty Ltd)
Penguin Group (USA) Inc.
375 Hudson Street, New York, New York 10014, USA
Penguin Group (Canada)
90 Eglinton Avenue East, Suite 700, Toronto ON M4P 2Y3, Canada
(a division of Pearson Penguin Canada Inc.)
Penguin Books Ltd
80 Strand, London WC2R 0RL, England
Penguin Ireland
25 St Stephen's Green, Dublin 2, Ireland
(a division of Penguin Books Ltd)
Penguin Books India Pvt Ltd
11 Community Centre, Panchsheel Park, New Delhi – 110 017, India
Penguin Group (NZ)
Cnr Airborne and Rosedale Roads, Albany, Auckland, New Zealand
(a division of Pearson New Zealand Ltd)
Penguin Books (South Africa) (Pty) Ltd
24 Sturdee Avenue, Rosebank, Johannesburg 2196, South Africa

Penguin Books Ltd, Registered Offices: 80 Strand, London WC2R 0RL, England

First published by Penguin Books Australia Ltd, 2002
This paperback edition published by Penguin Group (Australia), 2006

10 9 8 7 6 5 4 3 2 1

Text copyright © Stephanie Alexander 2002, 2006
Illustrations copyright © Simon Griffiths 2002, 2006

The moral right of the author has been asserted

Designed by Danie Pout Design
Cover design by Jay Ryves © Penguin Group (Australia)
Cover photograph by Simon Griffiths
All photographs by Simon Griffiths except for those on inside back flap, by Earl Carter, page 17, by Jean Grelet (reprinted by permission of Semitour Périgord), and pages 183, 203, 219, 233, 235, 239, 259, 260, 264–5, 267, 269, 270, 273, 274, 276–7, 280, 294, 297 (top left and right), 298, 300–1, 306, 310, 316, 333, 334, 351, 352, 355, by Jac'Phot
Map drawn by Danie Pout Design
'Le Canalé' recipe on page 69 reprinted by permission of Régis Marcon
Typeset in 10.5/16.5 pt Garamond by Post Pre-press, Brisbane, Queensland
Printed and bound in Singapore by Imago

National Library of Australia
Cataloguing-in-Publication data:

Alexander, Stephanie, 1940– .
Cooking & travelling in South-West France.

Includes index.
ISBN 1 920989 24 2 (pbk).

1. Cookery – France, Southwest. 2. France, Southwest – Description and travel. I. Griffiths, Simon (Simon John). II. Title.

641.59447

www.penguin.com.au

Dedicated to the memory of
my much-loved friend Graham Little (1939–2000),
who came on the first adventure

Contents

BEURRES :: ŒUFS :: FROMAGES

Country of Enchantment

*W*hat is it about France and me? I am a passionate Australian and could not contemplate living elsewhere – and yet France is never far from my thoughts. Working with food, of course, there is the obvious connection, and I have never disguised my fascination with and admiration for French country cooking. Certainly the smells and signs and cafés and other well-known French images are familiar and very powerful, and Paris is always seductive, but what is in my mind's eye is almost always the countryside.

In the countryside the rhythm of daily life is important and valued. The formal greetings and thank-yous, the shopkeeper's advice on how best to cook cardoons or their inquiry as to whether the customer would like a high-baked loaf or one a little less crusty – such details seem to matter. Commerce still slows or stops for lunch. I am more moved by a worn mortar for pounding some savoury mixture, or a slightly chipped soup tureen, or a long-handled iron pan, than I am by imposing buildings.

In France I am a voyeur or, more accurately, an eavesdropper. I can listen and understand and I can enjoy, although I no longer have any French acquaintances. The long-ago friendships made when I was an *au pair* and later, when I taught English at a French teacher-training institution in the Loire town of Tours, were somehow allowed to lapse. I am sad about that. Now when I visit it is with Australian friends, most of whom have visited only once or twice. I have a feeling of returning to a cherished second home – but the French do not let people into their inner circle easily and I will always be looking on and listening. Nonetheless, when I see someone riding slowly on a bicycle with a baguette tied firmly to the rear of it, along a road lined with poplars, or trail my hand in a fast-flowing river and look up at a castle built several hundred years ago, or spread out waxed-paper parcels on a grassy picnic spot, or happen upon an unselfconscious country market, or listen to the sing-song exchange in a local bakery, my heart soars.

Of course, it is all changing I am told, and no doubt it is. (I read recently that there are those who want to cut down the poplars – too easy for mad French drivers to smash their heads on when driving at silly speeds.) But deep in the countryside change is rather slow, and I secretly hope and believe that it may never be total in my lifetime. I am never comfortable theorising for too long and trust my feelings more than theories anyway. For me, two or three weeks immersed in an

OPPOSITE, TOP LEFT Autumn colours glow against a weathered stone house in the picturesque town of Limeuil.
OPPOSITE, TOP RIGHT Astonishingly luxuriant geraniums spill from window boxes at the Hôtel de Ville in the market town of Sarlat.
OPPOSITE, BOTTOM LEFT The many lookout spots, including the ramparts of castles, offer marvellous and ever-changing views of the magnificent Dordogne River. This vista was photographed from the village of Domme.
OPPOSITE, BOTTOM RIGHT A bicycle with a baguette tied firmly on the back reassured me that some things do not change in rural France.

environment such as the south-west of France is a bit like sinking into a deep, cushioned couch that quickly eases tensions and is always anticipated with great pleasure.

This book is a personal response to a beautiful part of France that deserves to be better known and has much to offer the visitor, especially the food-loving visitor. The person I am writing for will be uplifted by the incredible landscape, will love to explore the countryside – above and below ground, its awesome caves as well as its food markets – and will delight in its savoury and satisfying cuisine and listen carefully to stories of times long gone.

I have holidayed in the south-west of France on many occasions: in spring, early summer, high summer, mid-autumn and early winter. In my old notebooks I find constant references to the intense green of the region's dense forests of oak, chestnut and beech, and of cultivated pine plantations pierced by shafts of sunlight. I read of the lushness of the roadside verges, with flowering elder and robinia and brilliant gorse bushes, and of the pleasure gained from walking along narrow, cobbled streets in villages with stone houses built hundreds of years ago. I experience that gasp of surprise as yet another castle comes into view, seemingly leaning into space from a rocky hilltop, surrounded by ancient fortifications. I am very conscious of my Australian 'otherness' at such moments. My own rural experiences have been so different – all sparseness and stretching plains and slender trees with gaunt elbows and knees, drooping leaves and bark in muted grey and lavender and drab olive, worn wooden fences and sheds and rusted iron.

These old notebooks are a surprising resource. I am so sure I will remember, but I do not. I read and then recall a special holiday in 1975 with my husband Maurice, our new baby, Holly, and our dear friends Graham and Jenny Little. We marvelled at the rugged Gorges du Tarn, a miniature Grand Canyon, and felt certain that time had stopped in the little hamlet of Le Rosier at the bottom of the gorge, where we ate a simply served meal of vegetable soup, a trout caught from the rushing Aveyron River and a roasted chicken. On another holiday in 1977 my husband and I sat disconsolately in a bar in Nantes in Brittany watching the rain stream down and longing for the greenery we had left behind in the south-west. We looked at each other and then with shared resolve headed back to be enchanted all over again by the golden stone houses, tiny villages, smiling faces and extraordinary vistas. A few lines record a pastoral moment as we picnicked somewhere beside the Dordogne River and admired the toffee-coloured cattle munching steadily as they stood hock high in a field of white daisies.

There is another holiday noted in 1987 when we travelled a little further to the east, into the *département* of Aveyron in the Midi-Pyrénées, and lunched at the pretty town of Millau. Years later I read *Spider Cup*, a novel by Australian author Marion Halligan, and experienced a certain frisson when she explained that the tissue-soft gloves widely featured in Millau's boutiques are made from newborn

OPPOSITE A peaceful corner of the village of Beynac displays many of the delightful features of the region – towers and chimneypots, golden stone, cobbled laneways and a sun-crisped grapevine.
OVERLEAF For two weeks in October 2000 we watched the changing autumn colourings in the landscape around the small market town of Le Bugue.

lambskin, a by-product of the industry that produces perhaps France's greatest cheese, Roquefort. I noted at the time that we enjoyed a Roquefort and walnut salad for lunch.

At Lamastre in the Auvergne we lunched in a small country restaurant. I was on one of my Elizabeth David pilgrimages, which involved following a long-ago trail to a restaurant she had once found irresistible – a foolish and romantic thing to do, and almost always doomed to disappointment, although I have come across some lovely villages on such journeys. Here in the Hôtel du Centre I had a memorable omelette generously stuffed with *mousserons*, those tiny mushrooms that are often called 'fairy-ring mushrooms'. The omelette was certainly special – buttery and made with richly flavoured eggs, and the mushrooms had just the right amount of garlicky juices – but the lunch was most memorable for its encapsulation of the best of bourgeois French dining. It was a cold, early spring day. The dining room was warm and cosy. The tables were well spaced, each laid with a beautifully ironed cloth and matching napkins. The rush-bottomed ladderback chairs were of softly gleaming walnut wood, and there was a tiny posy of cottage flowers on every table. The patrons appeared to be exclusively local and had their own napkin rings and, in some cases, their own partially drunk bottle of wine (left from a previous meal, I assumed). There was a hum of pleasant, connected conversation. The waitresses were middle-aged women who knew exactly how to manage a busy room. Every dish came from the kitchen on a simple oval serving platter. Madame would serve a portion and there would always be just a little extra that the diner was warmly encouraged to finish up. In planning a more recent trip to rural France in 2000, I wondered whether I would find such establishments any more.

The same holiday saw us travelling in the valley of the Lot River, where I recorded my pleasure at seeing the high escarpments and the silver flash of the water, and the rioting wildflowers: spikes of blue and pink, clumps of pink stars falling over rocks, shivery grass and rock roses. I noted a meal of tripe and saffron at Saint-Cirq Lapopie and a dinner in Sarlat where I had my first taste of *le tourin*, the popular onion soup that seems to be made everywhere in the region. I was delighted by the villages of Limeuil and of Trémolat, where a shaft of sunlight illuminated a vase of glorious peony roses in front of the altar in the Romanesque church. The last entry in this notebook is a memory from Souillac of a hot *pâté en croûte*, a savoury pie filled with coarsely minced ham.

I had three trips to the south-west during the 18 months from July 1999 to November 2000. During the European summer of 1999 I holidayed and kept house in a restored barn, La Vieille Grange, with my friend Julie Gibbs; in late November and early December of the same year I spent just a few concentrated days with Maggie Beer, determined to join a truffle hunt and to explore fully the production of *foie gras*. The third experience was hosting a house party for 10 people when we cooked, photographed, walked, laughed, shopped and talked for two whole weeks in October 2000. We stayed in a lovely house deep in the Dordogne, in the hamlet of Lavalade. What follows is from the notebooks of those three trips, describing some of the tourist sights I enjoyed at different times of the year – not to mention details of meals cooked and meals eaten! It records my daily experiences, mingled with historical bits and pieces so that the reader will move between the daily doings and the other things buzzing in my head that give depth, layers and meaning to my gastronomic travelling.

There are a few 'what ifs' and here and there I have pointed to relationships and connections with my own experience in Australia. It is not intended as a comprehensive investigation into the cooking of the region, which has been undertaken by writers such as Jeanne Strang (in *Goose Fat and Garlic*), Paula Wolfert (*The Cooking of South-West France*) and Anne Penton (*Customs and Cookery in the Périgord and Quercy*), whose books are based on research spread over several years. Nor can it be a personal hymn to the region based on childhood and adolescent memories, such as can be found in Pierre Koffmann's *Memories of Gascony*. These books have been invaluable to me as references and as practical handbooks. Their recipes have often been the springboard for my own attempts to recreate something I have seen or tasted.

I am interested in traditions: how they endure as much as how they change. What happens when the very nature of life changes out of all recognition? Do the villages die? Who cares? Where does tourism fit into all of this? What, if anything, is retained? Is rural life, as it has been known until recently, finished in France? Can traditional pursuits endure only if they become tourist attractions? Will the gastronomy of the region, based as it has been on specialised skills and products, continue only if it can be sold to tourists?

I wanted to look, to understand, to ask questions, as well as to taste and sip. And I wanted to encourage other food lovers to visit and walk the walks through green forests, linger in tiny villages and shop in the market and drink in the bar, and experience the sights, smells and flavours of this most beautiful and gentle part of France.

The South - West Today

*T*he entire south-west area is a gastronomic paradise. First and foremost in interest is the raising of the ducks and geese that provide the region with much of its income. *Foie gras* production is big business and with it comes commerce in every other possible morsel of these birds, from the neck to the gizzards, fresh and *confit* (preserved). Corn is grown everywhere to force-feed the birds, but also as food for chickens and other farm animals.

The region is also famous for its delicious farm cheeses, usually of goat's milk but also of cow's milk, and firmer cheeses made from ewe's milk. Groves and groves of walnuts produce aromatic walnut oil and walnut meats to be incorporated in all manner of dishes. Not too far away from the Dordogne, in the *département* of Lot-et-Garonne, are the plum orchards around Villeneuve-sur-Lot, whose fruit is dried to create the famous prunes for *pâtisserie* and used fresh to make the fiery *eau-de-vie de prune*. Add to this apples and Armagnac, chestnuts, apéritifs made from peaches or walnuts, massive crusty loaves of bread from the nearby Auvergne, sausages and raw hams from the same region and from Bayonne, and Roquefort cheese a bit further away in the Rouergue, and you have just a few of the specialities.

Paula Wolfert, one of the best modern food writers, offers some interesting theories in her excellent book *The Cooking of South-West France*. I was particularly intrigued with this one: she distinguishes between 'front of the mouth' food, or dishes that appeal to the tips of our tongues but have no real depth and that we have no real desire to eat again, and what she calls 'evolved food', or dishes rooted in historical traditions with natural taste affinities and their own logic. Such dishes have come about to meet the needs and lifestyle of a hardworking and healthy people who, in the main, cook what they produce and waste very little. This is the food I love to eat. Its deep flavours result from the slow melding of ingredients. Simple vegetables acquire marvellously subtle layers of flavour as they simmer together; sauces glisten in all shades of brown.

There is a recognisable look to the people of the south-west. They are smooth and round of cheek, black-eyed, brown-skinned, nuggety rather than rangy, with a stern composure that suggests purpose and attention to the task and faces that light up readily if someone compliments or enjoys or appreciates. They are quick to respond to enthusiasm and, if you show genuine interest, it is difficult

REGIONAL NAMES

Before reading on it will be helpful to understand that modern-day France is divided into 22 régions *and each* région *is subdivided into* départements. *The south-west today contains two* régions, *Aquitaine and Midi-Pyrénées, and each of these has several* départements. *The names of these* départements *do not, however, correspond to the old names of the area, which are frequently used by locals in preference to the modern names. It sounds confusing and it is confusing. The people speak to you of the Périgord and Quercy rather than the Dordogne, Lot and Lot-et-Garonne. And the boundaries of the present* départements *do not exactly correspond to the old regions. To my ear, the former names evoke the stories and traditions better than the bureaucratic names for the* départements, *and I am not alone in thinking this: 'Périgord' and 'Quercy' are most definitely used to sell the products of the region. It is best to become familiar with both terms for a locality.*

to shop at the market without gaining a new bit of food lore. Not once have I experienced any impatience with my imperfect language, such as can be found in areas ground down by armies of insensitive tourists.

On recent trips I couldn't help noticing that most people I met or engaged with in any form of commerce were well over 40 years of age. The young have left in search of work and opportunities elsewhere. For many of the locals, life has changed out of all recognition. In times gone by, a farm would provide a livelihood for an extended family, but now there are few peasant farmers left. Some still live on their farm holdings, but usually the amount of land is much reduced. Frequently the owners of properties are no longer the original families, but English or French people who have decided to retire to the region. Large agricultural concerns have also bought up numbers of small farms and manage them to maximise efficiency of production. Much of the land that was once forested has been cleared for pine plantations or to permit the cultivation of strawberries or sunflowers. Plastic tubing for the strawberry farms crisscrosses many a field. The observer has the pleasure of a blazing field of sunflowers in summer, to be followed in autumn by the less exhilarating sight of the withered flowerheads drooping on their stems before they are cut down to repeat the cycle.

The south-west has for decades been cut off from the major roads and railways that service much of rural France. As a consequence, cultural and culinary traditions have been largely maintained, even in the face of the declining population. It has been important that two of the world's most highly sought after gastronomic luxuries – black truffles (*Tuber melanosporum*) and *foie gras* – are found here, and they are very big business. The isolation of the *départements* is being challenged by the construction of a new freeway that will link the Dordogne with the main north–south artery road between Paris and the south of France. Some people feel this will bring disaster, in the shape of mass tourism; others believe it will permit some form of industrial infrastructure, which might offer opportunities to some of the young people who at present flock to Toulouse, Périgueux and other big towns.

Périgueux has a large hospitality training college, L'École Hôtelière, and its co-director, Roger Haigh, agreed to be my guide during my five-day visit in late 1999 to facilitate my meeting specialist growers and help me learn as much as possible. Over our first lunch Roger expressed his view that life is privileged in Périgord – that, in fact, the inhabitants have been living in a bubble. Far from autoroutes (at least until the new road becomes a reality) and with limited access to the fast-train system, the area is still well placed to benefit from the increased interest in all sorts of *tourisme de vert*, or 'green tourism'. Accommodation abounds, in the form of *gîtes* (self-catering options of varying size and character) and *chambres d'hôte* (what we know as bed-and-breakfast establishments). Roger described the locals as self-contained and hardworking, traditionally involved in all manner

PAGE 13 A picturesque farm-shop sign (translating as 'The White Goose') offers two of the region's gastronomic specialities – *foie gras* and truffles.
OPPOSITE, TOP LEFT The raising of geese and ducks for *foie gras* is big business and every farm shop sells a surprising range of preserves made from all parts of the birds.
OPPOSITE, TOP RIGHT A cheese vendor at Le Bugue market exhibits some of the region's famous goat's milk farm cheeses at various stages of maturity.
OPPOSITE, BOTTOM Fields of blazing sunflowers such as this one near Souillac are later harvested for the seeds, which are crushed to produce the domestic oils that have to a large extent supplanted the animal fats traditionally used in cooking.

of agricultural pursuits, but who are now, like the people of many other rural villages and towns in France, facing the reality of considerable unemployment.

Roger believes that Périgord's future must involve its controlled development, raising its profile from many different angles, especially by having its culinary specialities better known and promoted and their authenticity protected. In particular, he says, the residents need to do whatever is possible to encourage the revival of the black truffle industry which, while it is important now, is a fraction of what it was 100 years ago, when it brought considerable financial rewards to many country people. Annual harvests have drastically diminished from more than 800 tonnes at the beginning of the 20th century to 40 tonnes in the 1990s.

We discussed the place of traditional cookery in any appreciation of the region. Roger reinforced what I later heard from Henriette Deroeux (see page 58): it is the grandmothers who understand the culinary traditions and maintain them, but they represent the last generation with such knowledge. Their daughters might or might not know how to, or be bothered to, prepare the traditional country dishes of their childhood, and it is pretty certain that the daughters of the daughters cannot do so and have little interest in the past.

Roger admitted that it isn't easy to convince the locals they need to adopt a more entrepreneurial approach. Change is viewed with suspicion and cooperative ventures are few and far between. The World Cookbook Fair held in Périgueux every two years is becoming an important event. So far there have been five fairs, well supported by English-speaking and European publishers. The École Hôtelière also hopes to train young chefs to use the magnificent local ingredients with imagination.

I thought about what Roger said and it seemed to me that against this background of concern for vanishing traditions and vanishing opportunities for young people must be set the reality of the trend towards globalisation, as evident in France as it is in other European countries. France is well aware of the prestige and income it has long attracted as a country with a rich and diverse culinary history and, especially in the south-west, as a producer of high-cost, difficult-to-mechanise products. To grow bigger, push for new markets and promote efficiency and corporate culture would seem to spell death for the sort of artisanal production I had come to see. The questions that hang rather uneasily are these. To what extent, if at all, can the traditional output be made to 'pay its way' without compromising the very things that have made it great? Even more importantly, is there still a viable market to support and sustain any increases in current production?

The large-scale sale and renting of houses, big or small, permits what can be called 'cultural tourism': visitors come to experience something different in order to increase their understanding of the place and its people, as well as to offer themselves a change of lifestyle. There is no sense of exploitation of the local inhabitants or resources, nor is there any sense that they are part of any sort of 'theme park'.

There is no shortage of sights to marvel at and no end to the trails to be walked and the activities to delight visitors of all ages. Those interested in history can start at prehistory and continue on (the Dordogne alone has more than 200 prehistoric sites). For me it is all of this, plus an area of such gastronomical richness that I am in a state of sensual overload for much of the time I am there.

As someone who loves to visit and hear stories of how it used to be, who cannot quite believe in the magical beauty of these quiet and untroubled villages and yet who will return to a world where commercial realities apply, I am sometimes confused about what to think. The reality is, of course, that it doesn't matter one jot what I think. The changes will continue. For some people they will bring a sense of dislocation and perhaps a reflection that their life has had no real meaning if it can be so readily set aside. For others they will offer real opportunities for a better life. For many, the changes will be accompanied by anxiety for the future.

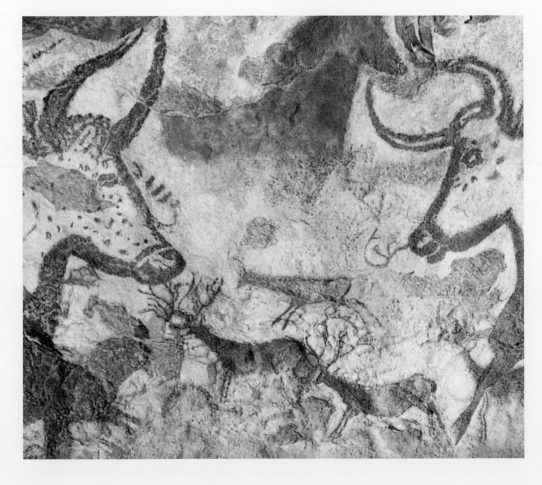

LEFT A visit to one of the many prehistoric sites in the Dordogne is an excellent way of appreciating the antiquity of the area. This picture features a detail from the marvellous Lascaux II replica paintings (see page 35).

Summer Notebooks

*I*n the wonderful guidebook *Southwest France* by Dana Facaros and Michael Pauls (Cadogan), the authors introduce the area by saying: 'If southwest France could croon a tune, it would have to be that old Ink Spots hit, "I don't want to set the world on fire, I just want to be the one you love".' I happen to own that very same Ink Spots recording, and feel that Facaros and Pauls got the feeling just right. After I read the phrase, the melody stayed in my head on and off throughout my trip in the European summer of 1999.

For a long time I had been quietly reflecting on the many experiences I have had in France and my reflections all seemed to lead me to or near the Dordogne Valley in the south-west. It was not that difficult to persuade my friend Julie Gibbs to come on a research trip to the area. We had travelled together in other years and made a good team: Julie the fearless and capable driver and 'big picture' girl with an eye for *brocante* (second-hand treasures), and me the navigator, linguist and fossicker for detail. We excitedly decided on the first two weeks in July.

I have commented in other writings on the charms of France's D roads. Well away from most trucks and those motorists determined to travel at frightening speeds on the N roads and autoroutes, the D roads are well surfaced, tend to meander and allow both driver and passenger to enjoy the experience of getting there as well as arriving. We started our adventure at Bordeaux airport, where we picked up our hired car and were quickly on the D936. Pretty soon we were admiring villages of honey-coloured stone, houses with weathered tiles in all shades of pink and brown, window boxes bright with geraniums and petunias, gateways and walls heavy with flowering wisteria or purple clematis. Almost every house and certainly every bar had some evidence that the residents were rejoicing in the summer weather – usually an umbrella, a table and a few chairs set in a shady part of the garden, or even almost on the road. Roadside signs offered cherries and peaches for sale and we passed peach orchards with the fruit a blur of pink through the leaves, and fields of blazing sunflowers and cornfields with the new corn growing strongly, and noticed the flash of scarlet poppies among the grasses at the verge.

We had our first view of the Dordogne River at Branne. The Dordogne is 490 km (304 miles) long, making it one of the most important rivers in France. Here it was wide and slow-flowing and shining green under the hot sun. This beautiful

river is a favourite with canoeists and there were quite a few slipping and gliding over the water. As the paddles dipped and lifted the water sparkled and rippled. Here and there the banks were wide and sandy, creating 'beaches' where children played and shrieked and splashed. We resolved that one of our expeditions would have to be a riverbank picnic.

The *départements* of the Dordogne (in the *région* of Aquitaine) and the nearby Lot (Midi-Pyrénées) are favourite holiday destinations, with many of the visitors being English. Every village has a camping spot and we saw a large number of cyclists with laden bicycles intent on a camping holiday, including one couple on a tandem, towing a smart suitcase on a purpose-built luggage carriage.

The weather was glorious. It was a long time since I had been in Europe in high summer and I was quickly reminded of how lush this part of the French countryside is. The woods were deeply green and the trees magnificent, their trunks encircled with ivy. This is, of course, black truffle country, so I looked with special interest at the dense forests. All growth was luxuriant, all gardens seemed to be rioting and all hedges seemed to be sprouting out of control.

Our Barn: La Vieille Grange

Our summer holiday in the old barn was arranged through a colleague in Australia who now owns the house and is happy to rent it out to others. The house had a terrace edged with stone walls and beyond these a thick tangle of stinging nettles and ivy, an old apple tree, a fig tree and a massive oak. It was here that we enjoyed our daily breakfast of sliced white peaches followed by thick, hard slices of toast made from the local sourdough (*pain au levain*), with sun-ripened tomatoes. We had a rooster and two hens for company. The rooster crowed triumphantly; the hens were very beautiful, one the colour of marmalade, the other a mix of russet, cream and gold feathers with a spectacular scarlet comb. They enjoyed our scraps of lettuce. Birds sang lustily at all times.

The house had stone walls and heavy beams. From the outside we could see the ends of the beams where they were thrust deep into the stone. The roof was a high gable of new terracotta tiles. Bedrooms and bathrooms were upstairs and the living area was downstairs. We opened the windows wide to the fresh air and to the view. Someone had left us a welcome posy of pink hydrangea, purple-tipped artichoke, golden yarrow, violet buddleia and a leggy spray of an unknown pink and white flower. So pretty.

The outbuildings were as yet unrestored and showed how things once were. They had rough stone floors, lofts with crumbling partitions, sagging crossbeams and very old roof tiles that here and there let in a sunbeam. Nearby was a stone

OPPOSITE, TOP LEFT *Citron pressé*, a refreshing French speciality, was the perfect drink after an afternoon's sightseeing. It is mouth-puckeringly sour *au naturel*, but the drinker can add sugar depending on personal taste.

OPPOSITE, TOP RIGHT Window boxes filled with geraniums seemed to be a feature of every village in summer.

OPPOSITE, BOTTOM LEFT An increasingly rare example of *lauzes* – a roof made from limestone slabs.

OPPOSITE, BOTTOM RIGHT Strawberries were abundant in the summer markets. We bought a bagful of medium-sized ones to dip into while strolling through the Sarlat market. The stall-holder recommended that they be used for making jam. They were deeply red right to the centre, juicy and so sweet.

trough in which grew a rosemary bush (used for our first meal of roasted chicken). Near the loft where we parked our car, was a massive *tilleul* (lime-linden) tree. Our neighbour Henriette told us that we had just missed its scented flowering. Other than the birds, the occasional clip-clip of Henriette's pruning shears and the murmurings from the hens, it was totally quiet. Not once did we hear a car, a siren or a dog.

Our hamlet of Mercadiol had no facilities at all, but 3 km (2 miles) down the road was Saint Julien-de-Lampon, with a bank, a bakery, a post office, a church dating from the 12th century with frescoed murals from the 16th century, and a general store where we bought essentials such as water, wine (rosé from Bergerac) and cheese. Men played *boules* in the small village square, just as they do in every village in France. To the onlooker it seems a most amiable and unhurried pursuit. Saint Julien-de-Lampon has a bridge connecting it with Rouffillac, on the opposite bank of the Dordogne. This is the only river crossing in the area, and it is the existence of the bridge that assures the village its relative bustle.

Sights

Driving in this countryside was a joy. We had a good map and plenty of time and the sun was shining. We drove through long avenues of leafy woods, where sometimes the trees met overhead in a thick canopy. Then there were stretches where the road hugged the river bank and was edged by a low stone wall, offering glimpses of life on the river: canoes, kayaks and flat-bottomed cruise vessels – *les gabarres* – that were once used as cargo punts. Sometimes we drove alongside a sheer cliff that rose above us and quite often we saw perched in the near distance, gleaming in the sunshine, a village built snugly into the cliff, and often a castle as well. The road usually narrowed as it curved through the tiny villages, so we could almost touch the flower boxes and pretty hollyhocks that some householder had planted less than a metre from the road.

Sometimes we climbed quite high to explore a special place, perhaps one of *les plus beaux villages de France* ('the loveliest villages in France'), so named by an association that was formed in 1981 to identify and market those villages seen as noteworthy and beautiful. The aim was also to preserve and restore, and to spread the word, both within France and beyond, of this inestimable national resource. Currently there are 142 villages so designated. Domme, La Roque Gageac, Limeuil, Beynac and Saint-Cirq Lapopie were five that we visited.

MAPS
To enjoy a rural retreat such as this you need a very good map. We bought one with a scale of 1 cm to 250 m. These local tourist maps, the Séries Bleue *or Blue Series, published by the Institut Géographique National, are available at all good bookshops and newsagents and are a sure way of navigating the myriad lanes and pathways that traverse the rural landscape. Villages around here are so tiny they do not appear on even the larger-scale, yellow Michelin maps, which are indispensable for touring and offer a scale of 1 cm to 2 km.*

OPPOSITE, TOP This converted barn, La Vieille Grange, in the hamlet of Mercadiol, was the base for our very happy summer holiday.
OPPOSITE, BOTTOM The locals gathered every afternoon to play a relaxed game of *boules* in the small square alongside the medieval church at our closest village, Saint Julien-de-Lampon.

DOMME

At Domme we admired a wide view over the valley. The river was far below, the colourful canoes and kayaks bright splashes in an otherwise profoundly green landscape. We went underground here to explore illuminated chambers of stalactites and stalagmites. The air was surprisingly fresh and, for one like me who admits to a touch of claustrophobia, the caves were beautiful and impressive and not at all scary.

CHÂTEAU DE MARQUEYSSAC

There are more than 1000 châteaux in the *département* of Dordogne, and many of them are listed on signage as *Monuments Historiques de France*, presumably maintained by the state in some way. In contrast, the Château de Marqueyssac is in private hands, having been bought from the Marqueyssac family – who had owned the property since the late 17th century – by a Parisian businessman, M. Kléber Rossillon, in 1996.

The château and its extensive park are just a few minutes from Domme, across the river at Vézac. Although it rates only a glancing reference in most guidebooks, we found it an enchanting place. The present château dates from the end of the 18th century and is charmingly described in its brochure as a 'pleasure residence'. It was not open to the public, although we could walk around the exterior of part of it. The château had been maintained to the highest standard. Its roof was constructed using the traditional stone, and the doorways and window shutters had been painted with a pinky violet lime wash, which set off the pale stone walls and dark grey roof to perfection.

Visitors come here principally to admire the garden, designed and planted at the end of the 19th century by Julien-de-Cerval in the Italian style and restored by José Leygonie, a box expert and the garden manager of the nearby Manoir d'Eyrignac, famous for its geometric garden design. At Marqueyssac there are more than 150 000 box trees, which edge long promenades, form bushy secret spaces, describe geometric figures or are pruned into witty shapes. The paths are raked gravel and the effect is of order, symmetry and calm. The views over the valley of the Dordogne are spectacular. These are billion-dollar views! From different vantage points we could see La Roque Gageac and the châteaus of Castelnaud, Fayrac and Beynac. In the other direction we gazed down onto a blindingly green patchwork quilt of springy cornfields, with the winding river gleaming silver in the sunlight.

In the elegant tea pavilion we enjoyed a *citron pressé*, that most French of drinks – freshly squeezed lemon juice served with a pourer of powdered sugar, iced water and long parfait spoons for stirring – and resolved to return another day for a longer walk and perhaps a light lunch.

OPPOSITE The lime-washed violet shutters at Château de Marqueyssac were so beautiful set against the pale stone and the charcoal-grey of the *lauze* roof. **OVERLEAF** The extensive sculpted box gardens at Château de Marqueyssac were overgrown and uncared-for in 1996 when their new owner began the painstaking process of restoration. Visitors can now spend an entire afternoon strolling along the half-hidden pathways of the splendidly restored gardens and gazing down at the Dordogne River 130 metres (426 feet) below.

CHÂTEAU DE BEYNAC

Around a curve in the road we found Château de Beynac silhouetted just above us. It clings to the rockface high above the road and commands a strategic view in all directions. Forbidding and impressive, it is not difficult to imagine how such a place would have struck fear into the hearts of its enemies, who seem to have been numerous. Like many of the local castles, Beynac has a long history of feudal wars, wars of religion and, later, wars against the English, in this case since the 12th century. History books tell that the 12th century was a prosperous time for the lords of the south-west of France, and massive stone churches and castles were built in almost every town and village. For many visitors it is this fascinating and rich legacy of the past that draws them to the region.

LA ROQUE GAGEAC

What a vertiginous existence it must be being a citizen of this village. It is built right into the cliff and has an extensive area of troglodyte dwellings to explore. They are reached by an extremely long and winding staircase. I declined the

opportunity and even Julie decided it was just too hot. We sat on the river wall across the road, from where we had an excellent overview of the tightly packed houses seemingly flattened into the cliff face.

Many of the houses were very old and seemed in remarkably good repair. One had an enchanting round tower topped by a pointed stone roof. Set into the roof was a tiny attic window and I thought it would be the perfect setting for a re-enactment of the fairy story of Rapunzel, who let down her hair for her lover.

CHÂTEAU DE HAUTEFORT

Another day, another garden. This one was in the grounds of the Château de Hautefort. Classed as one of the Historic Monuments of France, the château has undergone the usual complicated history of destruction, rebuilding and modification since the 12th century. The existing structure, essentially a creation of the 17th century, passed through various hands until it and its gardens were restored by the curiously named Baron and Baronne de Bastard. Completed to the Baronne's satisfaction in 1968, the property then went up in flames that, according to reports, could be seen across half of Périgord. With amazing persistence and devotion, the Baronne recommenced and it is this rebuilt vision of splendour and loveliness that people can now visit.

The walks and secret garden rooms of Château de Marqueyssac (see page 26) seemed positively unruly compared with the precision here at Hautefort. Two gardeners were at work trimming, which I presume would be a full-time occupation. Their tools included tape measures, spirit levels, stakes driven into the ground and taut string to ensure that not one leaf deviated from the correct angle. This formality fascinated me and evoked admiration but no leap in the breast as happens when I wander beside a gently rioting English herbaceous border. This French garden consists of geometric shapes: cones (some with balls balanced on top), columns, rectangles, squares, diamonds and here and there a semicircle, all in box or variegated box and yew. It is a mathematician's delight, where symmetry is all. Such gardens are designed to be overlooked from windows or balconies high in the château, from where the patterns can best be admired. I could imagine myself straightening my shoulders, smoothing my hair and thinking logical thoughts as I gazed down on those correctly laid-out, perfectly groomed garden beds.

Along the walls were *terrasses fleuries*, where the green box edging was filled in with massed plantings of impatiens, begonias and petunias in all shades of pink, purple, red and white. They looked sumptuous, like richly decorated rugs. A west-facing wall had a row of flowering *Magnolia grandiflora*, gloriously scented on this warm day, its glossy green leaves a lovely contrast to the creamy stone.

OPPOSITE, TOP At La Roque Gageac the buildings are pressed up against the cliff face and seem strangely two-dimensional – like a stage set, as many have observed. Visitors can climb to inspect the troglodyte caves in the cliff above the village, but the way up is very steep.
OPPOSITE, BOTTOM Château de Hautefort, a rather forbidding structure, was rebuilt in the mid-17th century on the site of an earlier fortress dating from the 12th century. Its paths and entranceway are of raked white gravel, with not a pebble out of place. The day we visited the formal garden beds were filled with flowering begonias.

CHÂTEAU DE FÉNELON

One of our morning walks was to this château, reached from La Vieille Grange via a track that wound and climbed past fields of ripe wheat and fast-growing corn and through dense woodland, with the lichen-covered stone walls of the château at the other side of the track. Now and then I noticed smallish patches of wild strawberries. I had a very good look and only found two fruit – no wonder they are so costly to purchase. (I found out subsequently that *fraises des bois* are now cultivated. Another blow to romance!) Near our house I saw overhanging branches of *myrtilles* (bilberries), the berries fully formed and with a distinctive blue blush. They are a fruit of the autumn and right now were extremely sour. In autumn the blackberries would also be prolific, but at the moment the fruits were tight little green clusters.

Château de Fénelon dates from the 14th to the 17th century and its story is the familiar one of disputed ownership between the French and the English, destruction during the Hundred Years War and eventual partial reconstruction. These castles were sited so that the owner would have good warning of enemy approaches and, as always, there was a splendid view over the valley from the ramparts. The towers of Rouffillac Castle could be seen on the next hilltop.

This château is one of the few historic buildings in the area to have retained its stone roof made of *lauzes* – a word that does not refer to a particular variety of stone, but specifically to the cut limestone slabs used as roofing material in the region.

SAINT-CIRQ LAPOPIE AND ENVIRONS

We spent a glorious day touring in the valley of the Lot River en route to Saint-Cirq Lapopie, another of *les plus beaux villages de France*. It had rained overnight and the poppies had blossomed. The drifts of scarlet in the ripe wheat, with the sun shining, reminded me of the famous Monet painting of a young girl with a parasol walking among the wheat and poppies.

When you look at a map of France it is surprising how much of it is still shaded green. There are great swathes of countryside that remain thickly forested, and nowhere are they seen more splendidly than in this valley. It is much wilder and craggier than the valley of its sister river, the Dordogne. The scenery was breathtaking, the polished silver cliffs awesome. Up closer and with the sun directly on them they were more colourful, streaked with creamy limestone, orange and yellow ochre from the iron, and black magnesium – the colours of the prehistoric cave paintings that are the hidden treasure of so much of this region.

The Lot River is wider and deeper than the Dordogne. We saw no canoes, but there were a few larger pleasure boats. At Bouziès-Bas we crossed the river via a single-lane bridge and climbed up and up and up to a lookout from where we had a magnificent view. There was a simple wooden seat placed strategically, no other cars and the air was clear but cool. We sat and felt our hearts fill with the wonder of it all.

French writer André Breton once said, in writing about Saint-Cirq Lapopie: 'Every morning when I get up, I have the impression of contemplating the very best of art, nature and life'. Remnants of the original châteaus cling to the cliffs and the 16th-century church is still intact, but it is the streets of half-timbered medieval houses with their curved, pointed roofs that draw most of the admiration. The town is rigorously protected and preserved and is now the home of many artists. It has 187 inhabitants and goodness knows how many visitors per year. As with other superb sites, there is the paradox of how to support it and continue its existence without spoiling it.

Visiting outside the main tourist season was a definite advantage: we could wander and dawdle at will, sit on a stone step and read our guidebook. But there was no question that the economy of the town depends on its visitors. Boutiques selling *produits de la région* lined the streets and the quality of the produce was excellent. I bought some walnut mustard, which I planned to try on something – the proprietors suggested grilled duck. Well, they would, wouldn't they, given the importance of ducks to the economy of the area?

OPPOSITE, LEFT We could walk to Château de Fénelon along a lovely wooded path that, according to our neighbour Henriette, has been there since Roman times.
OPPOSITE, RIGHT High above the River Lot, a seat is perfectly placed to look at the view. We never tired of seeing the stunning river valleys of both the Lot and the Dordogne rivers and of breathing in the clear, crisp air from these elevated lookouts.

CUSSAC
A major new cave discovery in the small village of Cussac, in the western Dordogne, was announced in early July 2001. This cave has vivid prehistoric engravings dating from as early as 28 000 BC, and several human graves. It has been hailed as being 'as important for engraving as Lascaux is for painting'. There are reportedly hundreds of metres of engravings depicting animals, including bison, horses and rhinoceroses, and human figures. At the time of writing, it was too soon to know whether the public would be permitted to view the cave.

We lunched at the Auberge du Sombral on the Place Sombral, attracted by its pale green damask cloths, scarlet geraniums and smiling waitress. The meal was perfection (see page 346). Later in the day, further south, we passed through the tiny hamlet of Montjoi and Julie observed that it looked like 'the medieval town from central casting'. One of the smallest of the *bastide* towns (fortified towns founded in the Middle Ages), it has only two streets and dates from the 13th century. It was quite lovely and there was not a tourist or a tourist shop in sight.

GROTTE DU PECH MERLE

Two-thirds of the world's known decorated caves (those with paintings or markings on the walls) are in south-west France. The most famous of these are Lascaux and Font de Gaume in the Dordogne and the Grotte du Pech Merle in the Lot. After being preserved for up to 20 000 years, the biggest threat to the continued existence of the cave paintings is human breath. Since the caves at Lascaux were closed to prevent further deterioration, those at Pech Merle and Font de Gaume (at Les Eyzies) have been considered the two finest viewable examples of prehistoric art in Europe. At the Grotte du Pech Merle tourists are limited to 700 per day to see these spectacular underground attractions. I wonder how long visits will be possible.

The caves at Pech Merle were discovered in 1922 by two young boys. The idea of these children scrambling through tiny openings and along narrow underground tunnels is too horrible to contemplate! The boys tumbled into a vast cavern which, as seen today with careful lighting, is jaw-droppingly beautiful. There are 2 km (1¼ miles) of passages, caves and ledges, some decorated with images of bison, mammoth and bears and all displaying ornate and fantastic rock formations, stalactites and stalagmites. Many of the rock columns are marked and shaped so that they resemble carved temples such as the time-worn marvels at Angkor Wat in Cambodia.

Perhaps the most extraordinary relic is the imprint of feet – probably those of a young person or a woman, it is thought – caught in the muddy clay of the cave floor. It is quite unsettling to think that people once passed this way, leaving their handprints on the walls and their footprints on the floor. The footprints are said to be at least 10 000 years old. (To put this into perspective, the oldest evidence of indigenous habitation in Australia comes from Lake Mungo in south-west New South Wales, where human remains have been dated at about 60 000 years old. Human activity in the Kakadu National Park may have extended back 55 000 years and the outstanding rock-art galleries of northern Australia have been dated at 25 000 years old.)

LASCAUX II

The cave paintings at Lascaux are widely regarded as the Sistine Chapel of prehistoric art, although some people suggest that it might be more appropriate to speak of the Sistine Chapel as the Lascaux of renaissance art! They were discovered in 1940 by four young boys – a remarkably similar story to the discovery of Pech Merle. Our tour guide told us that two of the boys are now in their seventies and still visit regularly. The treasure was soon evaluated by an expert in prehistoric art, a priest called Abbé Breuil. By the mid-1960s one million people had visited the caves and the paintings were becoming obscured by a calcium deposit and fungal growth resulting from the introduction of light, warmth, humidity and, above all, human breath. The caves were closed to the public in 1963 and to the present day only five people per week have been permitted to visit them, those five needing to have scientific qualifications (or else be politicians, said our guide).

However, the local departmental council, under the auspices of a tourist body, La Régie Départementale du Tourisme de la Dordogne, and with assistance from the European community, has constructed and reproduced the two most important caves using identical proportions to the originals. This painstaking work took 15 years and is a masterpiece. The paintings were undertaken by a French-woman, Monique Peytral, who mixed the same ochres and oxides and used the same techniques and exactly the same dimensions as those used by the prehistoric artists. The result is breathtaking.

Like many others I had seen reproductions of the paintings in books, but I was totally unprepared for their size and the power of the images. These enor-mous works are 2 metres (approximately 2 yards) above the floor of the cave and, if depicting a bull or bison, often more than 4 metres ($4\frac{1}{3}$ yards) in length. It needs to be remembered that the only light available to the prehistoric artists was a small clay saucer filled with burning animal fat and that, at least in the narrowest cave, there was very little room to move, certainly not backwards to check their progress. The contours of the caves were used by the artists to suggest movement: the foot of a horse seems to stamp and the animals chase each other across the walls.

ROCAMADOUR

We had been warned of impossible July crowds in the perched town of Roca-madour, said to be the second most visited site in France after Mont Saint Michel in Normandy, so we rose early and had the pleasure of seeing the morning sun light up the towers and roofscape of this extraordinary site from the deserted lookout spot at L'Hospitalet. There were no crowds to spoil our visit and only a couple of tour buses had arrived by the time we left.

Since the late 11th century Rocamadour has been an important pilgrim staging point on the way to Santiago de Compostela in Spain. All sorts of claims are made for the mystic powers of the Black Virgin, said to have been carved from walnut wood in the 11th century, that is displayed above the altar of the Chapelle Notre Dame. The statue does have considerable presence, with the Virgin's slight body held stiffly, her expression severe. We climbed to the ramparts of the castle,

OVERLEAF The morning we visited the spectacular cliff-clinging village of Rocamadour, the cloudy sky seemed to emphasise the solemnity of the site. Once in the village itself, where the main street is thronged with shops, it is difficult to recapture this feeling until you enter the Chapelle Notre Dame, where the 11th-century statue of the Black Virgin is displayed.

following the Stations of the Cross, and had an awesome, if rather unsettling, view way, way down into the valley of the Alzou River. In the oldest and least restored section of Rocamadour, the Quartier de Coustalou, no house seemed to have a straight angle. The roofs were tilted and the walls curved inward. Nowadays many of these houses are the studios and workshops of artists.

Rocamadour's main street was lined with the inevitable souvenir shops, their brightly coloured wares and leather bags at odds with the charm and patina of many of the small houses. 'Walnut boutiques' offered anything and everything that could possibly be made from a walnut – oil, cakes, biscuits, walnuts in honey, mustard, woodwares and more. There was also plenty of opportunity to purchase Cabécous de Rocamadour, the delicious flat discs of goat's cheese that are produced around about (although not in the village itself) and considered so important gas-tronomically that they have AOC status (see below). We had already purchased and enjoyed *cabécous* at all stages of maturity, from the sweetest, softest and youngest through to those that retained a little creamy centre but were firm skinned, to the well aged, which were quite hard, with beige skins.

If you see wines or certain foods that are designated 'AOC' (Appellation d'Origine Contrôlée), you can be guaranteed that the item has been produced in the region claimed and that its production has followed established methods. For wine, AOC also establishes the grape varieties or percentage of a particular variety permitted for the appellation.

A highlight of our visit, although unrelated to the Black Virgin or to seeking penance, was a viewing of two tapestries designed by Jean Lurçat that hang in the Hôtel de Ville. Lurçat is credited with the revival of French tapestry by introducing modern themes and designs into what had become a largely moribund art form. These dramatic designs of local flora and fauna were woven in the Aubusson workshops in 1960 and look absolutely contemporary now. Brightly patterned and coloured butterflies float in the upper panels, a turtle swims, a snake challenges a bird, a clump of flag irises rises up one side of the work. The designs are in gold, blue, red and green against velvety black and the effect is sumptuous. One of Lurçat's vivid tapestries hangs in the Powerhouse Museum in Sydney.

Summer Eating

Oh, those peaches! In Australia we are starting to see a revival of the white varieties of peach and nectarine that were the flavours of summer in my childhood. In France they seem never to have gone away. Peeled and sliced with the fruit held strategically over a plate to catch the copious juice, they are sublime.

My best holidays are always those where I have a base, a place with a kitchen where I can actually use the seductive ingredients seen in the markets. This is also the way to save your liver and wallet in France. It is quite difficult to avoid an overdose of fat if you eat all your meals in restaurants, no matter how simple they are. And if you are a food lover, it doesn't seem quite right to exist on ham sandwiches or chips or pizza slices when you ought to be experiencing the glories of French food.

Whichever meal you have at home each day will be memorable. This is the time to try out the cheeses. They cost very little to buy in the market or in a village *fromagerie* and you can enjoy making the selection and, depending on your language skills, asking questions of the shopkeeper. The same thing applies with the *charcuterie*. Buy some *rillettes* (see page 321) or *grillons* (page 309), or a *saucisson sec* (salami-style sausage), or a slice of terrine or raw ham and, together with some tomatoes, radishes, olives and cornichons (pickled small cucumbers), a container of celeriac rémoulade (grated celeriac in a mustard mayonnaise) and a baguette, you have a great food experience for only a modest outlay.

Julie loves chicken and claims it is her comfort food, so for our first dinner at La Vieille Grange I roasted a fine, gold-coloured chicken with rosemary, garlic, a slice of lemon, potatoes and carrots. With this we had a big leafy salad and our first *fromage fermier de chèvre* – a tiny *cabécou* – and our first bottle of south-western rosé, Vin de Pays des Côtes du Tarn. We both found the weight of these rosés perfect for summer drinking. They were dry, fruity and low in alcohol at 11.5 per cent, and the colour was glorious.

Our second dinner at the old barn was another bird – this time plump quail bought at the market at nearby Sarlat. Julie built a fire in a sheltered corner of the courtyard using a small log and some of the bundled vine prunings stored in an outbuilding, and pretty soon the quail were crisping to perfection. To protect the breasts we sat the birds on vine leaves, on a piece of old chicken wire that was to hand. I made a *salade composée* (see page 44) of sautéed small potatoes, a gently warmed *confit* winglet (*manchon*) of duck, some exquisite green beans grown at Sarlat and some cultivated *girolle* mushrooms, with plenty of floppy salad leaves. Later, when reading *La Bonne Cuisine du Périgord* by the inspiring La Mazille (see page 57), I found her version of grilled quail with vine leaves and a variation that featured a grilled woodcock wrapped in a vine leaf. We followed our quail and

ACCOMMODATION
The rent for an apartment or a house in rural France is a fraction of what you will pay for a room in a comfortable hotel, and the benefits are many. You can rent a palatial home or a much more simple gîte. Gîtes *are listed by all French tourist offices and are to be found all over the countryside, often as adjuncts to a farmhouse where you can buy eggs, milk and, sometimes, farm-produced cheese.*

salad with a small chestnut-leaf-wrapped Banon cheese, enjoyed with more rosé and some yellow cherries.

Like every other tourist, I was intrigued by the massive duck breasts on sale in the markets, a consequence and valuable by-product of the *foie gras* industry, so on another occasion I decided to grill my first-ever *magret de canard* (see page 48). Ours weighed 400 g (14 oz), plenty for two people. Julie lusted for cabbage, so I bought one of them as well. Still on the poultry theme, we were to have a guinea fowl the next night. That experience commenced with the purchase of the bird two days before. It was seasoned and trussed by the butcher, and the gizzard, neck and liver were included as a matter of course in the parcel.

Every variety of bird I bought on this and subsequent trips was excellent. I tended to buy from a specialist vendor or from a market stall where someone was selling his or her own birds. In all cases the birds were full-flavoured and muscular but not tough, and the skin was dry and supple and crisped beautifully. (I describe in some detail the cooking of a guinea fowl on page 288.)

We finished our *magret* dinner with La Mazille's strawberry salad (see page 50) and sat on the terrace feeling mellow and well fed as warm rain started to fall. There were many more meals cooked and many picnics. But we also wanted to experience dishes cooked by others, and some of these are described in the chapter called 'Eating Out'.

OPPOSITE A dish of sliced white peaches such as this was a major component of our favourite summer breakfast at La Vieille Grange.

A Word about Bread

No meal in France could be contemplated without bread. Even the smallest French village still has a baker, who produces a considerable variety of loaves on a daily basis. Not all bakeries produce fancy pâtisserie but they will all bake croissants, brioche and several other speciality items. The shop will be warm and smell of freshly baked loaves, and Madame will smile as she wraps your order, having first inquired whether your preference is for a crunchy crust or one a little less so. In larger towns, the supermarkets and general stores also sell bread – but it is in the small bakeries that the longest queues form every day, at about 15 minutes before noon.

The baguette, so synonymous with France the world over, is the least popular style in the countryside here, and *pain de campagne* is the bread of choice for many older residents in the south-west. This massive crusty loaf usually weighs 2 kg (4½ lb) and is also known as *une tourte*. In earlier times the peasants' *tourtes* weighed more like 6 kg (13 lb) and one *tourte* would have been eaten over a week. The dense, creamy-coloured dough has a slight sourness, achieved by incorporating some of the previous day's dough. It is quite acceptable to ask for half a loaf. *Pain de campagne* is essential for making a good bread-based soup and in many homes is still served at every meal, often *trempé* (soaked, dunked or dipped) either into a soup or a braise.

Pain au levain means that the bread is raised using a natural starter – as it would have been made traditionally – rather than commercial yeast. Thin breadsticks are *ficelles* and fatter ones are sold as *pains* or *gros pains*. There are special names for other shapes, such as *couronne* (a circle, illustrated opposite), *épi* (a loaf with small pointed 'ears' like a wheat sheaf), and so on. *Pain de seigle* is made with a percentage of rye flour, *pain complet* with a percentage of wholewheat flour. And *feu de bois* means the bread was baked in a wood-fired oven.

Our experience with bread was positive on the whole, but here and there (especially in supermarkets) the traditional baguette disappointed, being floppy, with little crust and little flavour. Our preference was always for small village bakers.

Salades composées

Salades composées are a delightful way to begin a meal, especially in the warmer months (although often a country *auberge* or restaurant will first offer a homemade pâté or terrine). The custom of serving such combination salads is fairly recent and would surprise the cooks of 50 years ago. Most home cooks I met on my travels through the region would probably prefer to start their main meal of the day with soup. But the ingredients for such salads are all readily available in prime condition and in every case are worth star treatment.

There are no precise recipes because the fun lies in being impromptu. The cook can select from a wide range of seasonal green leaves and then choose smaller quantities of delicious morsels, such as ham from Bayonne, chunks of sautéed bacon, steamed *écrevisses* (see page 47), *confit* of duck wingtips or gizzards, smoked duck breast, grilled slices of *boudin noir* (blood sausage), garlic-rubbed croûtons, crispy curls of duck skin, garlicky potatoes, roasted chestnuts, sliced wild mushrooms tossed with garlic and parsley, slices of creamy Roquefort with new season's walnuts, grilled *cabécou*, not to mention *foie gras*! Restraint is called for.

Because many of the specialities are rich, the dressings tend to be quite sharp. At home I would use around 5 parts extra-virgin olive oil to 1 part wine vinegar. In Périgord I was more likely to use 1 part walnut oil, 2 parts extra-virgin olive oil and 1 part wine vinegar or *verjus*. And if a *confit* was to be part of the salad, I would add a few drops of the duck fat to the salad bowl and reduce or omit the olive oil.

OPPOSITE *Salades composées* are a delightful challenge for the cook. Here, the *salade* features duck livers (not *foie gras*), bacon chunks, wild mushrooms, broad beans and crispy potatoes.

Yabbies with Fennel Broth

Such is the enthusiasm of the French population for *écrevisses* (which Australians call yabbies and Americans call crawfish) that French rivers have been largely emptied of these small crustaceans. They are now imported from North Africa and further afield. In Australia we are belatedly realising the culinary value of our *écrevisses* and, to supply the demand, more and more yabby farms are appearing. They are also becoming a big export business, with seemingly infinite markets in Asia.

Country children still catch yabbies in dams by dangling bits of meat from a hook on the end of a piece of string. The country cooks I know prefer their yabbies straight from the dam, intestinal tracts intact. Farmed yabbies have already been purged in fresh water and do not need to have the intestinal tract removed before cooking. French cooks extract the tract whilst the creature is still alive. I know that yabbies have very simple nervous systems, but I cannot do this.

Unless you catch the yabbies in your own dam or live near a yabby farm, finding live creatures is quite difficult. A good fishmonger may be able to order them for you. Live yabbies put in the freezer for 1 hour go to sleep and can be tipped into boiling water or a steamer with no flailing of claws or unnecessary trauma – for either the yabbies or the cook.

The yabbies I obtained for testing and photographing this dish were exceptionally large, each one weighing around 120 g (4 oz). With yabbies of this size, 5 per person is sufficient and I allowed a few extra minutes' cooking time.

This is a simple and more or less classic way of preparing these small shellfish. It is ideal for outdoor eating, with plenty of paper napkins and warm water for rinsing fingers. A fancier dish results if the yabbies are shelled and only the tails are served, lightly dressed with a full-flavoured vinaigrette including some walnut oil, perhaps with chilled slow-roasted tomatoes and plenty of torn basil.

Stun the yabbies in the freezer for 1 hour before you begin cooking.

When you are ready to eat, put everything except the yabbies and fennel leaves into a large pot and bring to simmering point. Simmer for 15 minutes, then add the yabbies and cover the pot. Turn the heat to high and boil for 8 minutes. The yabbies will turn bright red.

Tip the yabbies and the broth into a large, heated bowl and scatter with the fennel leaves. Serve at once, offering spoons for the juices and plenty of good bread.

Serves 4

40 × 60–70 g/2–2½ oz live yabbies/crawfish

1 medium carrot, peeled and finely sliced

6 shallots, finely sliced

1 leek, finely sliced and well washed

4 cloves garlic, sliced

1 hot chilli, seeded and finely sliced (optional)

1 large bouquet garni (thyme, bay leaf, parsley stalk, wild fennel stalk)

½ teaspoon sweet paprika

1 bottle (750 ml/26 fl oz) dry white wine

sea salt

freshly ground black pepper

1 head of wild fennel, well washed and cut roughly with scissors

1 handful soft fennel leaves, roughly chopped

OPPOSITE When eating yabbies I find that a strong nutcracker is helpful for extracting the sweet meat from the front claws.

Grilled Magret of Duck

Serves 2

1 × 400 g/14 oz magret
sea salt
1 bay leaf
3 cloves garlic
1 tablespoon extra-virgin olive oil
2 shallots, finely chopped
2 tablespoons finely chopped young
    parsley (preferably flat-leaf)
freshly ground black pepper
6 small onions
250 ml/9 fl oz chicken stock
2 cups sliced cabbage
6 small carrots, peeled
4 small waxy potatoes, peeled or not
    as you prefer

The *magret* is the breast fillet taken from a fattened duck. Once upon a time a fattened duck would have been cut into quarters for preserving and the breast meat would thus have been quartered. Nowadays the prime *confit* is the leg joints and the *magret* is served as another speciality – and it is delicious. Cooked mostly on the skin side, the considerable fat is encouraged to render. Some fat lubricates the very lean meat but most disappears in the cooking. A *magret* is always cooked rare or medium–rare and is served thinly sliced.

An average *magret* weighs 400–500 g (14–18 oz). A duck breast fillet in Australia rarely weighs more than 200 g (7 oz) and the ratio of fat to lean is quite different. The nearest equivalent is the breast fillet from a Muscovy duck and, in my experience, while they are wonderfully flavourful, they are not as tender as the French birds. I have included this recipe as most cooks will want to give it a go when they are *in situ*. In Australia or elsewhere, you must allow 1 breast fillet per person. The method can still be followed, but once the skin has crisped for about 5 minutes, it will need just 1 minute on the flesh side before being put aside to rest. Slice the breast on the diagonal to achieve long, even slices.

With a sharp knife, crisscross the fat on the duck breast, then rub it with salt. Crumble the bay leaf and crush 1 garlic clove, then mix these with a little of the olive oil and brush the meaty side of the breast with the mixture. Mince the remaining garlic cloves and mix with the shallot and parsley and plenty of pepper. Set aside.

Simmer the onions in the chicken stock until tender and set the pot aside. Blanch the cabbage in plenty of lightly salted water and drain well. Boil the carrots and potatoes in lightly salted water until just tender. Cool, then cut into thick slices.

Heat a heavy-based, cast-iron ridged grill pan to very hot. Put the *magret* on it skin-side down, reduce the heat a little and let the breast hiss and sizzle for 5–6 minutes without disturbing it. Pour off and reserve the fat once or twice. Meanwhile, in a separate pan heat a little of the reserved rendered duck fat and sauté the cabbage, carrots and potatoes. As the vegetables start to colour, add the onions together with any reduced cooking juices. Toss quickly to mix and to prevent the vegetables catching. Stir in most of the shallot mixture and move the pan away from the heat.

Turn the duck breast and cook for 3 minutes on the flesh side. Transfer to the top of the vegetables to relax for 5 minutes. Transfer the *magret* to a board and slice thinly. To serve, divide the vegetables between 2 hot plates, then divide the *magret* slices and fan them out. Scatter with the remaining shallot mixture.

OPPOSITE In addition to the method of serving given in the recipe, grilled *magret* is also good with a wedge of *galette sarladaise* (see page 284) and a dollop of *aillade toulousaine* (page 205), as seen here.

Quail in Vine Leaves
Inspired by La Mazille

Serves 2

2 plump quail, cleaned
sea salt
freshly ground black pepper
handful of unripe green grapes
  (if available)
livers from the 2 quail *or* 1 chicken
  liver, trimmed
1 tablespoon walnut oil *or* olive oil
2 thin slices pork fat, large enough
  to wrap over the quail breasts
2 fresh vine/grape leaves
2 thick slices of bread, about the
  same size as the quail

In its original version this quail would have been skewered and cooked in front of a wood fire, with the bread sitting in a dish underneath the bird to catch all the juices. If you have a spit in the oven or on your barbecue, the quail can be roasted on this and the bread could sit in a heavy frying pan or similar underneath. If you have neither, try the method given here.

Preheat the oven or barbecue to very hot (250°C/475°F). Season the quail well inside and out. Tuck half the grapes and 1 quail liver (or 1 piece of chicken liver, if using) inside each bird. Brush the skin of the quail with a little of the walnut oil and cover the breast of each bird with a slice of pork fat. Brush the vine leaves with the rest of the oil and wrap 1 leaf around each quail, tying with string.

Put the slices of bread into a heavy ovenproof pan and place each bird on a slice of bread. Roast for 10 minutes. Remove the birds to a warm dish and allow to rest for 5 minutes while you return the bread to the oven for 5 minutes. Retrieve the bread and settle the birds on top of it again. Cut and discard the string and open the parcels. The fat should have crisped and basted the birds and the bread should be well roasted and deliciously flavoured.

Chicken livers
It is not very practical to buy a single chicken liver. Sauté a few extra and serve as a garnish.

Strawberry Salad
Inspired by La Mazille

Serves 4

500 g/1 lb 2 oz ripe strawberries,
  hulled (or a mixture of regular
  strawberries and fraises des bois)
½ cup castor/superfine sugar
60 ml/2 fl oz eau-de-vie de prune *or*
  eau-de-vie de pêche *or* Armagnac
  or mature red wine

Macerate the strawberries with the sugar and liqueur for 30 minutes without stirring. Stir gently to mix just before serving. Arrange in a pretty glass dish and accompany with a crisp biscuit – La Mazille suggests *les gaufres* (see page 89) flavoured with aniseed, as pictured opposite.

Henriette & Women's Business

I learned to cook at my mother's knee. There is no substitute for this way of learning, and those who apply themselves in later life will never 'get it' in quite the same way. I even tuck the pastry over the edge of a tart tin the same way Mum did, and mash carrot with potato for a glorious golden mash as she did.

Writing this, I am trying to think of some evidence of culinary rebellion. Mum used to thicken milk sauces for cauliflower and the like with a bit of flour mixed with water, not because she hadn't heard of a roux but because butter was somewhat of an extravagance, even though we had our own cow. The hand-churning was physically tiring and maybe butter was for more obvious uses, like on homemade bread rolls smothered with Mum's blackberry jam. And I remember a favourite task when I was about 10 of feeding green beans through a cast-iron slicer that was clamped to a bench and delivered slivers of the beans in a most satisfying and efficient manner. I now prefer to leave my green beans whole. Other than these trivial differences, Mum's influence is still very strong.

A roasted leg of lamb was a family favourite (memory tells me that it was fairly well cooked, though) and Mum used to stick it with bits of garlic and, surprisingly, anchovy. I don't know where she had read of this. She had not yet travelled, but her cookery library offered vicarious influences from all around the globe. The morning after the roast she could be found in the kitchen carefully turning over the congealed fat in the baking dish to get at the layer of mahogany jelly underneath. This treasure, together with a little of the fat, was spread on fresh wholemeal bread and sprinkled with a very little salt. I was soon initiated into this marvellous treat.

It was with a special thrill of recognition, then, that I read an interview in a French magazine (*Périgord Magazine*'s 'Gastronomie' special issue 81) with a local woman named Patrice Gibertie, in which she described one of the special *trucs* (hints) of the Périgourdine housewife. It was a most luxurious dish: a goose neck stuffed with *foie gras* and then cooked in goose fat. When the goose neck was retrieved from the *confit* crock, there was a layer of delicious jelly at the bottom of the dish. 'This,' she said, 'is the base of some of our best sauces. A spoonful added to a dish of *cèpes* will transform them into something heavenly.'

Her recipe idea is one that will remain in the mind's eye unless you are in the south-west with the means and the sense of adventure to have a go. For what

OPPOSITE An arrangement of autumn glory, gathered from the woods around the farmhouse we rented at Lavalade and from our neighbour's fig tree.

it is worth, I repeat her very sketchy instructions: 'Macerate a *foie gras* with a little salt, pepper and a small glass of *eau-de-vie*. Divide the *foie gras* and slip each half into a goose neck, adding some truffle. Sew up and *confire* [cook slowly] in barely simmering goose fat for 1 hour. Transfer to an earthenware pot, ensuring the neck is well covered with fat.'

The *foie gras* referred to would be raw and cleaned (see page 307). Would this dish be eaten cold as a sort of luxurious terrine? I imagine so. And I imagine, too, that the *confit* neck would be gently warmed in a little of its own fat to crisp the skin and then be allowed to cool completely before being sliced.

Gibertie stated that the cooking of her childhood was that of the home – women's cooking. Women learned to cook by observing, listening to and helping their mothers, aunts and grandmothers, just like I did. It was not just skill in preparation they absorbed in this way, it was understanding the evolution of a dish, the tiny detail, the gathering of something special to include (maybe the jelly from the bottom of the dish!). There was no butter or cream available so they used what they had and succeeded magnificently. While Gibertie admitted that after the Revolution the French planted potatoes all over the country and no-one was hungry any more, it was only in Périgord that the potatoes became *pommes sarladaises* (see page 284). (I imagine other regions in France might dispute that *pommes sarladaises* is the only potato masterpiece, but . . .)

Often what the women had available was influenced by what their husbands or sons brought in from the hunt or from the fields – birds stole grain and had to be shot; weeds invaded the crops and had to be pulled out. There would have been little meat, but there might have been a hare or a partridge, a basket of wild mushrooms or a handful of dandelions or nettles, and these special extras were celebrated and treated with reverence. The widespread planting and use of haricot beans was sensible for small peasant farmers as the beans' cultivation did not require animals or costly equipment; women, old people and children could, and did, gather in the crop; and the beans were sustaining and nourishing. For the people of Périgord, their culinary patrimony – the truffle, the *cèpe* and *foie gras* – was considered their *panthéon gourmand* (their collective culinary heritage to be preserved) and a gift from God.

The Gibertie interview concluded with a litany of remembered dishes. There were no details given, but with a bit of imagination I could almost catch the aromas, and some of the dishes mentioned are very well known: broad-bean soup with a fricassée of fried bits and pieces (the local tradition was to extract some of the vegetables from the soup pot, fry them in a little duck or goose fat and put them back in the pot), rabbit soup, simple stews of dried beans with a bit of pork for flavour, sorrel sauce with a stuffed goose neck, roast veal stuffed with *cèpes*, rabbit stuffed with goose *confit*, apple pancakes and pumpkin *clafoutis* and walnut tarts.

This wonderful interview left me intrigued and frustrated. I wanted to ask questions of Patrice Gibertie. Who is she? Or who was she? In the same magazine were details of a leg of lamb stuffed with garlic and anchovies and left in the oven for seven hours (see page 85). I had to try this in memory of my mother's roast.

La Mazille

Beneath many English-language collections of recipes from the Périgord bubble the lively, authoritative words of La Mazille, the penname of Mme André-Adrienne Mallet-Maze. Her extraordinarily comprehensive collection of more than 400 recipes, *La Bonne Cuisine du Périgord*, originally published in 1929, leaves little to discover. Here is a treasure-house of 'women's business'! I was introduced to it by food writer Paula Wolfert, who is a good friend. I knew the name La Mazille from the bibliographies of Elizabeth David and others who had recognised her authority concerning the cuisine of Périgord and its neighbouring areas, but had not realised her primal importance.

André-Adrienne Mallet-Maze, also known as 'Danielle' as well as 'La Mazille', was born near Paris in 1891 of a Périgourdin family. They came originally from a tiny village called Planèze, not far from Brive-la-Gaillarde in Limousin, next to the Dordogne. André-Adrienne claimed that it was her heritage and the fact that she visited the region frequently during her growing-up years that enabled her to understand the minds of the local cooks: 'They cook instinctively without really knowing why they do something, and how they create their culinary masterpieces.'

In 1922 La Mazille married an erudite bookseller who came from the same village as her own family, and it was he who suggested she write her first book. There did not exist at this time any published collection of Périgourdin recipes, although André-Adrienne was very familiar with a collection of family recipes that had been put together by the governess of a paternal aunt. Apparently she taught herself to cook as a result of writing her book. The youngest of her three daughters was reported as saying, 'She couldn't boil an egg before, but after writing the book she became an excellent cook.'

Widowed in 1935, La Mazille spent the next 22 years as a public servant working for the Ministère des Anciens Combattants in straitened circumstances. She remained optimistic and visited Neuvic frequently with her daughters, where she was warmly welcomed. She had become well known as a result of her book and later wrote another, *Histoires périgourdines au coin du feu*. She died in 1984, and in 1991, on the 100th anniversary of her birth, a plaque was erected in her honour in a street in Planèze. Her importance in documenting Périgourdin traditions has been recognised by the city of Périgueux, which has named the major award of its biennial international Cookbook Fair the Prix La Mazille.

The French edition of *La Bonne Cuisine du Périgord* is still in print in facsimile. Apart from the wonderful recipes, the book vividly evokes the country households of two generations ago. It includes personal opinion, *trucs* and *tours de main* (personal tricks), even alternative versions of the same dish, all offered in a warm, practical and personal voice. The cuisine that emanated from these country kitchens was savoury, its dishes gently simmered with a little of this and a little of that, lubricated judiciously with the suave flavours of goose and duck fat. It is a cuisine that is a revelation for those who have not tried it.

The recipes are marvellous, but it is La Mazille's authoritative voice and her insight into the whys and wherefores that make this little book such a jewel. From it I have understood the relationship and differences between *rillettes de Tours* and *grillons périgourdins* (see page 309); received sensible advice about clearing the fat for proper sealing of *confits* (page 311) and how to deal with *cèpes* in the Périgourdin manner (page 168) as opposed to the Tuscan; thought more about garlic in cookery; registered the importance of a tight-fitting lid for a good braise and of choosing a warmed plate on which to serve salad leaves if they are to be topped with warm food – and so on and so on. The book is so conversational in tone that there is no sense of reading of another time or age, despite its having been written more than 70 years ago.

Henriette and André

The dishes and experiences recorded by La Mazille would have been very familiar to Henriette Deroeux. Henriette and her husband, André, were our neighbours during our 1999 summer holiday, and in fact 'our' house, La Vieille Grange, had once belonged to them. It used to be the barn attached to the main house but was converted to a separate dwelling some years ago. The two properties are now divided by a narrow lane, but André's little Renault was parked in one of the outbuildings alongside our house, and Henriette hung her washing on the same line as we did. The hens took no notice of the lane or any other demarcation and wandered at will between the two properties.

Henriette was 79 when we met, André several years older. She was tiny, neat and lively, with curly grey hair, eyes like shiny black buttons and a lovely smile. She was born in the stone house in which she still lives and is a priceless repository of stories and reminiscences. Like me, Henriette learned to cook at her mother's knee. Our conversations were all too brief and there was much more I could have learned from her, but I was fearful of seeming too nosy.

The Australian owners have become great friends with Henriette and André and the feeling is certainly mutual. Henriette showed me her scrapbook with many

OPPOSITE Henriette Deroeux stands at her front door wearing the traditional apron that has just one wide band of firm fabric over one shoulder. I loved listening to her stories of how life used to be and how it had changed – for the good and the bad.

happy snaps of her being hugged by several different little girls. André brought out a bottle of his homemade walnut wine (see page 197) and Julie and I sipped it cautiously, unsure at our first taste of this curiously flavoured, slightly medicinal sweet liqueur.

Henriette and André live a very quiet life. André is not very well and can no longer take any active part in tending the trees or garden. Henriette does what she can and certainly takes a close interest in any comings and goings. She told us that whereas once there were 28 families living and farming in Mercadiol, there are now just four. (Fifteen months later, when we met again, these four had dwindled to two.) She said it is very difficult for the older people to meet these days. Unless they drive, there is no other form of transport. Formerly they would meet regularly to participate in the tasks associated with the farming year, helping each other to harvest and plant and coming together for celebrations and special days. The church is still an important gathering place that permits the members of the small community to watch out for one another.

From Henriette's perspective, the rural heart of France is dying. The young people leave the farms as soon as possible, the old die or decide to follow their children to the towns, and the houses are sold to the English as holiday homes. Her references to a largely vanished life of rural cooperation and sharing are repeated in many accounts of life in the south-west. There are still plenty of small farms that offer demonstrations of *gavage* (force-feeding of ducks and geese; see page 296) and then sell the tourists the products in their farm shop, but the picture of hardworking peasants living in tune with the seasons, caring for the land and being largely self-sufficient, is now more and more a fantasy. It has been replaced by the reality of huge farming concerns that contract farmers to grow tobacco or corn or strawberries. Agribusiness must bear responsibility for destroying the habitats of game birds and animals and of polluting rivers so that fishing has been dramatically reduced and wild *écrevisses* are largely a thing of the past. River sand is now mined in areas where fish once laid their eggs. With the changes have come considerable unemployment and the associated social consequences.

I asked Henriette to help us locate a suitable *foie gras* farm, where we could see the *gavage* of the birds in order to have a more complete understanding of the process. She did better than this and accompanied us. On the way she pointed out houses that had once been farms and are now holiday residences. She told me she used to keep a few ducks, as did all housewives, in order to prepare her own *foie gras*, just enough for the family. The women took the fattened livers to a small artisan who packed them in special tins and sterilised them for long keeping. The other parts of the birds were prepared as *confits*.

Julie and I had remarked to each other over and over again as we drove through the countryside that we never saw a duck or a goose. What we did see were plywood signs hanging on stands placed on the roadside advertising the sale

OPPOSITE, TOP LEFT Henriette's well-waxed floorboards, gleaming walnut-wood door and polished grandfather clock were evidence of her care, energy and respect for her heritage.
OPPOSITE, TOP RIGHT This handsome old water pump is a reminder of the days when all water – for both the household and the garden – had to be pumped by hand and carted in buckets.
OPPOSITE, BOTTOM LEFT I bought these well-worn copper pots at a market in Sarlat to remind me forever of French country cooks and country cooking. Sadly, my purchases were lost in a never-delivered air-freight parcel and this photograph is now my only souvenir.
OPPOSITE, BOTTOM RIGHT The old wooden bench alongside Henriette's kitchen table was mostly tucked underneath as it is rarely used. A rush-bottomed chair is much kinder on André's back.

of *foie gras* and related foodstuffs *à la ferme*. Many farmers buy in ducklings from a breeder, feed them, process the livers and the rest of the birds and sell the final products, which is why you cannot drive down any small road in this part of France without seeing a sign advertising '*Élevage. Gavage. Vente directe à la ferme*' ('Breeding. Force-feeding. Sales direct from the farm').

Arriving at the selected farm I expected to see birds everywhere. I did not, but finally I understood why: summer is too hot for ducks, the farmer told us. The *gavage* season runs from September to May only, so there are no ducks to be seen in summer, other than a few kept for breeding and demonstrations.

The quantity of *foie gras* prepared and sold is staggering – without even considering the output from the large manufacturers – but there are many people who are so horrified by the process that they cannot consider the end product. Each bird is force-fed once in the morning and once in the evening (more often and for longer for geese). The feed is corn that has been soaked in boiling water to soften it. I have to report that the ducks I saw seemed quite indifferent and waddled away from the farmer's enclosing arm with no signs of distress after swallowing their dose of corn. Henriette assured me that they do not suffer. 'A bird in distress cannot make a good liver,' she said, with an eye to the practical.

Paula Wolfert quotes another Périgourdin cook, who said of the ducks and geese, 'It is their destiny to provide us with livers'. The birds are regarded with affection and certainly with respect by the inhabitants of the south-west. No-one I spoke to expressed any misgivings about the time-honoured practice of *gavage*. It was discussed as an Australian farmer might discuss sheep-drenching or some other aspect of farming that is little understood by the non-farming public. I write in more detail about duck farming and *gavage* in the 'Foie Gras & Confit' chapter.

In October 2000, Henriette and I met again. She greeted me with kisses on both cheeks and grasped my hands in her own warm ones. On this visit I was again accompanied by Julie and photographer Simon Griffiths. We sat in the front parlour at a large table covered with a smooth cloth and set with etched wine glasses, a bottle of Monbazillac and a platter piled with one of Henriette's specialities: rolled wafer biscuits known as *gaufres* (see page 89) and cooked in a special iron (*un gaufrier*) over the coals. These biscuits, now made with butter, were once made with pork fat.

Later we moved to the kitchen to admire the fireplace. The floorboards had the smooth patina of wood well waxed over time. The table was made of walnut wood, smoke-darkened over the years, as were the ceiling beams. Once again I asked Henriette about how it used to be and she spoke of her mother and how 'Maman' had run the household. The fireplace had been the centre of the house, around which all the family used to gather to keep warm and to share tasks. In the evenings they cracked walnuts or stripped corn husks or shelled chestnuts.

OPPOSITE, LEFT Henriette cooks *les gaufres*. She has had a 'modern' stove installed in the fireplace but prefers to cook the wafer biscuits over the coals using a traditional two-handled iron press.

OPPOSITE, RIGHT André poured Monbazillac and offered it with great courtesy. It was quite delicious with the crisp *gaufres*.

OVERLEAF In Henriette's kitchen, with her mother's copper preserving pan displayed, little has changed since Henriette's mother's day.

While we talked, the fire was burning and drawing perfectly. As in most traditional houses, Henriette and André have a strip of cloth suspended from the mantelpiece to help draw the smoke up the chimney, and a deep hearth so that someone can step inside to tend to a cooking pot or simply to keep warm. Henriette had her best clothes on to receive us but agreed to slip on her one-shouldered apron to show me how she stood inside the hearth to cook the *gaufres* over the coals.

André pointed to the cavities in the walls to the side of the hearth where *daubières* (heavy cast-iron or earthenware casseroles) could be put, with coals heaped on the lids, to continue their slow cooking or to keep hot. Such stews would have had bits of pork fat – trotters, skin or belly – added to ensure richness and would have been moistened with water or wine, not stock.

I asked Henriette how the remaining local residents spent their time during the winter. 'They don't do very much at all,' was the answer. 'It is the time to gather and dry the walnuts and bundle the dried tobacco, for those who still work these crops. And there is always TV. It gets dark early so one goes to bed early and does not get up until it is light.'

Twenty-five years ago tradesmen visited from the nearby village of Masclat in their vans (even longer ago the vans were drawn by horses). 'We had a butcher twice a week, the baker twice a week and the grocer twice a week,' remembered

André. This no longer happens and although there is a 'Mercadiol' sign just near Henriette and André's house, there is no village of that name, just a few stone houses and a crumbling lane.

Henriette described all these changes philosophically, without anger or resentment. She was quick to admit that in many important ways life has improved a great deal. The houses now have heating, electric light (electricity arrived in 1933) and modern sewerage, and tourism has provided a stimulus to restore and maintain old houses that might otherwise have been abandoned. This has created a bit of an industry in itself. Many French people buy houses here and come to retire (or buy them to restore and then to rent or sell to the English). But unlike the local bureaucrats, Henriette does not see that the future of the area lies with tourism. She considers that the Dordogne is not a prime spot for tourism: 'The young want the sea or the mountains.' I reminded her that there are the castles, the history and the exceptional gastronomy, not to mention the beauty and tranquillity of the forests and villages. She just gave a shrug of her shoulders when I asked what she thought would become of hamlets such as Mercadiol.

I wanted to know if the locals still ate *confit*. 'Absolutely,' was the answer. Of course, being substantial, it is not a dish for every day, but it is still highly regarded in the region. Henriette was firm and clear when I asked how she thought food had changed in her adult lifetime: 'The quality of ingredients has diminished. Eggs from the supermarket have no flavour, and as for the colour of the yolks . . .!' She made a very dismissive gesture. (Henriette and André's own hens look fat and healthy.) She continued: 'One should eat strawberries the day they are picked or perhaps the next day. It is not normal to keep strawberries for a week, and they do not have the same flavour.'

Henriette makes soup every night, usually with puréed vegetables, and it is always eaten with bread in it. She and André eat plenty of egg dishes and salads, and not very much meat. She said that everyone now prefers to do everything quickly. The old dishes took time and often lots of hard work. 'When my mother made the *confit* she used the huge copper basin that still hangs over the fireplace. *Confit* was cooked very slowly for two days over the fire and then stored for five to six months after the harvest. There was no need to sterilise anything. We had no heating, so it was stored in the house. The young have no interest in maintaining these traditions in their homes – nine out of ten prefer McDonald's. Or they prefer to eat from cans and buy frozen foods.' We both agreed that if the mother does not or cannot cook, it is likely that the children will not, either.

We moved outside to inspect the original bread oven, housed in a building a short walk away. With an agility that put me – 20 years her junior – to shame, Henriette scrambled up a grassy bank at the entrance. The oven was last used around 1945. During the war the bread was baked at night to stop the Germans taking it all. She can still remember the smell on the night air (I wondered why the Germans

SOUPE AND POTAGE
La soupe *is different from* le potage. *Traditionally, the former was often the main meal and the poultry or game or meat that gave the soup its character was eaten as a separate course after the liquid. A potage was altogether more delicate, perhaps a smooth cream of vegetable. The vegetables in* la soupe – *the familiar root vegetables and cabbage and haricot beans – would have been grown in the kitchen garden.*

La soupe *was almost always ladled over a slice of* pain de campagne *(see page 42) or one of the substantial dumplings made expressly for simmering in* la soupe *(page 350). The practice of adding a small amount of separately sautéed ingredients at the end of the cooking added depth of flavour, too. This fricassée was sometimes fresh vegetables with a bit of bacon, sometimes the vegetables from the soup, drained and fried with a bit of goose fat with maybe some parsley added for freshness.*

couldn't smell it too). Each loaf weighed 4 kg (9 lb) and the oven took six loaves at a time. The families in Mercadiol cooperated and combined their bread-making efforts. When one farmer could not access his fields easily because of the position of the bread oven, the families got together to rebuild the oven in a more propitious spot, where it now stands. The wooden peels used to thrust the loaves deep into the oven were still resting on racks high up the wall, thick with dust and spider's webs.

Bread, affirmed André, is the base of all cuisine. Henriette believes that bread should be made only with wheat, salt and water and cannot see any reason to put walnuts or raisins in it, for example. 'Good bread,' she said, 'lasts one week.' (I was reminded of this remark a few days later when I bought bread from an artisanal baker at Le Bugue market. His wife told me that the loaf had been made by her husband 'with love' and should be stored in a cotton cloth, where it would last for eight days. It was reassuring to know that some things do not change.)

André showed us the barn where the animals had lived. The date '1876' was chiselled into the stone. The animals inhabited the bottom level and feed was stored in the top storey. Henriette returned to the theme of how things have changed: 'A few families still raise their own pig each year. There is a proper way to handle a pig after it is killed: it must be left on an angle and allowed to bleed thoroughly and cool down slowly so that the muscles are relaxed before the meat is butchered to make the hams and sausages.' Nowadays, she said, the pig must be killed at an abattoir and, although the meat will be returned to the family, the killing and subsequent handling are quite different. There is insufficient time or care taken to permit slow cooling and resting, and this, combined with inferior industrial feed, means that the sausages and hams no longer have the same flavour as before.

We returned to the house for afternoon tea and to sample the *gaufres* Henriette had made for us. Julie, Simon and I ate them with enthusiasm and André carefully poured glasses of 1996 Fleur d'Or Monbazillac. Henriette told us that her dining table could extend to accommodate 20 people. As she and André have no children, I could only imagine that in times gone by there were many occasions when family and neighbours gathered together to share a meal. I hoped so.

I asked about truffles and wild mushrooms and chestnuts and Henriette replied with a story: 'A very lucky local man was walking his dog on the path to Château de Fénelon one winter's day when his dog became agitated and started scratching at the ground. Lo and behold, there were truffles.' She did not mention whether the man found one or ten, but clearly the implication was that there are still truffles in the vicinity.

It had not been a good year for wild mushrooms, which were usually plentiful in the chestnut woods during September and October. One local theory was that the terrible storms of the previous winter had disturbed the roots and spores. Another was that because of the exceptionally hot summer the ground was too hard for the mushrooms to sprout. I found all this a bit confusing, especially since the fields around the house we were staying in were sprinkled with the white caps of what we would call field mushrooms. The French seem to have no interest in this variety, although during our holiday we took one to the local pharmacist, as instructed to do, and she confirmed that it was edible.

Many chestnut forests have been cut down and replaced with pine, which offers a fast cash crop. I love chestnuts but had to realise that for the old-timers in the Périgord and Quercy, chestnuts are synonymous with terrible hunger and poverty, similar to the way many Australian country people feel about wild rabbit. Henriette and André made no mention of chestnuts when describing the foods they particularly enjoyed.

We said goodbye and I tried to communicate how privileged I felt to have been invited into Henriette's home. Her response was to fling her arms wide and say that her mother had always told her to open her arms to the world and to people. André kissed my hand, then pressed a tin of truffles into it as a very special gift. I found Henriette and André to be an inspiring couple, both so interested and courteous, eager to share their experiences and thoughts with a near-stranger. Those musings were all delivered with buckets of old-world charm and absolutely no trace of resentment towards those who have, to some extent, taken over their territory and who have certainly helped change their lives forever.

LEFT A portrait of Henriette and André. It was a privilege to be welcomed into their lives and their home.

Canelés de Bordeaux

The tradition of sharing recipes and general culinary wisdom is at the heart of much 'women's business'. Paula Wolfert (see page 12) and I saw each other in early 2001 and discovered that we were both immersed in investigating the food of south-west France, me for this book and Paula for a new edition of her fine work *The Cooking of South-West France*. She offered to share her version of *canelés de Bordeaux*, the delightful little fluted cakes that are to be found all over the south-west. They were part of the petits fours selection in all the restaurants we visited and they were delicious, with a curious but rustic charm. Paula was given her version by a pastry chef from the city of Bordeaux.

Canelés are spectacular to watch during the baking process, rising like soufflés and then settling gently back into the moulds (providing you are not using a convection oven, which leads to very misshapen cakes). They are notoriously difficult to make and my first attempts were not very successful. They should be glossy and dark and crunchy on the outside and smooth and almost custard-like inside. They are always powerfully flavoured with rum or, in some cases, *eau-de-vie*. Several colleagues rolled their eyes and threw up their hands when I mentioned that I was having difficulties making them. 'It has to be in your blood,' declared Phillippa Grogan, a friend who is herself an accomplished cook and the owner of a high-class bakery and *pâtisserie* in Melbourne.

Suitably challenged, I continued my experiments. Paula and I exchanged several e-mails and compared notes on the efficacy of using the traditional moulds versus silicone-moulded *canelé* sheets, whether or not a cook could hope to succeed with petits-fours-sized moulds (I knew that some cooks could, as I had enjoyed the results), time and temperature of baking, and methods of preparing the moulds. Through much trial and error, I discovered that attention to the details of *canelé*-making is very important.

After an initial success with the silicone sheets I rejected them, as each successive batch of the little cakes became more and more hourglass-shaped and they did not colour or caramelise as they ought. The copper moulds worked brilliantly, but so did cheaper non-stick moulds, which I found far easier to clean. Paula advised against washing copper moulds and suggested cleaning them with ketchup and kitchen paper. The non-stick moulds need to be washed in soapy water and thoroughly dried.

I baked and rebaked, working with three recipes. The one that came with the copper moulds I purchased at Bordeaux airport was the least successful (the *canelés* came out spongy and full of holes) and I dismissed it early on. Paula's recipe worked well and her cakes were the lightest and had the glossiest crust, although I did alter some of her baking and timing instructions (the recipe is on

CANELÉ OR CANNELÉ?
The making of canelés *clearly arouses strong emotions and is regarded by the Bordelais with great seriousness. There is even an association, the Confrérie du Canelé (Brotherhood of the Canelé), which was founded to protect the traditions associated with this little cake. My editor discovered a web site devoted to the* canelé *(http://perso.wanadoo. fr/gilles.castadere/Caneles-Bordelais) and it was by perusing this site that one of the other mysteries associated with the cake was explained to me. The origin of the name is the verb* canneler, *which means 'to flute, channel or groove', referring to the shape of the moulds used. But during my research I had found that some recipes spelled the name* canelé, *others* cannelé. *The author of the web site says this about the spelling:* 'Écrit originellement avec 2 "n", il en a perdu 1 (pour surprendre!) lors de la fondation de la Confrérie du Canelé le 24 mars 1985' *('Written originally with 2 n's, it lost 1 (surprise!) at the time of the founding of the Confrérie du Canelé on 24 March 1985').*

page 70). However, the best results were achieved with a recipe recommended by Phillippa and taken from a book on desserts by Michel Roux, in which he credits the recipe to a pastry chef from the town of Libourne, east of Bordeaux. It resulted in cakes that slipped easily from the moulds and had a smooth texture.

And then, just as I was putting away my moulds with a sense of relief, Phillippa telephoned with the news that she had a 'new' recipe and it was just marvellous, very straightforward and the cakes tasted superb. I had to try it, and am so pleased I did – it was the nearest to the taste memory I could conjure up. The recipe is below.

When I wish to make large sized *canelés* I use my non-stick moulds, which each hold approximately 90 ml (3 fl oz) batter. The small copper ones hold 30 ml (1 fl oz) batter. The rules that I regard as essential are these:

1. Do not use a convection oven, as the forced air seems to encourage the cakes to 'escape' from their moulds rather than rising gently and evenly.

2. Grease your moulds exceptionally well. A mixture of sweet almond oil and melted butter seems to work better than just butter, but if no almond oil is available, double-butter the moulds as described below. (Michel Roux recommends a mixture of beeswax and melted butter, but I could not locate a supplier of pure beeswax and I didn't think my readers would be able to either.)

3. For the last 15 minutes of baking, cover the cakes loosely with a sheet of foil to prevent any charring of the top.

Le Canelé

This is the recipe Phillippa Grogan recommended as the best one of all. It is from Régis Marcon, winner of the 1995 Bocuse d'Or international cookery competition. Phillippa said that the batter improves with standing around – she made a batch of cakes on each of four days and says the best batch was baked on day four! She and I both adjusted the baking temperature from the original.

Makes 12 large-sized cakes

125 g/4½ oz plain/all-purpose flour
250 g/9 oz castor/superfine sugar
1 egg
2 egg yolks
1½ tablespoons rum
1 drop pure vanilla extract
500 ml/17½ fl oz milk
60 g/2 oz unsalted butter

Mix the flour and sugar in a food processor. In a separate bowl, lightly whisk together all the other ingredients except the butter. With the motor running, pour the egg mixture into the food processor. Pour the batter into a bowl and leave for 24 hours.

Preheat a non-fanforced oven to 180°C/375°F. Brush your moulds with some of the butter, then invert them on a baking sheet and chill for 30 minutes. Barely melt the rest of the butter and use this to grease the chilled moulds again. Fill the moulds with batter to within 2 mm/¹⁄₁₀ in of the tops of the moulds. Bake for 1 hour and 15 minutes. Turn out at once.

Paula Wolfert's Canelés de Bordeaux

Makes 10 large-sized or approximately
25 petits-fours-sized cakes

375 ml/1¾ cups milk
190 g/1 scant cup castor/superfine
  sugar
115 g/¾ cup plain/all-purpose flour
pinch of salt
30 g/1 oz unsalted butter, diced
4 large egg yolks
3 tablespoons/¼ cup whipping
  cream
3 teaspoons rum *or* eau-de-vie
few drops of pure vanilla extract

As noted on page 68, I have made minor adjustments to Paula's baking and timing instructions.

Prepare the batter 1–2 days in advance of baking. Bring the milk to scalding point (84°C/180°F) in a saucepan. Meanwhile, combine the sugar, flour and salt in the bowl of a food processor and process briefly. Scatter the butter bits on top and process again briefly. Lightly whisk the egg yolks with the cream, add to the flour mixture and process briefly, stopping the motor before the batter forms a ball. With the motor running, quickly and steadily add the hot milk. Pour the mixture immediately through a sieve set over a bowl. Stir in the rum and vanilla and allow to cool. Cover and refrigerate for 24 hours.

When you are ready to cook, preheat a non-fanforced oven to 200°C/400°F. Spray the interior of your chosen moulds very well with non-stick baking spray or brush them with melted butter or a mixture of oil and butter. Invert them on a tray lined with kitchen paper for 5 minutes. Give the batter a gentle mix, but do not agitate it or you will create air bubbles. Fill each mould nearly to the top, leaving just 3 mm/⅑ in. Bake the *canelés* for 30 minutes, then turn the tray 180 degrees. At this point, if you are making full-sized *canelés*, bake them for a further 25 minutes, then cover the cakes loosely with foil to prevent any charring of the tops and bake for a further 15 minutes. If you are making petits-fours-sized *canelés*, bake them for a further 20 minutes.

Remove the *canelés* from the oven and turn out at once onto a wire rack. Allow to cool a little and harden (the outside should be crunchy). Serve warm.

Paula's tips

1. After a few hours at room temperature, the *canelés* will become soft. Crisp them by putting them in a 225°C/425°F oven for 5 minutes and allowing them to cool.
2. Baked *canelés* can be frozen, wrapped individually. To serve, unwrap and put the frozen *canelés* in the oven at 250°C/475°F for 5 minutes. Remove from the oven and rest for 30 minutes. Return to the oven for another 5 minutes, then allow to cool.
3. Before using copper moulds for the first time, season them generously with sweet almond oil (or another neutral basting oil) and put them in the oven at 180°C/375°F for 1 hour.
4. Never wash or scrub the insides of copper moulds. To remove any debris, put them in a hot oven (200°C/400°F) for 15 minutes. When they are cool enough to handle, scrub away the debris with kitchen paper.

OPPOSITE, TOP LEFT I find *canelés* difficult to remove from copper moulds such as these, even after double-greasing. There are all sorts of *trucs* suggested. My own is to use non-stick moulds – less decorative, but cheaper too!
OPPOSITE, TOP RIGHT *Canelé* batter must rest for at least 12 hours before you fill the twice-buttered moulds.
OPPOSITE, BOTTOM LEFT The little cakes rise considerably in the oven and larger *canelés* will take at least an extra 15 minutes to achieve the deep bronze colour desired.
OPPOSITE, BOTTOM RIGHT The finished products should have a gloss and crunch on the outside once they have cooled a little. They are at their best 10 or 15 minutes after unmoulding.

Velouté of Batavia or Escarole Lettuce and Radish Tops

Serves 6

1.5 litres/2½ pints water
3 large potatoes, cut into 4 cm dice
fresh tops of 1 bunch radishes,
    washed (total weight
    approximately 200 g)
200 g/7 oz salad greens (see recipe
    introduction), washed and roughly
    chopped
150 g/5 oz trimmed sorrel leaves
    (stalks removed), roughly chopped
1 bay leaf
150 ml/5 fl oz pouring cream
freshly ground black pepper
sea salt
60 g/2 oz unsalted butter

The Batavian endive or escarole salad vegetable is not seen very often in Australia, but it is one of my favourites. In France it is opened out on the market stalls to display its gold and pale green interior in the same way as the French display the heart of the more 'bitey' *chicorée frisée*. Both vegetables are blanched during the growing period – that is, light is excluded from them to keep the centres pale and tender. Escarole has broader leaves with a slightly frilly edge. It is very crunchy and stands up well to being tossed with warm ingredients without wilting into a tired heap.

There is enormous confusion in both French and English over the names of these salad vegetables. In France what is called *escarole* or *Batavia* might be called Batavian endive in English, while in some Italian shops in Australia the same thing might be called Romagna. It is closely related to the more bitter salad vegetable known in France as *chicorée frisée* or simply *frisée*, but sold in Australia as curly endive or, sometimes, frisee. But in France *endive* means what we know as witlof and Americans know as Belgian endive!

This soup is an excellent way to utilise the coarse leaves of any variety of lettuce. Other green leaves could be added or substituted: silver beet, rainbow chard, turnip tops, watercress, and so on.

Put the water, potato, radish tops, salad greens, sorrel and bay leaf into a large pot, cover and simmer gently for 1 hour. Extract the bay leaf and discard. Purée the soup in a food processor, then strain back into the pan through a coarse strainer. Return to simmering point, add the cream and adjust the seasoning. Just before serving, stir in the butter.

PREVIOUS PAGES Pink and white French radishes are deliciously spicy and crunchy. I just love biting a radish in half, adding a smear of unsalted butter and a single flake of sea salt and eating it – and continuing like this through an entire bunch.

La Soupe de lapin avec sa fricassée

RABBIT SOUP WITH ITS FRICASSÉE

Serves 4–6

2 × 1.5 kg/3 lb farmed rabbits
1 leek
1 stick celery, with leaves attached
2 carrots, peeled and diced
2 turnips, peeled and diced
2 potatoes, peeled and diced
2 cloves garlic, chopped
1 tablespoon plain/all-purpose flour
2.5 litres/4½ pints water
1 large onion, stuck with 2 cloves
1 bouquet garni (thyme, bay leaf, parsley stalks)
sea salt
freshly ground black pepper
6 slices substantial bread

Fricassée
reserved onion
30 g/1 oz bacon *or* pancetta
reserved celery leaves (optional)
reserved rabbit's kidneys
1 tablespoon reserved rendered rabbit fat *or* rendered duck or pork fat

In the past, a hearty soup such as this might well be the only dish served at an evening meal other than a salad and maybe a piece of fruit. The portions were quite large and the custom of ladling the soup over a thick slice of bread meant that the dish became a substantial one.

For this soup, you need the forequarters and kidneys of the rabbits, plus trimmings from the ribcages and belly flaps. Joint the rabbits, removing the legs and saddles (reserve these for use in another dish – for example, see pages 156 and 246). Pull out the kidneys and remove the soft fat around them and chop it. With kitchen scissors, trim away the rabbits' belly flaps and any excess bony ribcage bits. Chop each forequarter into 3 or 4 pieces.

Discard the dark green part of the leek and slit the remainder lengthwise, leaving the leaves attached to the root end. Turn the leek 90 degrees and slit again. Hold it under running water and rub firmly to dislodge any dirt. Cut off and discard the root end. Pat the leek dry and slice across into dice. Remove the leaves from the celery stick and reserve them, then dice the celery.

Put the soft rabbit fat into a heavy-based soup pot (4 litres/3½ quarts in capacity) and render over gentle heat for 1–2 minutes. The fat pieces will become golden and crispy and the fat will run quite quickly. Scoop out the crispy bits and set aside. Reserve 1 tablespoon of the rendered fat for the fricassée.

In the same pot, sauté the rabbit forequarter pieces over medium heat until they are well browned, then remove to a plate. Do this in 2 batches if the pan is not very wide. Add the leek, celery, carrot, turnip, potato and garlic and sauté, stirring regularly, until they start to colour. Sprinkle on the flour and gradually add the water, stirring until smooth. Return the rabbit pieces and any juices to the pan, along with the onion and the bouquet garni. Add some salt and pepper, then cover and simmer for 1 hour.

Carefully lift the rabbit pieces out of the pot with a slotted spoon and set aside. When the rabbit pieces are cool enough to handle, strip off all the meaty bits and return them to the soup pot with the simmering vegetables. Simmer for another hour, removing the onion when the potato is cooked. Remove and discard the cloves from the onion and set it aside for the fricassée.

To make the fricassée, chop the onion, bacon and celery leaves and slice the kidneys. Sauté the bacon in the reserved rabbit fat (or duck or pork fat) for 1 minute. Add the onion, kidney and celery leaves and sauté, stirring often. When the fricassée is well coloured, tip it into the soup and adjust the seasoning to taste. Simmer for 10 minutes.

To serve, preheat wide soup bowls and put 1 slice of bread in each. Ladle the soup over the bread and eat immediately.

Vegetable Soup for André

When Henriette was recounting her and André's favourite evening meal, she described a soup very like this one. André has diabetes and has some trouble digesting chunky foods, so a substantial soup that slides down easily, yet is full of nourishment, is their preferred choice. This recipe is loosely based on *la panade de légumes*, as set down by La Mazille, which she suggests is an ideal dish for fragile stomachs.

Make no mistake: this is *une soupe*, not *un potage* (see page 65). It is very thick, a real rib-sticker and quite marvellous. It even resembles the countryside – all speckled brown and green, with dark fragments contributed by the famous du Puy lentils from the Auvergne. If it is too powerful for your household, you can, of course, add more water.

Du Puy lentils, once only available in Australia as an expensive import, are now being grown successfully in the Wimmera in Victoria. They have an intense flavour and keep their shape when cooked, making them ideal to serve in salads or as a garnish for poultry or game.

Soak the lentils in water for 2–3 hours, then drain and rinse. Bring 3 litres/5⅓ pints of clean water and the ham bone to a boil in a large pot (5–6 litres/4½–5 quarts in capacity) with the bouquet garni. Skim. Add the beans, lentils and garlic and simmer very gently, covered, for 1 hour, skimming once or twice. Add the potato, carrot, turnip, celeriac and bread and simmer for a further hour.

Test to see that everything is very tender. Remove and discard the ham bone and bouquet garni. Add the peas and simmer for 15 minutes or until cooked. Pass the soup through the coarse disc of a food mill, pressing firmly to extract as much flavour as possible. Taste and adjust the seasoning and serve at once.

Makes 10 generous portions

200 g/7 oz lentils (preferably du Puy)
water
1 ham bone
1 bouquet garni (thyme, bay leaf, parsley stalks)
200 g/7 oz haricot beans, soaked overnight, drained and rinsed
4 cloves garlic, peeled
200 g/7 oz potatoes, diced
200 g/7 oz carrots, diced
150 g/5 oz turnip, diced
150 g/5 oz celeriac, diced
150 g/5 oz pain de campagne or good sourdough, cut into cubes
300 g/10½ oz shelled fresh peas or 100 g/3½ oz dehydrated peas
sea salt
freshly ground black pepper

Stephanie's Cassoulet

Serves 12 generously

1 kg/2 lb haricot beans, soaked
    overnight
4 tablespoons rendered duck *or*
    pork fat
1 fresh pork neck
1 kg/2 lb skinned, boned salted
    belly pork
3 fresh pork hocks
freshly ground black pepper
5 litres/4½ quarts veal stock
1 cup chopped, seeded tomato
    (fresh *or* canned)
2 whole heads garlic, unpeeled
1 bouquet garni (thyme, bay leaf,
    parsley stalks)
rind from ½ loin of pork, left in
    1 piece
4 large onions, chopped
6 medium carrots, peeled and
    chopped
250 g/9 oz minced pork fat, worked
    with 1 tablespoon chopped garlic
sea salt (optional)
2 boiling sausages
12 confit duck legs, skinned (reserve
    the skin)
2 cups fresh white breadcrumbs

PREVIOUS PAGES The ingredients for a fine
cassoulet: fresh pork, sausage, rolled
pork rind, *confit* duck legs, aromatics
and the all-important beans.

Here is my own tried and true recipe of the most famous of the many bean dishes of the south-west. There are as many versions as there are cooks, and the renowned *cassoulet* towns of Toulouse, Castelnaudary and Carcassonne all include significant variations. In ordinary households beans will often be the mainstay of the meal, but a *cassoulet* is always special and will be prepared with a wide variety of meats. La Sobronade (see page 82) is an example of a more everyday bean stew.

Little nuggets of gelatinous pork rind are to be found in many bean recipes. Rolled, trimmed pork rind, already cooked in pork fat, is widely available in south-west markets and butchers' stalls, but in Australia your butcher may need advance notice to supply it. For further information about preserved pork rind, turn to page 314.

Instead, you might want to stir in a spoonful of 'Gascony butter' or *hachis*, a pounded mixture of fresh garlic, pork fat and parsley. (This mixture is sold at French local markets and has many other uses in soups, stews and stuffings.) A further option is to transfer cooked, drained beans, with or without meat or extra vegetables, to an earthenware gratin dish, add a layer of coarse breadcrumbs, drizzle over some of the reserved cooking juices and return the beans to a moderate oven until the crust is golden brown.

I find it simplest to cook this dish in a large, deep baking dish or, failing that, a stockpot, and then to assemble the *cassoulet* in two or more deep pottery casseroles for serving. If you do not have anything large enough for the initial cooking, either halve the quantities of ingredients or divide the ingredients and cook the *cassoulet* in two separate pots. It can simmer either on top of the stove or in a moderate oven (180°C/350°F), again depending on your facilities.

Drain the beans, then put them in a saucepan and barely cover with cold water. Bring to simmering point and simmer for 10 minutes. Drain and rinse in a colander. Set aside.

In your selected pot or pan, heat half the duck fat until it is rippling. Brown the pork neck, then the belly pork and then the hocks, removing each piece of meat to an oven tray as it has been browned. Return the browned meats to the pot, grind over a generous amount of black pepper and pour over the stock. Add the tomato, garlic and bouquet garni and lay the sheet of pork rind on top. Simmer for 1 hour (or cook for 1 hour in an oven that has been preheated to 180°C/350°F).

Meanwhile, lightly brown the onion and carrot in batches in the remaining duck fat. After the meats have simmered for 1 hour, add the sautéed onion and carrot, the beans and the paste of pork fat and garlic. Simmer for a further 45 minutes, then test to see if the beans are tender. If not, continue to simmer until they are cooked.

Remove the pieces of meat to an oven tray. When cool enough to handle, remove and discard the skin from the pork hock and chop all the meat into chunks. Cut the pork rind into thin strips, about 1 cm × 6 cm/½ in × 2½ in. Fish out from the pot the whole heads of garlic and squeeze them through a coarse sieve, letting the garlic purée drop back into the beans and juices. Taste the juices for seasoning and add a little salt if necessary.

Bring a saucepan of water to the boil, then reduce to a bare simmer. Drop in the sausages and cook for 30 minutes to 1 hour depending on the variety. Lift out and, when cool enough to handle, remove the skin and slice thickly.

To assemble the *cassoulet*, settle a layer of the beans and vegetables on the bottom of your serving dish or dishes. Scatter over half the meats and sausage slices and some strips of pork rind, so that guests serving themselves will find a selection. Add some more beans and vegetables. Scatter over the remaining meats and sausage slices and more pork strips. Poke in the duck legs and cover with the rest of the beans and vegetables. Now ladle over the juices to come almost to the top of the dish. Cover with a thick layer of breadcrumbs and then moisten the crumbs with a little more juice. Reheat slowly in a moderate oven (180°C/350°F) for at least 45 minutes. Serve as soon as the juices are bubbling and the crust is a deep-gold colour.

Put the reserved duck skin on an oven tray lined with baking paper. Crisp in a moderate oven and crumble over a green salad for a delectable and perfect accompaniment to *cassoulet*. Any excess beans and juices can be served a few days later (when the memory of the *cassoulet* has faded a little) as a gratin on the side of some other dish.

Note
Some cooks insist on pushing the crust of the *cassoulet* down into the juices once or twice and waiting for the crust to re-form. I prefer not to do this as it can make the *cassoulet* stodgy – each time the crust is pushed down, more juices are absorbed.

La Sobronade

HARICOT-BEAN SOUPY STEW

Serves 8

250 g/9 oz haricot beans, soaked
    overnight
450 g/1 lb belly pork, skinned, boned
    and diced
cold water
1 tablespoon rendered pork or
    duck fat
1 turnip, peeled and cut into
    1 cm/½ in dice
1 onion, chopped
3 carrots, peeled and cut into
    1 cm/½ in dice
500 g/1 lb 2 oz celeriac, cut into
    1 cm/½ in dice
1 bouquet garni (thyme, bay leaf,
    parsley stalks)
2 × 250 g/9 oz Toulouse sausages or
    other fresh, pure pork sausages
350 g/12½ oz waxy potatoes, peeled
2 cloves garlic
4 tablespoons fresh, young parsley
    (preferably flat-leaf)
sea salt
freshly ground black pepper

On pages 80–1 is my recipe for *cassoulet*, the ultimate haricot-bean dish. Here is a simpler bean dish. I have tried but failed to find the actual meaning of the word *sobronade* and a French-speaking friend could not find the word in any of his dictionaries or encyclopedias either. A search of the Internet yielded a single response under 'La gastronomie (Périgord et Quercy)': '*La sobronade est une soupe épaisse où se mélangent jambon, porc, haricots blancs et oignons*' ('*La sobronade* is a thick soup that blends ham, pork, white haricot beans and onions'). La Mazille describes the dish as a soup, but one so thick that you can stand a spoon in it. Other writers have suggested it is more like a stew.

Drain and rinse the beans, then put them into a large pot with the belly pork. Add cold water to come 2 cm/1 in above the beans. Bring slowly to a boil, then skim and reduce to a simmer.

Meanwhile, heat the pork fat in a frying pan and sauté the turnip, onion, carrot and celeriac until just starting to colour. Add these vegetables to the simmering beans with the bouquet garni. Cover and simmer very gently for 1 hour.

Cook the sausages in the same frying pan you used for the vegetables, without additional fat, for a few minutes to 'stiffen' them. Cut the sausages and potatoes into 4 cm/1½ in chunks and add to the beans. Simmer for 30 minutes, uncovered. At this stage the bean mixture should still be very moist but not sloppy. If it is looking at all dry, add a little hot water. Chop the garlic with the parsley and stir into the pot. Taste and adjust the seasoning.

Allow the dish to stand for 20 minutes before serving – it will continue to thicken up. La Mazille advises that dishes such as this one would traditionally have been served over bread.

Seven-hour Leg of Lamb with Anchovy and Garlic

Once upon a time this dish was probably cooked in the communal village oven after all the bread had been baked and the oven was cooling down. A relic of the past, you might think – but it fits perfectly into a modern lifestyle. After 20 minutes' preparation you can put the sealed pot into the oven and leave it untouched for 7 hours. At the end of the cooking time, you will have a succulent and most beautifully perfumed piece of meat that slips from the bone at the first touch of a knife. It is reminiscent of the roast lamb my mother used to cook (see page 54).

A 'Frenched' leg of lamb refers to the way in which the butcher cuts off the knobby end of the shank bone and a little of the shank meat to leave a clean bone protruding, which can later be grasped for easy carving. A Frenched leg will also fit more neatly into a lidded casserole dish, an essential item for this recipe.

Select an ovenproof dish that will hold the meat snugly and has a tight-fitting lid. An oval-shaped, enamelled cast-iron pot is ideal. If your dish is round, test it by forcing the meat in before you start any further preparation. If the lid does not close completely, choose another pot.

Preheat the oven to 120°C/250°F. Pat the anchovy fillets free of excess oil and cut each one into 3 pieces. With a sharp knife, make 12 incisions deep in the meat on both sides of the leg of lamb. Force 1 piece of anchovy and 1 piece of garlic into each incision. Grind over some pepper and rub the joint with a little salt. Heat the olive oil in a heavy-based frying pan and seal the lamb on all sides until it is a rich golden brown. Put the pork rind in your selected pot, fat-side down. Add the bouquets garnis and the lamb, then pour over the stock and wine. Put on the lid. In a small bowl, mix the flour and water to a paste. Smear this paste around the join where the lid fits into the pot, to seal it well. Be generous with this step and enjoy it! Stand the pot on a baking tray to catch any drips and put it in the oven. Forget about it for 7 hours.

When ready to serve, remove the pot from the oven. It is most spectacular to crack the sealing crust at the table, but be careful – the pot will be very hot. Lift out the meat and transfer to a hot serving dish. Pour the collected juices into a jug. Cut a little of the pork rind into small slivers so that diners can enjoy its succulence. Gently carve the meat (it will be very tender and will break up). Moisten it generously with the cooking juices and serve with something comforting, such as *l'aligot* (page 131), potatoes with dried or fresh *cèpes* (pages 171 and 173), or separately baked potatoes and whole garlic, as pictured opposite. To follow, I particularly enjoy a soft-leaved green salad turned in the juices left on my plate.

Serves 6

4 anchovy fillets
1 × 1.8–2 kg/4–4½ lb leg of lamb, Frenched
3 large cloves garlic, peeled and quartered
freshly ground black pepper
sea salt
1 tablespoon olive oil
1 × 200 g/7 oz piece of pork rind, with 5 mm/¼ in of fat attached
2 bouquets garnis (thyme, bay leaf, parsley stalks, small piece of celery)
250 ml/9 fl oz full-flavoured veal, lamb or chicken stock
250 ml/9 fl oz dry white wine
1 cup plain/all-purpose flour
125 ml/4½ fl oz water

Les Jacques

APPLE PANCAKES, PÉRIGORD STYLE

Makes 6–8

2 eating apples
1 tablespoon eau-de-vie de prune
   (preferably La Vieille Prune)
unsalted butter *or* rendered duck fat
sugar

Batter
1¼ cups plain/all-purpose flour
pinch of salt
150 ml/5 fl oz milk
150 ml/5 fl oz water
1 teaspoon eau-de-vie de prune
   (preferably La Vieille Prune)
2 large eggs, lightly whisked

An essential ingredient for many of the very simple country desserts in Périgord is a slosh of one of the potent liqueurs or *eaux-de-vie* distilled from a wide range of fruits and berries. The bone-dry, super-charged aroma is so true to the fruit used that a small amount goes a long way. Probably the most famous is *poire William*, distilled in Alsace. We visited an artisanal house at Montech where the owner, M. Jean Delpont, proudly showed us stacked crates of William pears ready for distilling into his own *poire William*. I purchased a bottle of La Vieille Prune, an outstanding *eau-de-vie de prune* made by the Louis Roque Distillerie (see page 151) in the lovely town of Souillac. In New Zealand you can obtain high-quality *eau-de-vie* distilled by Prenzel (see 'A South-West Pantry' for contact details).

This recipe is not intended to produce thin, lacy crêpes. Rather, these are relatively thick pancakes, even a touch leathery, but with wonderful crispy edges. *Les Jacques* are usually served one to a portion and flat, with the apple slices (which still have texture) uppermost. A final sprinkling of sugar adds crunch.

You could substitute Armagnac or Calvados for the *eau-de-vie de vieille prune*. My *eau-de-vie* was 42 per cent proof.

Peel, core and thinly slice the apples. Turn them in the *eau-de-vie* to coat, then set aside until needed.

To make the batter, put the flour and salt into a food processor. Mix the milk, water and *eau-de-vie* in a jug. With the motor running, add the eggs to the flour. Add half the milk mixture and beat really well. Stop the machine and scrape the sides of the bowl to ensure that there are no bits of flour adhering. Add the balance of the liquid and mix again. Let the batter rest for 2 hours.

Heat an 18 cm/7 in non-stick frying pan and brush it with a little butter. When the fat is sizzling, *slowly* ladle in enough batter to nearly cover the base (not as thinly as you would if making crêpes). By doing this slowly, the batter will start to set around the edges and you can make a pancake of about 16 cm/6 in diameter. As the edges start to look golden, carefully place 6–8 slices of apple on the uncooked part and dribble over another tablespoon of batter. Adjust the heat so that the pancake is cooking steadily and leave for 4 minutes. Slip a wide lifter under the pancake and turn it over. Cook for 3 minutes, then turn out onto a warmed plate so that the scorched slices of apple are showing. Scatter with sugar and serve.

Henriette's Wafer Biscuits Over the Coals

LES GAUFRES

Henriette's wafer-biscuit press had an intricate pattern on each side and very long handles for use over an open fire. My first tests of this recipe, back home in Australia, were made using an electric waffle iron. The waffles were thick and heavy and I was certainly not able to roll them. Then I remembered an Austrian gadget inherited from my mother among her eclectic collection of kitchen tools. I rummaged and found it: a much smaller, but very similar, wafer-biscuit press to the one Henriette had used. Mine had a diameter of 11 cm (4 in) and even had the same pattern. Now I was in business! The wafer biscuits cooked in this press came out as thin as *tuiles*, those thin biscuits often served with ice-cream. *Les gaufres* are perfect with a glass of dessert wine or as an accompaniment to ice-cream or other creamy desserts that would benefit from a bit of crunch.

Sift the flour and salt into a bowl. Whisk the eggs with the sugar until thick, then beat in the cooled butter and the water or liqueur. Fold in the sifted flour.

Prepare your work surface. Have ready a large sheet of foil, a knife and a jug of warm water with 2 dessertspoons resting in it. The knife is needed to quickly scrape the edges of the press (which will be held over the foil for a moment) to remove any excess batter that oozes out and will burn. There will be a good deal of dripping of batter from the spoons. The water and the foil will deal with most of the mess.

Heat a wafer-biscuit press to very hot. Grease it lightly with the pork fat or buttered paper and, holding it over the foil on your work surface, spoon 1 dessertspoon of batter onto one side. Close it firmly, scrape away any ooze and put one side to the flame for 25 seconds. Turn the other side to the flame for a little less time (say, 20 seconds) and then remove from the fire. Tip the wafer biscuit out and at once roll it loosely around a piece of dowel or the handle of a wooden spoon. After a few seconds, slip the wafer biscuit off the dowel and leave it to cool completely. Continue in this way until all the batter is used.

Variation

If you do not have access to a special wafer-biscuit press, line a baking tray/sheet with greaseproof paper and, using the back of a spoon, spread the batter into 10–12 cm/4–5 in circles on the tray. Bake at 180°C/375°F for about 5 minutes until golden brown at the edges. Leave for a few moments and then roll around the handle of a wooden spoon or slip over a curved bottle for a traditional *tuile* shape.

Makes 6–8 using an electric waffle iron or 20 using an iron press

200 g/7 oz plain/all-purpose flour
tiny pinch of salt
3 large, farm-fresh eggs
150 g/5 oz castor/superfine sugar
125 g/4½ oz unsalted butter, melted and cooled
1 tablespoon water (*or* brandy *or* orange-flower water *or* eau-de-vie)
small piece of pork fat (*or* a buttered or oiled piece of kitchen paper)

Quince Jam as Described by La Mazille

'This jam presents as beautiful chunks of amber bathed in a red jelly and is of a remarkable finesse,' says La Mazille in *La Bonne Cuisine du Périgord*. I was impatient to try it once the quince season arrived. I have translated and paraphrased La Mazille's recipe, with a few additions and comments of my own regarding the size of the fruit and testing the jelly in the usual manner. Her 'jam' ends up rather like a Greek 'spoon sweet' – chunks of quince with wonderful crunch from the retained core, and a thick red–amber syrup.

Take ripe quinces, wash and dry them. Do not peel or core the fruit. Cut each fruit into 6–8 pieces depending on size. [All the quinces I saw in France were considerably smaller than those we see in Australia. I cut my Australian quinces in half and then cut each half into 6 pieces, making 12 pieces from a single fruit.] Put them into a copper jam-making pan [or a large stainless steel pot] and cover with cold water. Cook until the quinces are very tender.

Remove the fruit, weigh it and take the same weight of sugar. Put the sugar into the liquid in the pan, stir until the sugar has completely melted and then bring to a boil. Throw in the fruit and skim. Cook over a moderate heat for approximately 45 minutes, skimming several times, or until the fruit is just starting to break and the liquid sets to a jelly when tested on a cold saucer. Let it cool a little before bottling into clean, sterilised jars. Seal at once. Enjoy with yoghurt, crème fraîche or the very best cream.

Autumn Notebooks

*A*s a child I was enthralled reading of the country house parties that featured in many English crime stories – the body in the library or conservatory and other permutations on the theme! I found the interaction between the characters fascinating and the rituals that marked the day – breakfast, croquet, 'tea', preparing a bath, dressing for dinner, and so on – often surprising but always intensely interesting. Because of this, re-creating in some way the sort of environment where anything might happen is, for me, a very exciting project.

Hosting or participating in a house party in a foreign country is a wonderful way to experience another culture. Essential ingredients are friends who are comfortable with each other, tolerant of each other's foibles, interested in their environment and in new experiences and always ready to laugh. The October 2000 house party at Lavalade was my sixth such adventure and, apart from myself, the participants were my personal assistant, Anna Dollard, friends Angela and Duffy Clemens and Maggie and Colin Beer, cheese expert Will Studd and his wife, Bonnie, special friend Julie Gibbs and photographer Simon Griffiths.

We all had different things to do while we were there. My task was to work on this book, completing the necessary research and cooking lots of food, refining the recipes and working with Simon on photographing the dishes. Anna and Julie had been involved in planning the trip since early on. Anna had searched out a suitable house to rent – a task of primary importance – and located relevant maps, as well as establishing on-the-ground contacts and attending to a thousand other important details. Julie, who has a great eye for lovely plates and linens and bits on which to display food, was in charge of sourcing props for the photographs, including antique-shop research and borrowings. Simon established indoor and outdoor 'studios' and was reassuringly laid-back about his stuff being swept aside when we needed the table for lunch or dinner.

Maggie and Colin were supposed to be relaxing, but found this hard to do – Maggie was a great friend in the kitchen and cooked some fantastic food, while Colin, with his professional interest in game breeding, scoured the countryside looking at birds (the feathered variety) and interesting agricultural machinery. Will, a regular visitor to Europe, indulged us all with a nightly 'cheesefest' that often featured cheeses unobtainable in Australia. Bonnie searched our immediate surroundings hoping for significant finds of *cèpes*, but in vain. She did, however, keep

OPPOSITE Angela, Maggie, Julie, Colin and I toast the house party over lunch in the garden. When we arrived at Lavalade, the ground was already thick with fallen leaves. As the days passed, the weather became crisper and soon it was too cold to eat outside.

the kitchen stocked with fresh chestnuts and walnuts. Angie and Duffy were the walkers and shoppers and our 'reality check'. They always had time for a long walk, an apéritif at the local bar or helping with the dishes. Great friends, all of them!

The adventure began with Will and me meeting Simon at Toulouse airport, where we picked up our car and set out immediately to meet Jean and Lorraine Lagarde, an experience described on pages 142–8. Three days later our task was to shop till we dropped for perishables – cheese, meat and poultry – at the excellent market at Montauban's Place Nationale and then to start some serious driving in order to be united with the rest of the group. As we drove from Montauban to Lavalade, the car bursting with our combined luggage and the food, I imagined the other house guests also on their way: some still in the air from Australia, some on the fast train from Paris, others already in the region and on their way to meet the train. It was an exciting feeling.

I had compiled a four-page shopping list for the obliging Angie and Duffy, whose holiday had commenced one week earlier not too far away. They were to arrive with dry goods and fruit and vegetables. I wondered how they would manage with all of this plus collecting Maggie and Colin, and their luggage, from the Paris train at Angoulême, a two-hour drive from the house. I need not have given it a thought. The resourceful Clemenses had already driven past the house, estimated the distance and decided to leave the shopping at Simply Périgord, the house rental agency, to be collected later.

Three hours after leaving Montauban we arrived at Lavalade. The house, chosen sight unseen from the agency catalogue, had heavy wooden doors less than a metre from the country lane, but behind this rather abrupt entrance was a lovely surprise: a delightful house with spacious living and cooking areas, sufficient bedrooms and bathrooms to accommodate the ten of us comfortably and, through wide French doors, a sunny courtyard and rambling garden. Beyond this were mind-soothing vistas of farmland and rolling hills.

Anna, Julie and Bonnie, the first arrivals, had arranged purple buddleia and pink roses and autumn leaves to greet us. It had been a major organisational effort not only to gather us all here (with only three items of lost luggage) but to arrange supplies, such as boxes of handpicked local wines and thick linen tablecloths from a roadside *brocante* warehouse, and an introduction to an obliging antique dealer who would help us with beautiful plates for photography. We had two cars bulging with shopping: in one, fruit and vegetables from Le Bugue market, and in the other, fresh pork, *confit*, aromatic cheeses and new season's pink garlic from Montauban market. I had packed insulated bags and sachets of gel ice to ensure that the food travelled well.

Dinner on the first evening was simple: roasted farm chicken with plenty of that pink garlic and fresh bay leaves, potatoes and baby beans the size of my little finger. We all went early to bed – the adventures could start tomorrow.

OPPOSITE, TOP LEFT Pink roses and buddleia had been put in a vase to welcome us. There were plenty of late roses still in bloom, tumbling over doorways or rambling on trellises against weathered stone walls.

OPPOSITE, TOP RIGHT I flung my bedroom window at Lavalade wide each evening to enjoy the crisp night air. The only disadvantage was that I heard the calls of the rooster and nearby donkey loud and clear very early each morning.

OPPOSITE, BOTTOM LEFT This heavy linen and worn cutlery were 'finds' at the *brocante* market at Le Bugue. There seemed to be an inexhaustible supply of magnificent tablecloths, bedsheets, curtains and table napery at these markets.

OPPOSITE, BOTTOM RIGHT There were fine local wines to learn about and to enjoy, including the south-western appellations of Bergerac and Montravel.

OVERLEAF A Citroën 2CV was parked outside a neighbour's house at Lavalade, near walls draped in a thick curtain of Virginia creeper. There are still plenty of these bouncy little cars around. They are affectionately known as *deux chevaux* (meaning 'two horses') and first came onto the market in 1949. Apparently the 2CV was designed as a simple vehicle for farmers and one of its design specifications was that it be able to 'cross a ploughed field without breaking any eggs carried in a basket'.

Working and Eating

Making and photographing the dishes for a book is not as simple as it might sound. Experience has shown that it takes a long time to set up each shot, not to mention the time first of all to cook the dish. Processes often have to be repeated, quantities must be altered to make a dish of the correct size for the chosen plate, slices of meat have to be cut just so, loaves of bread must be ripped apart to scatter the scene with crumbs, stuffed birds may need to be sliced to display the stuffing, or a dish may have to be 'brutalised' in some other way. Sauces must be kept to one side and spooned just as the shutter clicks; occasionally step-by-step photographs are necessary – and so on and so on. I started early each morning, cutting, peeling, chopping while the rest of the household busied themselves in various ways: reading, walking, touring, scouring the house for props or, in Maggie's case, finding a spot where she could send e-mails to Australia and keep tabs on her many enterprises.

Being poultry farmers, among many other things, the Beers were particularly interested in the quality of the French birds and the farming methods used in the local industry. They planned to pay a visit to a farm to observe how the birds were raised and we started a game to see who could find the quirkiest duck or goose signage. Just down the road Colin had spied a large farm raising game birds (partridges and pheasants) that would later be released into the wild to accommodate the national passion for *la chasse* (hunting), and they resolved to investigate this, too.

Anna sat at the computer ready to record any changes in recipes – 'Was that one clove of garlic or two?' she would ask, checking against the early version already in the computer – and springing to the stone sink whenever the mountain of dirty dishes threatened to slide. The photographs took absolute priority for Simon and me and, while we all certainly hoped to eat what was still edible after the shoots, the team was ready to cook more, or something else, if there was nothing. In fact, almost all the food remained edible, and it was so good that we had to be very firm about holding the enthusiasts back until Simon pronounced that he was absolutely finished with it. The day's food then became our lunch or dinner, sometimes combined in different ways, or expanded.

On one occasion a stuffed cabbage extravaganza was cut into 10 generous wedges and accompanied by the marvellous potato dish *l'aligot*, whipped with generous amounts of cream, butter and *tomme fraîche de Cantal* (see page 131). The next day I made a huge pot of *le tourin*, the local onion soup served in many small restaurants (page 121). It has no cheese, but stirred-in egg whites separate into fine shreds giving the impression of cheese (for less cost, which I feel must have been a consideration in earlier times). I grilled some slices of dark *pain de*

OPPOSITE I cannot help being a kitchen romantic. Old pots, a waxed wooden table, shining shallots, a few prized *cèpes* and branches of gathered bay leaves just seem to fall into a still-life that reinforces the beauty of the everyday.

campagne and we commented on how the quality and character of the bread added a special note to the soup. White bread (which is referred to dismissively by the inimitable La Mazille as 'town bread') simply would not do this.

Other dishes included bean casseroles, creamy ham and cheese gratins, dumplings, birds of all sizes, and tarts, pancakes and fritters using autumnal fruits. A nearby quince tree yielded several small fruit that we thought we would cook with a game bird. I was intrigued by a recipe from La Mazille for quince jam (see page 90), but there was not enough fruit to try it. The small purple figs from an old untended tree became fritters for dinner (page 138). A curious sight before dusk each evening was our neighbour's hens roosting high in the fig tree.

This is hearty food, closely linked to the earth and its harvest and intended for a population that rose early, worked in the fields and came home for a substantial lunch with plenty of chewy bread, then did more physical work before a lighter evening meal and early to bed. We tried to compensate for our softer lifestyle by some vigorous country walks, but we did wake early, usually aroused by the 'sobbing' of a nearby donkey or the 'barking' of a turkey.

While dinner every evening had special emphasis due to my project, we had plenty of time for frivolity, too. There was the 'Night of the Eel', when a dinner guest went to top up her water glass only to retreat with piercing shrieks as two tails flapped at her from the water jug. Someone had slipped the sinuous creatures into the jug while the table was distracted. There were screams, recriminations, accusations and remorse and tears of laughter. Then there was the 'Song and Dance Night'. The red wines were so seductive on this particular evening that several guests took to singing and one of them was even seen doing the bossa nova with a broom!

And there was the 'Big Night', when we invited those outsiders who had helped the project in some important way to share the pork cooked with André's truffle (see page 281). We heard about the big storm of winter 1999–2000, when one couple had had to borrow a chainsaw and cut their way home through the fallen trees in fear of their lives as roofing flew through the air as easily as Mary Poppins and her brolly. All of the Dordogne had been without power for 17 days and we heard of freezers full of spoiled food. One of our guests said it had taken her a full nine months to be able to look without horror at a candle – which was just as well, because we had gone to a lot of trouble to create an autumnal centre-piece of candles jammed into a day-old baguette surrounded by autumn leaves and chestnuts and the occasional wild mushroom.

OPPOSITE The autumn colours deepened every few days on 'our' road near Lavalade. It was rare to meet anyone on our daily walks, although once or twice we exchanged a greeting with a farmer riding a tractor and once a red squirrel dashed across in front of us.

Sights

WALKS AND RIVER TRIPS

From our guidebook I learned of the network of long-distance walking trails – the *sentiers de grande randonnée*, or GRs for short – which cover some of the most glorious scenery in south-west France. These paths are marked with red and white signs. Each GR is described in a Topoguide, which has maps and details about camping sites, *refuges* and *rando-étapes* (inexpensive shelters) and is available in some bookshops and in larger tourist offices. Walkers take note: at the office at Le Bugue we obtained a useful folder that contained 10 or 12 separate small sheets describing walks in the area, with shelters and other points of interest noted. Each sheet was written in both French and English.

Duffy had bought the Séries Bleue 1936O and 1936ET maps, on which walking tracks were marked. As mentioned earlier (see page 25), these excellent maps have a scale of 1:25 000, or 1 cm to 250 m, and if you want to explore the myriad country lanes (and few have numbers), a Séries Bleue map of the region is absolutely vital. The alternative is a better-than-even chance of becoming hopelessly lost, as Julie and I had in the summer. These very minor roads all look the same and are so narrow that bushes brush the sides of the car. On that occasion we were returning from a simple dinner less than 2 km (1¼ miles) from our barn. The light had gone and all landmarks had disappeared. We vaguely glimpsed stone walls and houses and smelt cows, but saw no-one, nor did we meet another car. After half an hour we started to cross and recross a railway line and became quite alarmed. Eventually we found a sign and realised we had succeeded in achieving a large circle. Safely home, we agreed that a torch and a better map were essential and confessed we had both seriously wondered if we might have to spend the night in the car.

The GR6 was marked on our Séries Bleue map 1936ET and one day the more intrepid of the group (or those not involved in cooking and photography) walked 15 km (9 miles) along it from Le Bugue to Limeuil. On another day a less ambitious walk nearer to home ended at the local bar at Sainte Alvère, where the walkers enjoyed a reviving apéritif.

The trees bordering the rivers were just taking on their autumn colouring, tints of gold mingling with green. Both the Dordogne and the Vézère – another important river that flows into the Dordogne at the village of Limeuil – were shining bronze in the afternoon sunshine. Some of our group took to the Dordogne in canoes, which can be done at various landing stages. In summer you will often drive along the narrow roads behind a van towing a trailer laden with canoes. (Wooden barges also ply the river, so the less adventurous can still get out on the water.) Our canoeists started at La Roque Gageac and were swiftly out of sight, to be collected two hours later and returned to their car.

OPPOSITE, TOP LEFT This window has almost disappeared under the encroaching Virginia creeper.
OPPOSITE, TOP RIGHT Some of the house guests were eager to try the canoeing experience and reported that the river flowed very fast. Certainly they were quickly out of sight of the watchers on the banks.
OPPOSITE, BOTTOM LEFT Simon photographed another river view, this time of a wooden barge, from the ramparts of the castle at Beynac. Such barges – *les gabarres* – once carried freight but now carry tourists.
OPPOSITE, BOTTOM RIGHT This cheerfully painted little van was typical of the vehicles we shared the roads with. The driver always drove at a challenging speed, especially at midday, when it was time to head home to lunch or, as in this case, to get back to his restaurant for the lunch rush.

L'ACACIA

The robinia tree is known as l'acacia *in French and common English names are 'black locust' and 'false acacia'. In the springtime a French delicacy is* beignets d'acacia, *fritters made by dipping sprays of the tree's cream-coloured, pea-shaped flowers in a light batter, frying them in olive oil and serving them sprinkled with sugar. In at least one Australian cookery book I have seen cooks being encouraged to dip our own wattle flowers (the true acacia genus) in batter and fry them. This is not a good idea: I do not know if wattle flowers are dangerous to eat, but they are certainly not the flowers intended.*

OPPOSITE Here is one of the infrequently encountered tractor drivers, wearing a traditional beret. He made absolutely no attempt to hurry or pull over, rightly considering that he had prior claim to the road compared with mere tourists.
OVERLEAF These gorgeous scarlet–orange pumpkins lolled like garden gnomes in the vegetable patch of our neighbour's garden. Their flesh was far more vivid in colour than the varieties I am used to.

CHÂTEAU DE MARQUEYSSAC

A few days later we revisited the Château de Marqueyssac, last seen by Julie and me in high summer (see page 26). This time the pathways were scattered with pink–mauve wild cyclamen, a similar colour to that of the lime-washed shutters of the château. Its grounds are special in that they offer formal, trimmed box gardens, with wild gardens and walkways further away from the château that lead the visitor to an extraordinary view over the countryside. Just a few days had changed the colours. There was more gold in the forest, and here and there a pink tinge was appearing. We hoped we might even see the trees turn to flame before our holiday was over. The once lush stands of green corn were now golden and dried out and seen from above they resembled springy mattresses, standing high alongside harvested fields. As we travelled the roads we passed wooden structures containing tightly packed, stripped corn cobs, harvested and ready for winter feed, and heard the breeze rustling through the cornstalks.

FORESTS AND KITCHEN GARDENS

The forests were beautiful and somehow the foliage seemed gentle and feminine – clear colours, soft leaves with rounded shapes, delicate lichen on walls and boughs, and scrambling ivy tumbling over dry stone walls or encircling slender tree trunks. I identified oak, chestnut, hawthorn, maple and robinia (*acacia*) – such a contrast to our own angular eucalypts with their predominant colours of olive, silver-grey and ochre, and our bush with its open character and dry undergrowth of fallen bark that crunches underfoot.

The whole countryside was preparing for winter and the villages were quiet. Some of the houses were gloriously draped with crimson Virginia creeper. Firewood was stacked in mountainous heaps, smoke trailed from chimneys and the kitchen gardens had the last autumn tomatoes still hanging on blackened, bedraggled plants. In the garden beds I could see mostly cabbages, onions and garlic, and a few *salades*, with here and there the brilliant orange flash of pumpkins. Will is a keen vegetable gardener and was intrigued by one particular long-stemmed, cabbage-like vegetable. It resembled all the descriptions I had read of a very old variety of cabbage. Philip Oyler (see page 186) described it in his book *Feeding Ourselves* and identified it as the 'Jersey walking-stick cabbage'. He said it grows perfectly straight and the leaves are picked from the stem, always leaving a crown of green leaves at the top.

Almost every kitchen garden had a walnut tree, even if there was a walnut grove attached to the farm. And there were fruit trees, especially fig and quince and greengage plum. Families gathered the nuts in the walnut groves. Many of the farmhouses had a square tower either attached at the first floor or built to one side. These towers were once *pigeonniers* (dovecotes), where pigeons were bred for the table. There would have been a door from the tower to the main part of the house, enabling the master of the household to grab a plump pigeon quickly for dinner.

We enjoyed our misty walks and the smell of wood smoke as we walked through the villages. Now and then we surprised a pheasant in the woods and once two deer strolled across the road in front of us and, later, a red squirrel raced over a grassy slope. On Sundays there was an extra edge to these walks because this is the day for Frenchmen to be out with their guns and dogs, and shots rang out and echoed across the hillsides. The forest pathways were thick with fallen chestnuts and I wondered why anyone would bother to sell them when they were thick on the ground just for the gathering. The holly bushes had red berries already.

LIMEUIL

We visited Limeuil, which is about 20 km (12½ miles) from Lavalade and considered one of the most beautiful villages in France. People come there not only to admire the well-preserved medieval village but to gaze over the confluence of the Dordogne and Vézère rivers. Limeuil is perched on a hill and it is worth the climb through its cobbled streets to see the long view over the countryside as well as to admire the stone houses, some dating from the 15th century. (Should you see a sign advising that you are approaching or are near one of *les plus beaux villages de France*, it is always worth a detour. I have written earlier of another of these special places, Saint-Cirq Lapopie; see page 33.)

In Limeuil we saw just six people in the village and at least three were tourists, like us. The church of Sainte Catherine was securely locked but a notice advised that torchlight processions were held on a Thursday evening. I assumed this was only in summer although it did not say so. There was no movement in the tiny square other than the scattering and lifting of autumn leaves. The shuttered stone houses suggested the occupants had left with the warmer weather. Lovely single red roses still bloomed and trellises of vines that would have provided summer shade now offered purple bunches of grapes ripe for the picking beneath crisping, curling leaves.

The streets were narrow and very steep, the houses mostly with the traditional *lauze* roofing. We mused on the weight of such a roof and wondered at the thickness of the stone walls. Here and there part of a building was in a semi-collapsed state, allowing the interested observer better to appreciate the skill of the original stonework, even if it had not survived several hundred years absolutely intact.

OPPOSITE In Limeuil the picturesque, the old and the well-worn are to be seen up every street and around every corner. There is an old house built right into the hillside (top left), which fascinated us, and from the parapet of the stone bridge we had an excellent view of the meeting of the Dordogne and Vézère rivers. The beautiful medieval village is apparently packed with tourists in the summer, but in the autumn we had the steep streets and tiny squares almost to ourselves.

The Cheese Story

Dinner each evening at Lavalade concluded with a carefully selected cheese course. We did not restrict ourselves to cheese from the south-west, rather wishing to profit from the dual advantages of a resident expert and of cheeses we had never tasted before. All the cheeses we enjoyed were unpasteurised or, as they are described in France, made with *lait cru* (raw milk). This is another experience we would not be able to have at home because at present it is not permitted to make cheese from unpasteurised milk in Australia, as has been done for centuries in Europe. Whether the Australian policy should be changed is a complex and emotive issue and anyone interested in the debate should read the afterword in Will Studd's major work, *Chalk and Cheese*, where he discusses it in depth.

Will's status as a Maître Fromager de France (he is one of the few non-French members of the prestigious Guilde des Fromagers) opened many doors or, more particularly, many *fromageries*. Not only were we welcomed at La Coopérative des Fermiers de Rocamadour, a state-of-the-art production and distribution centre for local goat's cheeses, but we were also invited to visit several small artisanal cheesemakers.

Will questioned the farmers and producers closely on the techniques and philosophies of goat husbandry as well as of cheesemaking. He was in his element and ploughed on through complex technical vocabulary with only limited French, but plenty of understanding. My interest was mostly to do with flavour but I was intrigued to find that different farmers had different theories: goats kept inside all the time versus goats free to move outside at will; cultures added to the milk versus the necessary yeasts being naturally present in the whey of the milk at the smaller artisanal farms; the importance of hay in the diet, and so on. The goats themselves were very appealing, with intelligent, lovely faces and inquisitive natures. A less appealing story is that, as the French are not fond of eating kid, males are despatched within a week of their birth and exported, mostly to other parts of Europe. This seems odd to me when the French eat with relish all manner of birds, not to mention other unusual foods such as snails and frog's legs (both of which I love, before anyone thinks I am being disparaging).

In every market we visited, and in every cheese shop, there was an abundance of farmhouse cheese (or cheese that was at least claiming to be from the farm), all of it made with unpasteurised milk. I asked at the Rocamadour cooperative what the future for unpasteurised cheese in France was. While admitting the push from the European Union for tighter control and uniformity, the cheesemaker I spoke to was cautiously optimistic. He pointed out that some of the most famous of French cheeses – those with AOC – are required to be made with unpasteurised milk. Such cheeses include Roquefort and Brie de Meaux, and their status and

OPPOSITE Cheeses sold in the markets, such as this goat's cheese, are identified on their labels by variety, region and farm. The labels are also required to state the fat content. Not all market-sold cheeses are labelled, however – you will always find unlabelled ones, too, usually being offered by their makers, who will be only too happy to talk about their products.

reputation is such that it is unlikely they will be challenged. As long as this is so, the small cheesemakers of the south-west are safe.

CABÉCOUS DE ROCAMADOUR

Cabécous de Rocamadour are one of the cheeses with AOC status and these slim discs with their delicate, damp rind and more or less creamy interior are a true delight. Each *cabécou* is identified by a common label and, printed in smaller script, the farmer's numerical code and the name of the individual farm. Some farms fall outside the AOC area and their very similar cheeses are labelled '*Fromage de Chèvre*'. We visited the *fromagerie* and maturing rooms of M. Alibert, at his farm GAEC de Mordesson, at Rignac, who has been awarded many medals for his *cabécous*. I learned that a *cabécou* takes just six to seven days to mature from fresh curd, and that identical curd will produce different cheeses depending on the shape and size of the moulds and the different degrees of humidity in which they are matured.

It is a feature of the local markets that small farmers offer their own *cabécous* for sale. You can choose either *frais* (very fresh, when the cheese is soft and without noticeable rind), *mi-frais* (the centre is just starting to become creamy) or *fait* (fully developed and quite fragile), or you can buy cheeses that have been allowed to dry out. These are described as *sec* and are ideal for grating into gratins, soups and vegetable dishes. *Cabécous* can be eaten several ways: just as they are; semi-molten, having been passed under a hot grill, on toast or on leaves or on country bread and drizzled with local honey.

CHEESES EATEN AT LAVALADE

One of the stand-out cheeses we ate at Lavalade was a memorable Bleu des Causses. It was rich and sharp at the same time and matched perfectly with a glass of Monbazillac, the sweet wine produced in the area around Bergerac. Another highlight was an extraordinary Vacherin Mont d'Or, its pale apricot crust dimpled and cratered and the cheese within a semi-liquid aromatic treat. I have read of a way of enjoying Vacherin Mont d'Or in which you cut a hole in the centre, add garlic, pepper and a glass of full-flavoured white wine, wrap the cheese in aluminium foil and then bake it in a hot oven for 20 minutes and serve with boiled potatoes or *charcuterie*. Also exceptional was a sweet Gruyère with a slightly granular texture such as one would associate with the best Parmigiano-Reggiano.

From the Rocamadour cooperative we tasted the little-known local delicacy Pérail, a round, flattish cheese with a similar diameter to a Camembert and made from unpasteurised ewe's milk. The cheese was creamy and silky in texture with the faint but distinctive flavour and aroma of the milk.

A spirit of adventure is a great advantage when buying French cheese. The unknown will at the very least be interesting and will often turn out to be

OPPOSITE, TOP LEFT The small, flat discs of goat's cheese known as Cabécous de Rocamadour.
OPPOSITE, TOP RIGHT A ewe's milk cheese from the Pyrénées, Brebis Fermier, delicious with black cherry preserves.
OPPOSITE, BOTTOM LEFT We discovered this luscious Cabri-Ariegeois in Périgueux. It was best eaten by scooping some out with a spoon directly onto a piece of bread.
OPPOSITE, BOTTOM RIGHT Le Grain d'Orge, washed in Calvados (apple brandy).

marvellous. In the city of Périgueux Will found several wonderful cheeses, including one he had never seen before: Le Cabri-Ariegeois, Chèvre Fermier des Pyrénées. This was a goat's-cheese version of Vacherin Mont d'Or, similarly wrapped in thin strips of pine bark and with a washed rind. It is made only in late autumn and winter. We cut a small hole in the crust and found the centre of the cheese to be a luscious, flowing cream with subtle, smoky flavours.

Other purchases were a Brie de Meaux which, we all remarked, had that undeniable extra dimension that comes from *lait cru*, and a ewe's milk cheese from the Pyrénées, Brebis Fermier, probably one of the oldest cheese styles in the world. (*Brebis* is the French word for 'ewe'.) The vendor recommended a concentrated cherry jam be served with it. I wondered what he would have thought of my alternative suggestion, some sweet–sour pickled cherries I also enjoyed alongside local *charcuterie*.

Two further stand-outs were Le Grain d'Orge, a washed-rind, Livarot-style cheese washed in Calvados, and Gaperon, an intriguing ball of cheese still marked with the creases and folds of the cloth in which it had been hung to drain in a farmhouse in the Auvergne, the mountainous region adjacent to Périgord and Quercy. It was flavoured heavily with garlic and pepper and seemed to be the rustic ancestor of the similarly flavoured cheeses that are widely available in our own supermarkets. It is very low in fat, being made from skimmed milk or buttermilk. You can choose a creamy Gaperon or a drier variety. I was counselled by a cheese vendor never to refrigerate this cheese as it would quickly dry out.

OPPOSITE, TOP Cabécous de Rocamadour can be eaten in many different ways, including grilled and drizzled with honey (left) and grilled and served on salad leaves with fresh walnuts and tiny olives (right).

OPPOSITE, BOTTOM LEFT This unlabelled matured goat's cheese is typical of the many cheeses sold in country markets by the actual maker. Here it is served with rye bread, a particularly good match for strongly flavoured goat's cheeses.

OPPOSITE, BOTTOM RIGHT Gaperon is from the Auvergne and is flavoured with garlic and pepper. The name may derive from the local word for buttermilk, *gap* or *gape*.

La Soupe aux choux

CABBAGE SOUP

Serves 6

salt
6 large cabbage leaves
1 large onion, thinly sliced
1 tablespoon rendered duck *or* pork fat
8 slices 'real' bread (such as country-style sourdough), crusts on
150 g/5 oz Cantal cheese, coarsely grated
freshly ground black pepper
1.5 litres/2½ pints light chicken *or* veal stock

I made this soup in one of the brightly coloured earthenware gratin pots sold at country markets throughout the region. Mine is a shiny brown and measures 26 cm (10 in) in diameter. It looks most impressive brought directly to the table from the oven, although a thick heat mat is necessary as the pot gets very hot. If you have nothing suitable, the soup can be assembled in individual ovenproof bowls. Select the bread thoughtfully: it is an important ingredient.

Cantal cheese appears frequently in recipes for gratins and thick soups. It is a pressed cow's milk cheese made in the Auvergne with a greyish natural rind and a nutty flavour. In its fresh form it is *the* cheese for *l'aligot* (see page 131).

Bring a large pot of lightly salted water to a boil and immerse the cabbage leaves for 3–4 minutes. Drain well. Cut out and discard any thick central ribs and slice the leaves into strips. In a frying pan, sauté the onion in the duck fat until it is limp and golden. Set aside.

Preheat the oven to 180°C/375°F. Put 4 bread slices into the bottom of an ovenproof dish and sprinkle with half the onion, then cover this with half the cabbage strips and half the cheese. Grind on a generous amount of pepper. Repeat these layers, then pour in just over two-thirds of the stock. Bake, uncovered, for 25 minutes until golden and slightly puffed. (If you are using individual bowls, divide the ingredients in a similar fashion. The soup will be puffed and crusty after about 15 minutes.) Heat the remaining stock to very hot.

Remove the soup from the oven and allow to rest for a few minutes before taking to the table. During this time, trickle in the remaining stock. Most of the original liquid will have evaporated to create a wonderfully moist, pudding-like texture. The soup will be very hot, so wait for a minute or so before you tuck in.

Le Tourin

ONION SOUP

I can't help wondering whether this popular soup was the inspiration for the classic French onion soup served gratinée with cheese in so many Parisian bistros. I have tested and made it using chicken stock, but in many a peasant household it would have been made with water. Wine and water and *eau-de-vie* (see page 86) are all more important than stock in south-western cooking.

It is important that the onion and garlic are very thinly sliced. I use a Japanese vegetable slicer for paper-thin garlic slices, and a sharp knife for the onion. The character of the bread adds a most important element to the whole.

Melt the duck fat in a wide, heavy-based pan over medium heat. When the fat is hot, cook the onion slowly until it is limp and a deep golden colour (do not let it get any darker). Add the garlic and cook for a few minutes, then add the stock, bay leaf and thyme. Season with salt and pepper to taste and simmer over a very low heat for about 30 minutes.

Break up the egg whites lightly with a fork and slowly pour them into the soup, whisking gently. They will appear as 'threads'. In a clean bowl, whisk the egg yolks and vinegar, then stir in a ladleful of the soup. Return the mixture to the soup pot, stir carefully and turn off the heat. Taste and adjust the seasoning. To serve, put a slice of bread into each preheated bowl and ladle the soup over.

Serves 8

4 tablespoons rendered duck *or* pork fat
600 g/1 lb 5 oz onions, finely sliced
12 cloves garlic, thinly sliced
2.5 litres/4½ pints light chicken stock
1 bay leaf
1 generous sprig of thyme
sea salt
freshly ground black pepper
3 eggs, separated
2 tablespoons red-wine vinegar
6 slices pain de campagne

Stuffed Cabbage

Serves 10

salt

1 shapely green cabbage

100 g/3½ oz pork rind, in 1 piece

250 g/9 oz peeled chestnuts
  (optional)

1 carrot, thickly sliced

6 shallots, peeled

250 ml/9 fl oz dry white wine

375 ml/13 fl oz chicken stock

1 bouquet garni (thyme, bay leaf,
  parsley stalks)

Stuffing

250 g/9 oz mushrooms, chopped

2 cloves garlic, chopped

60 g/2 oz unsalted butter

2 tablespoons milk

4 tablespoons fresh breadcrumbs

750 g/1 lb 10½ oz coarsely minced
  pure pork sausage mixture

1 onion, diced

2 tablespoons freshly chopped young
  parsley (preferably flat-leaf)

sea salt

freshly ground black pepper

300 g/10½ oz reserved cabbage
  heart, chopped

1 large egg

OPPOSITE, TOP LEFT When the stuffed
cabbage is settled in its pot, the wooden
spoon makes an excellent handle for
easy removal.
OPPOSITE, TOP RIGHT The finished dish is
a feast for 10 hungry people.
OPPOSITE, BOTTOM LEFT A wedge of stuffed
cabbage is served with *l'aligot* (see page
131) and braised chestnuts from the pot.
OPPOSITE, BOTTOM RIGHT Extra cabbage
leaves and extra stuffing can be used
to make baby rolls like these.

Versions of this dish occur in every book of recipes emanating from or written about the south-west. And so they should – it is a magnificent recipe and provides an unforgettable meal for up to 10 food lovers. If you do not like to spend time in the kitchen, pass over this recipe as the dish is fiddly and takes a while to prepare. However, once prepared, the cooking takes care of itself.

European cabbages are often smaller than Australian ones. The one I chose weighed 2 kg (4½ lb) before I tore off the two damaged outside leaves. I like to use pure pork sausage mixture for the stuffing – my butcher supplies it already seasoned, but you may have to buy quality sausages and strip off the casings. Any extra stuffing can be frozen and used later to stuff big, meaty mushrooms or to make smaller individual cabbage rolls (see page 125).

Any leftovers make the most marvellous bubble-and-squeak. I fried mine with leftover potato and served it with a roasted guinea fowl and the house-party guests raved about the brilliant 'creation'!

Bring a large pot of salted water to a boil. Inspect the cabbage critically and tear off the outside leaves only if they are exceptionally coarse or damaged. Rinse the cabbage under the tap to dislodge any dirt. Slice the stem end neatly so it is quite level (the cabbage will eventually be presented end-up). Plunge the cabbage into the boiling water and simmer for 15 minutes, rolling it over with a fork halfway through this time. Carefully lift it out of the water and allow to drain for 5 minutes on a cake rack suspended over a baking dish or in a large colander resting over a baking dish. Turn the cabbage over to drain the other side. At all times handle it gently so as not to damage the outside leaves.

Put a clean tea towel on your workbench and cover it with a piece of muslin about 50 cm/20 in square. Lift the drained cabbage onto the centre of the muslin, stem down, and start opening each leaf completely so that the cabbage begins to resemble a flower. Once you get past the first 6 layers this will become more difficult and the smaller leaves may tear a little as they are eased away from the heart. When you can peel no more (the heart will probably not have been reached by the water), cut out the heart with a sharp knife. Cut it in half and discard the tough centre. Weigh the heart, then chop 300 g/10½ oz of it to add to the stuffing. Set the rest aside for another use (for example, a gratin; see page 129).

To make the stuffing, sauté the mushroom and garlic in a frying pan in 40 g/1½ oz of the butter. Cover the pan for the first minute or so until the mushroom has collapsed somewhat, then remove the lid and raise the heat. Shake the pan and transfer the mushroom and garlic to a large bowl. Do not wash the pan. Put the milk and breadcrumbs into a separate bowl with the pork mince, onion and

parsley and season to taste. Sauté the chopped cabbage heart in the mushroom pan in the remaining butter. Cover for the first minute until the cabbage has collapsed, then remove the lid and sauté briskly. The cabbage will take on a bit of colour. Remove from the pan and add to the stuffing mixture. Add the mushroom and garlic and stir in the egg, then combine the mixture well with your hands. Taste for salt and pepper (or, if you prefer, fry a little ball of the mixture and then taste it for seasoning).

Preheat the oven to 150°C/300°F. Take a large (hamburger-sized) lump of stuffing, form it into a ball and put it in the middle of your cabbage 'flower'. Fold a leaf over it. Take about half that quantity of stuffing and pat it onto the next leaf, keeping the stuffing as close to the centre as possible. Lift and press this leaf onto the central ball. Divide the rest of the stuffing into portions to match approximately the number of opened-out leaves you have (in other words, if you have 6 leaves, you will need 6 lumps of stuffing). There should be plenty (if you have any left over, it can be used as suggested in the recipe introduction). Continue patting stuffing onto the leaves and lifting them around the centre until all the leaves are back together. Take 2 diagonally opposite corners of the muslin and firmly pull the cabbage together. Tie firmly and slip a short-handled wooden spoon through the knot. Do the same with the other 2 corners. You will now have a bundle that would do Dick Whittington proud!

Choose a deep, lidded, enamelled cast-iron pot that will hold the stuffed cabbage very comfortably. Put in the pork rind, fat-side down, and tip in the chestnuts, if using. Settle the cabbage bundle on top and scatter the carrot and shallots around it. Pour over the wine and stock and add the bouquet garni. Top with a piece of baking paper and then the lid and cook in the oven for 3 hours.

When you are ready to serve, remove the baking paper. Using the wooden spoon as your 'handle', lift the cabbage into a colander positioned over a large metal bowl or baking dish. Allow to drain for 10 minutes. Meanwhile, heat a serving dish. Return any drained juices to the cooking pot, then lift out the pork rind and snip it into strips with scissors (lovers of the cooking of the south-west treasure these little nuggets of pork skin). Untie the muslin and tip the cabbage upside down onto the serving dish. Slice it into wedges and lift a wedge onto each diner's plate with a cake lifter. Offer the juices, pork rind and chestnuts all together in a separate container, with a spoon to catch the goodies, or arrange them decoratively around the cabbage before cutting it. Serve with regular mashed potato or the south-western speciality *l'aligot* (see page 131).

Small rolls

Individual cabbage rolls should be cooked for a far shorter time (maybe 45 minutes) in a similar manner to their big brother. Omit the pork rind from the recipe – it would not become soft and gelatinous in the shorter cooking time.

OPPOSITE, TOP Assembling the stuffed cabbage (left) and patting the last leaves into shape.
OPPOSITE, BOTTOM The tied bundle (left) is wrapped in doubled muslin with a wooden spoon for easy removal. The cooked parcel is drained in a colander.
OVERLEAF The flowerstalks and leaves of harvested corn catch the afternoon sun, beautiful against weathered stone farm buildings. One of our daily autumnal pleasures was looking at the wash of rich colour as the low sun lit up barns, walls, fields and monuments.

Gratin of Cabbage, Ham and Cantal Cheese

For this dish I used the leftover heart of the cabbage from the Stuffed Cabbage recipe on pages 122–5. I find it very satisfying to use leftovers creatively: a little of something left over becomes something quite different and yet there is a continuity that is part of the rhythm and character of a practical kitchen.

The quantities given here are approximate and the balance of flavours in the final dish can vary quite happily. There is no need for extra salt because of the ham and cheese.

Preheat the oven to 200°C/400°F. Bring a large pot of lightly salted water to a boil. Separate the cabbage leaves and blanch them for 5 minutes in the boiling water, then drain well and squeeze really hard in a clean cloth.

Paint the bottom and sides of a gratin dish (mine is a round one with a diameter of 20 cm/8 in and a depth of 6 cm/2½ in) with half the duck fat. Adding pepper as you go, layer the dish with one-third of the cabbage, one-third of the crème fraîche, one-third of the cheese and half the ham. Repeat the layers once, then cover with a last layer of cabbage and finish with the rest of the cheese and the rest of the crème fraîche. Scatter with the breadcrumbs and drizzle with the remaining duck fat.

Stand the gratin dish on a baking tray in case there is any overflow and bake for about 25 minutes until the crust is golden and the gratin is bubbling at the edges. To serve, cut through the layers with a sharp spoon.

Serves 4 as a luncheon dish
  or 6 as a side dish

salt
350 g/12½ oz cabbage
  (6–8 cabbage leaves)
2 teaspoons rendered duck fat
freshly ground black pepper
200 g/7 oz crème fraîche
100 g/3½ oz Cantal cheese
  (page 118), coarsely grated
200 g/7 oz cooked ham, cut into
  thin strips
4 tablespoons breadcrumbs

Potatoes Prepared as for l'Aligot

This dish is intended to be made with a soft, unfermented young cheese called *la tomme fraîche de Cantal*, found in country markets in its native Auvergne and throughout Quercy. I have read that the name of the dish derives from *aliquod*, a patois word translated as 'something'. The monks who first made the cheese were in the habit of offering 'a little something' – an *aliquod* – to the hungry: bread soaked in milk or broth mixed with cheese. Over the years the bread was replaced by potato. Whether this story is true or not I cannot say, but the *tomme* is so closely associated with the dish that it is often labelled *tomme fraîche aligot*.

The cheese is lightly pressed, quite white and acid and melts easily. It is the most important ingredient in *l'aligot*, but as the cheese is unobtainable in Australia you will be forced to experiment. I have quite successfully used a soft buffalo *tomme* and, most recently, a fresh buffalo mozzarella. The flavour is not as pronounced as when you use the traditional cheese, but it is delicious even so. Elizabeth David recommended to readers in England to substitute Caerphilly or Leicester.

David suggests that *l'aligot* is best as a first course accompanied by triangles of fried bread. I have served it alongside roast lamb and with *crêpinettes* (patties) of highly seasoned pork sausage mix, and have formed the leftovers into little croquettes and fried them – the creamy centre and crisp crust were irresistible. *L'aligot* can be made in advance and reheats wonderfully well, covered, in a microwave.

Boil the potatoes and garlic cloves in lightly salted water until quite tender. Drain the water from the pan, then shake the pan over a low heat for a few moments to evaporate any water. Pass the potatoes and garlic through a food mill or crush them with a potato masher. Beat in the butter and cream until the purée is smooth, adding seasoning to taste. While the potato is still very hot, add the cheese. Allow it to melt a little and then stir thoroughly. If using *tomme fraîche* or mozzarella, the texture will become a little elastic. Serve at once.

Serves 3–4

500 g/1 lb 2 oz potatoes suitable for mashing (such as Nicola, Spunta or Toolangi Delight)
2 cloves garlic, peeled
salt
50 g/1¾ oz unsalted butter
4 tablespoons double/heavy cream or crème fraîche
freshly ground black pepper
100 g/3½ oz tomme fraîche de Cantal or buffalo mozzarella or other soft melting cheese, diced

OPPOSITE, TOP LEFT Essential ingredients for *l'aligot* are butter, cheese and cream – it is an indulgent dish, but so good. I love the way the French wrap and present their best butters in foil or waxed paper and then settle them in wooden or pottery tubs and pots.
OPPOSITE, TOP RIGHT Potatoes prepared as for *l'aligot*, displaying the grainy, stretchy texture of the dish due to the cheese.
OPPOSITE, BOTTOM *L'aligot* can be served with fried bread or with grilled *crêpinettes* (right). The patties could be made from a mix such as was used to stuff the cabbage (see pages 122–5). Caul fat is an excellent wrapper, obtainable from a good butcher.

Goat's Cheese Tart

½ quantity Damien's Pâte Brisée
   (see below)
6 large eggs
1 clove garlic, finely chopped
3 tablespoons freshly chopped young
   parsley (preferably flat-leaf)
400 g/14 oz soft-rind goat's cheese,
   roughly grated, chopped *or* sliced
freshly ground black pepper

This recipe is really a generic one: it can be made with any combination of cheeses that are known to melt fairly well. I combined a few different cheeses, all of them local goat's cheeses with soft rinds. Be generous with the herbs. I have specified parsley, but do not feel restricted; others that combine particularly well with goat's cheese are chives, savoury, sorrel and lovage, the latter a little-used herb that grows easily and tastes like celery. Be careful when seasoning the mixture, as the cheese is often quite salty.

Preheat the oven to 200°C/400°F. Line a 24 cm/9½ in tart tin with the *pâte brisée* and blind bake for 20 minutes. Remove from the oven and reduce the oven temperature to 180°C/375°F. Whisk the eggs with the garlic and parsley, then stir in the cheese. Pour the mixture into the warm tart shell. Using a fork, move the cheese lumps around to distribute them evenly. Expect to see lumps of cheese sitting in the mixture: this is correct. Grind pepper over and bake for 15–20 minutes until golden and lightly puffed. Serve warm – the cheeses become tough and hard when cold.

Damien's Pâte Brisée

DAMIEN'S SHORTCRUST PASTRY

Makes enough pastry for
   2 × 24 cm/9½ in tart tins

180 g/6 oz unsalted butter
240 g/8½ oz plain/all-purpose flour
pinch of salt
3 tablespoons water

It was a joy to make pastry using French butter, which combines effortlessly with the flour without any need for overworking (Will Studd believes this is because the gentle culturing of the cream produces a softer texture). This is my all-purpose pie and tart pastry and was given to me by my good friend and fellow chef Damien Pignolet, from the wonderful Bistro Moncur in Sydney.

Remove the butter from the refrigerator 30 minutes before making the pastry. Sieve the flour and salt onto a marble pastry slab or your workbench. Chop the butter into smallish pieces and toss in the flour. Lightly rub to partly combine. Make a well in the centre and pour in the water. Using a pastry scraper (and being mindful of the technique you have observed of mixing cement), work the paste to a very rough heap of buttery lumps of dough. Using the heel of your hand, quickly smear the pastry away from you across the workbench. It will combine easily. Gather it together, press quickly into a flat cake, wrap in plastic film and refrigerate for 20–30 minutes. When you require the pastry, roll it out, dusting generously with flour as necessary. Line your tin and proceed as indicated in the recipe.

Partridge with Autumn Fruits

Serves 4

4 × 400 g/14 oz partridge (dressed weight)

sea salt

freshly ground black pepper

4 fresh bay leaves

4 large sprigs of thyme

2 tablespoons rendered duck or goose fat

4 thin slices pork fat

2 cloves garlic, unpeeled and lightly crushed

½ cup verjus

200 g/7 oz girolle mushrooms or small button mushrooms, halved

½ cup well-reduced poultry stock

1 cup wine grapes

4 escalopes/scallops of foie gras or 4 duck livers

1 teaspoon extra rendered duck or goose fat or olive oil

Compote

1 cup sugar

2 cups water

2 cloves

2 peaches, unpeeled

4 small figs, unpeeled

This is an attempt to re-create some of the flavours of a wonderful dish enjoyed in late autumn 2000 at Le Carré des Feuillants in Paris, a fine restaurant owned by Gascon chef Alain Dutournier. My recipe is far simpler than the dish we ate, which was accompanied by a tiny pie filled with the leg meat of the bird and walnuts. I also made a note at the time of the lovely wine we drank with the dish; it was 1994 Château La Grezette (Cahors).

The recipe given here is also in the spirit of a partridge dish we cooked at Lavalade with *girolle* mushrooms and *verjus*. On that occasion we drank a toast to the hunters whom we could hear not too far away and wished them luck. Nowadays many game birds are bred in captivity and then released into the wild. French partridge are the more highly regarded 'grey-leg' species and are larger than those available in Australia, weighing in the region of 500–600 g (18–21 oz) dressed weight. Australian partridge are known as 'red-leg' and it is rare to find one weighing more than 400–450 g (14–16 oz).

Preheat the oven to 200°C/400°F. Check the partridge for stray feathers. Rinse the birds and wipe them dry, inside and out, with kitchen paper. Season well with salt and pepper and put a bay leaf and a thyme sprig inside each bird. Melt a little of the duck fat and brush the birds with it, then wrap the birds with the pork fat. Tie neatly with string.

Choose an enamelled cast-iron pot that will hold the birds snugly and has a well-fitting lid. Heat the rest of the duck fat in this pot and brown the partridge very well on each side. Pour off and discard any excess rendered fat. Add the garlic and pour over the *verjus*. Allow it to bubble, then add the mushrooms. Cover tightly and transfer the pot to the oven for 15 minutes.

Meanwhile, make the compote. Dissolve the sugar in the water over moderate heat, stirring, then add the cloves. Score the peaches around their natural curve and drop into the just-simmering syrup for 5 minutes or until tender. Remove with a slotted spoon. Add the figs to the same syrup and poach for 3 minutes. Remove the fruit with a slotted spoon, reserving the syrup. Peel and halve the peaches.

Take the casserole from the oven. Remove and discard the pork fat and inspect the birds. Test to see if a skewer will easily pierce the thighs. If not, remove the breast fillets and the mushrooms to a warm plate and return the pot to the oven for 10 minutes. Take the pot out of the oven and lift the carcasses out of the pot, leaving the juices. Cut the legs off and put them on the plate with the breast fillets. Cut the carcasses into several pieces with kitchen scissors and put them back into the pot with any juices. Pour in the stock and boil hard on top of the stove for 5 minutes. Strain the sauce, pressing really well on the bones. Return the sauce to the pot and add the breasts, legs, mushrooms and poached fruit. Gently reheat, adding the grapes and a tiny quantity of the reserved syrup. Taste for salt and pepper and balance.

Season the escalopes of *foie gras* with salt and pepper. Heat the teaspoon of duck fat in a small, non-stick pan and sauté the escalopes for 30 seconds on each side. To serve, put 1 escalope on one side of each person's plate and 1 breast fillet on the other. Let the fruits, mushrooms and legs tumble in between.

Tripe and Trotters with Saffron and Radishes

Serves 8

2 large leeks
1 kg/2 lb cleaned, uncooked ox tripe
  (preferably honeycomb)
9 cloves garlic, peeled
2 pig's trotters/feet, split
250 ml/9 fl oz dry white wine
1 litre/1¾ pints well-flavoured stock
  (preferably veal)
1 onion, stuck with 2 cloves
3 large carrots, peeled and cut into
  even-sized chunks
1 stick celery, roughly chopped
1 teaspoon sea salt
1 bouquet garni (thyme, bay leaf,
  parsley stalks)
1 bunch radishes, trimmed
  (use the tops to make the soup
  on page 74)
2 tablespoons freshly chopped young
  parsley (preferably flat-leaf)
3 tablespoons Armagnac or brandy

Sauce

1 tablespoon rendered pork or
  duck fat
reserved white parts of 2 leeks, finely
  chopped
3 shallots, finely chopped
3 tablespoons plain/all-purpose flour
reserved tripe cooking liquid
good pinch of saffron threads

My friend Dany Chouet is originally from Périgord. I remember eating a glorious tripe dish she cooked in early autumn, at a table set in her splendid garden in Blackheath in Sydney's Blue Mountains, and was reminded of it when I cooked the following dish at Lavalade. I added saffron and extra trotters in memory of the tripe and saffron dish enjoyed at Saint-Cirq Lapopie in 1987 (see page 8).

Another food memory from the same trip comes from a dinner in the rose-brick town of Albi, in the *département* of Tarn in the Midi-Pyrénées. It was a case of my eyes being bigger than my stomach after a copious lunch elsewhere. What I needed for dinner was soup and a salad. What I ordered was a full-on dish described as a braise of salted pig's liver with saffron and radishes. It was all too rich and too challenging and I did not do justice to it. But I have remembered the interesting combination of the saffron-flavoured juices with the offal and the surprising texture of the cooked radishes.

Nowadays in Australia it is not possible to buy unbleached tripe, certainly not from a mainstream butcher, but you can order raw tripe. It will probably be the honeycomb variety. Many European recipes specify the thicker kind – what we know as blanket tripe. Again, it is possible to obtain this with advance ordering. However, it has a great deal more fat than honeycomb tripe and, because of its double seams, cooks more unevenly. Expect to cook both kinds of raw tripe for at least 5 hours before they are tender. If you are in any doubt as to whether what you have is raw or cooked, test it by pressing with your thumb. Raw tripe will offer considerable resistance, while cooked tripe will yield easily.

Preheat the oven to 150°C/300°F. Wash the leeks and cut them in half lengthwise, then cut off the white parts and reserve for the sauce. Tie the green parts together with string. Cut the tripe into 5 cm/2 in squares and lightly crush 6 of the garlic cloves.

Put the tripe and trotters into a large, enamelled cast-iron pot with a lid. Add the leek greens, crushed garlic, wine, stock, onion, carrot, celery, salt and bouquet garni. Bring to a boil and skim. Cover the pot and transfer to the oven. Cook for 3 hours, then remove the trotters and set them aside. Cook for another 2–3 hours until the tripe is tender.

Remove the pot from the oven, but do not turn the oven off. Allow the pot to cool a little, then strain the contents through a colander resting over a large bowl. Reserve the cooking liquid. Discard the bouquet garni and the leek greens. The carrot chunks should still be intact and full of flavour.

To make the sauce, rinse and dry the pot and then heat the duck fat over low heat until just starting to sizzle. Add the reserved chopped white parts of the leeks and the shallot. Cook very slowly until the vegetables soften. Stir in the flour and cook for 3–4 minutes, stirring, then gradually add about two-thirds of the reserved cooking liquid. Add the saffron and bring to a simmer.

Meanwhile, remove and discard the bones from the trotters. Cut the meat and skin into fine dice. Return the trotter meat and skin, tripe and carrot chunks to the sauce. Add more reserved cooking liquid if the sauce is too thick or there is not enough to cover the meat. Add the radishes. Cover the pot and return it to the oven for 45 minutes.

Finely chop the remaining garlic cloves. Remove the pot from the oven and check the seasoning, then add the chopped garlic, parsley and Armagnac. Serve very hot, accompanied by boiled potatoes.

Fig Fritters

Makes 12

300 g/10½ oz plain/all-purpose flour
1½ teaspoons instant dried yeast
pinch of salt
castor/superfine sugar
3 eggs, separated
1 tablespoon eau-de-vie or brandy
1½ cups water
500 ml/17½ fl oz unflavoured oil for
    frying (I use grapeseed)
12 small fresh figs, unpeeled

This recipe is ideal for small, very ripe figs and is a popular way of enjoying seasonal fruit. Try it in summer with apricots, plums or strawberries. The yeast batter is light and crunchy and the quick cooking time ensures the delicate fruit keeps its shape.

Mix together the flour, yeast, salt and 2 tablespoons castor sugar. Lightly whisk the egg yolks with the *eau-de-vie* and add the water. Make a well in the dry ingredients and tip in the egg mixture. Mix thoroughly, drawing the flour in from the sides to incorporate it (you may need a little extra water) to make a thick batter not unlike porridge. Rest for 1½ hours.

Whisk the egg whites until they hold soft peaks, then incorporate thoroughly into the batter. Heat the oil to 170°C/350°F in a heavy-based saucepan (or a thermostatically controlled deep-fryer) that is large enough to allow several fritters to be submerged with plenty of room between each one. Test the oil with a drop of batter; if it is hot enough the batter will turn golden brown very quickly (not dark brown).

Impale 1 fig on a fork and twirl it in the stiff batter, then drop it into the oil. Repeat with 2–3 more figs. Fry for 4–5 minutes and drain briefly on crumpled kitchen paper. Repeat until all the fruit has been used. Sprinkle with castor sugar to serve, if you wish.

Prunes & Plums

*F*rench country cookery has many recipes, sweet and savoury, that feature luscious dried plums, and the best prunes are considered to be *pruneaux d'Agen* – which are not, in fact, grown at Agen at all. An old friendship between Will Studd and Jean and Lorraine Lagarde allowed me the opportunity to find out more about *les pruneaux d'Agen*. Lorraine hails originally from Melbourne but she and Jean have made their home in France and their three children consider themselves more or less French. Jean is a marketing consultant for the Prune Council, which is known as BIP (Bureau Interprofessionel du Pruneau) and is the largest cooperative in the region.

As described earlier, my autumn adventure commenced in Toulouse, where Will and I had arranged to meet photographer Simon Griffiths. The three of us then collected our hire car and set out to rendezvous with Jean and Lorraine. We were to stay at their house in nearby Montauban for two nights, and Jean had kindly undertaken to organise visits and meetings with several small producers involved in the value-adding that is such an important part of the prune industry in the south-west. Lorraine had arranged a dinner party where a renowned local cook was to prepare her prize-winning speciality for us.

We discussed the program for the next day over lunch at Les Jardins de l'Opéra, in the centre of Toulouse. For my first meal on this trip to France I chose boldly: a salad of cockscombs and wild mushrooms (see page 180), followed by a *cassoulet* with broad beans *à l'ancienne* (in the old manner). Some authorities claim that an 'authentic' *cassoulet* uses broad beans rather than haricot beans, and by calling the dish '*à l'ancienne*' the chef was alluding to this. I am more inclined to the view that the origins of the dish are lost in the mists of time and the diner might as well enjoy sampling as many versions as come his or her way. The salad was a triumph and the *cassoulet* was excellent and generous. The chef outlined his food philosophy by asserting that 'life evolves, but good cooking must always proceed from a base of local knowledge and understanding'. A good thought to start with.

I had read of a herb garden in the cloister of the Musée des Augustins in Toulouse and this seemed an ideal place for a post-prandial walk. Light rain was falling and we were alone in the cloister. It was very lovely and I admired the basket-woven edging of the garden beds and noted that absinthe was one of the

herbs grown, along with wormwood and angelica and other more common varieties. We were quite close to Albi, the birthplace of painter Henri de Toulouse-Lautrec, who destroyed himself partly through his addiction to absinthe.

We drove to the Lagardes' home in the countryside in the southernmost *région* of the south-west, the Midi-Pyrénées. The rain had ceased and there was definitely a southern feel to the air. The leaves on the plum trees were changing colour and huge gold spangles flashed among the green. Each tree had been pruned to the shape of a pyramid, with its centre severely trimmed to allow the maximum sunshine to reach the fruit. Jean stressed that full sun is essential during flowering to ensure a quality plum crop. I had a momentary vision of how these serried rows would look in full flower – a brief five days of springtime splendour. One of my regrets is that I have never visited the area in the spring.

The Lagarde home is a charming old farmhouse with a terracotta stucco exterior and bold, dark blue shutters. The rays of the setting sun reflected and flickered like tongues of fire onto the stucco. For the dinner party Lorraine had invited their friend Zuzu Fel, a renowned local cook and winner of the prestigious 1999 Trophée Sofitel–*Le Figaro Magazine* with her recipe for *gigot d'agneau de lait et sa tatin aux cèpes* (leg of milk-fed lamb with wild-mushroom upside-down tart). Zuzu prepared the wild mushroom tart for us and shared the recipe with me (see page 322). Here in the Midi-Pyrénées it had been a poor year for wild mushrooms and Zuzu confessed that she had used frozen *cèpes*. The texture and flavour remained excellent.

Preserving the Fruit

It is worth a moment here to emphasise a very important linguistic distinction. What in English are 'prunes' are *les pruneaux* in French, while what are 'plums' in English are *les prunes* in French. On the trees the fruit are *les prunes d'Ente*. Once gathered and processed, the plums become *pruneaux d'Agen*. Really quite clear! (*Ente* is an ancient French word and the most popular explanation of the name is that the French verb *enter* means 'to graft', as it is certain that *les pruneaux d'Agen* are only produced from grafted plum trees. A more romantic explanation is that *prune d'Ente* is a corruption of *prune-datte*, the name given to the fruit by the 13th-century Crusaders, who returned with it from Syria.)

An intriguing fact is that *prunes d'Ente* are not grown around the town of Agen at all. Historically, the fruit was harvested in Lot-et-Garonne, Dordogne, Gers, Gironde, Lot and Tarn-et-Garonne and transported to Agen, an important river port. It was then sent by barge to Bordeaux for shipping to England, the packing cases stamped '*Pruneaux d'Agen*' ('Prunes from Agen'), and thus the name stuck.

OPPOSITE The farmhouse belonging to Jean and Lorraine Lagarde, near Montauban. We were in the Midi-Pyrénées, where roofs of stone slabs give way to pink and ochre curved tiles. **OVERLEAF** An old prune tin from Lorraine Lagarde's collection. The word 'Jasmin' on the label denotes a brand and not, as I had wondered, that the tin had originally contained tea!

The morning after our special dinner, Jean set about explaining to me the process of gathering and drying the plums. The fresh fruit is delicious and very beautiful: oval-shaped, with a violet coat muted by a purple–silver bloom and juicy yellow flesh. It is rarely sold fresh in French markets despite the fact that it makes delectable tarts and is lovely as a fresh fruit.

Of the approximately 50 000 tonnes (49 000 tons) of dried plums or prunes produced annually in France (in comparison, Australia produces 2000 tonnes), more than half are consumed in France. About one-tenth of the total production is value-added in some way: as liqueurs, confectionery, and so on.

Jean and Lorraine were intrigued to taste some of the spiced prune-plums I had brought as a gift. To their knowledge, this process of cooking fruits in a sweet, spiced vinegar syrup as a way of preserving them is unheard-of in France. (In fact, I did later find cherries preserved in this manner in a boutique at Rocamadour.) Jean rather tactfully pointed out that the size of the prune-plums I had processed would be unacceptable here. They would be considered undersized and would be lucky to receive 5 francs (A$1.50) a kilogram in the markets, as opposed to the 20 francs (A$5.50) a kilo paid for fruit of acceptable size.

We mused on the different cultural foodways used to preserve food for the colder weather. Drying in the sun was the traditional method in the southern region of the south-west, whereas in England the sun is not nearly as reliable or as fierce and acidulants such as vinegar, *verjus* and salt were needed to preserve the fruit – hence the English skill in bottling and making relishes and sweet–sour pickles, marmalades and the like.

Here in the south-west, drying in the sun has been replaced by more accurate drying ovens. The fruit is picked by mechanical means – the tree is shaken violently by a machine, much as I saw olives being gathered in Sicily two years ago – and the basic drying method consists of reducing the moisture content to 18–20 per cent. The process takes 20 hours and in this state the prunes can be stored for years. It takes 3.5 kg (7½ lb) of *prunes d'Ente* to produce 1 kg (2 lb) of dried *pruneaux*. To sell them, the producer adds water to partially hydrate the *pruneaux* so that the moisture content returns to 30 per cent. This results in the tender, moist prunes we buy in the shops.

There is a particular speciality of the area, known as *pruneaux mi-cuits*, which is much appreciated and eaten locally but has such a short shelf-life (one week) that it is of no commercial interest. '*Mi-cuit*' literally means 'half-cooked', but in this context means 'semi-processed': *pruneaux mi-cuits* are dried for just 10 hours and thus lose less moisture. They are intensely flavoured and very moist and the flesh retains its golden colour. They are clearly labelled *mi-cuit* at the local markets and no visitor in the autumn should miss out on this taste treat.

At a factory we visited after our first lunch in Toulouse I watched women twisting the stones from dried prunes and forcing into the cavity a paste made from

OPPOSITE, TOP LEFT Distillerie Lacheze (see page 151) produces an impressive range of fruit liqueurs, here made from prunes and blackcurrants.

OPPOSITE, TOP RIGHT Fresh prune-plums, their silvery bloom intact.

OPPOSITE, BOTTOM LEFT The local speciality of half-dried plums (*pruneaux mi-cuits*) can only be enjoyed in the autumn and in the locality. Because of the high moisture content, these prunes have a shelf-life of just one week.

OPPOSITE, BOTTOM RIGHT Armagnac is the brandy of the south-west and is fiercely championed by the local inhabitants. It is distilled at a lower strength than Cognac, resulting in more residual flavour compounds, and then aged in oak barrels that contribute further powerful aromas. Haut-Armagnac is of a lesser quality than Bas-Armagnac and is used to make liqueurs and to macerate fruit.

prunes, sugar, lemon zest and vanilla to create another local speciality: *les pruneaux fourrées*. I also ate prunes stuffed with almond paste and dipped in a light caramel, and for the chocoholics there were prunes stuffed with prune paste and dipped in dark chocolate. (Hearing about the prune/chocolate combination instantly brought to mind a luxury sweet I used to see in Melbourne years ago. Aptly named 'French plums', they were stoned prunes soaked in rum, I think, then dipped in chocolate and wrapped in a square of blue waxed paper twisted at each end like a tiny bonbon. They were sensational and so rich that I could only ever manage one.)

Another popular preserving method in the south-west is steeping the fruits of summer and autumn in alcohol. The next day we went to a small artisanal house, Distillerie Lacheze, at Le Tranchant, where the owner, M. Delmas, and his assistant proudly showed us barrel after barrel of perfectly peeled fruit steeping in *eau-de-vie* or young Armagnac. The smells were very heady indeed. M. Delmas used a handsome pierced-copper ladle to offer us a startlingly green macerated greengage, and then an apricot, and then a *pruneau*. The *pruneaux* are macerated in young Armagnac at 18 per cent alcohol and heated to enable the fruit to swell and thus absorb more flavour. The maceration takes place in stainless steel barrels or, sometimes, oak barrels. In the latter case the liqueur takes on extra colour from the oak. The fruit, sugar and alcohol mingle for three weeks before being ready for consumption.

M. Delmas assured us that such products are best consumed within a year as there is no significant improvement once the fruit and liquor are bottled. It is usual to offer a *pruneau* together with a small portion of the liquor as a powerful digestif – probably just the thing after a *confit* or, as we later experienced, to accompany a prune tart. Topped up with champagne, a *pruneau* with some of its liquor makes a delightful apéritif (see page 160).

The richness and full flavour of these macerated prunes are featured in many dishes in the regional repertoire. I have included a recipe for rabbit cooked with prunes (page 156) and one for eel with prunes (page 157). It is common to find chicken and pork also prepared with fresh or macerated prunes.

A few days later, at Souillac in the Lot, I visited the Distillerie Louis Roque to learn about the distillation process that results in their renowned aged plum *eau-de-vie*, La Vieille Prune, which has been made there since 1905. At home I have a treasured bottle of La Vieille Prune, purchased on an earlier trip to the region, that adds fiery magic to apple and almond tarts. Remembering the linguistic distinction (page 145), it was easy to understand that *eau-de-vie de pruneaux* and *eau-de-vie de prune* are significantly different.

There was a collection of handsome old alembic stills to look at, most of them made of copper. The process is really very simple. Selected fruit, with skin and stones intact, is mixed with neutral alcohol for two to three months. This ferments and is agitated to become a bubbling compote. The compote is transferred cold to

OPPOSITE, TOP LEFT At Distillerie Lacheze we were shown prunes macerating in young Armagnac with some added sugar. After three weeks the fruit can be enjoyed as an after-dinner treat, usually served in a small glass with a little of the liqueur.

OPPOSITE, TOP RIGHT AND BOTTOM RIGHT At a local factory the stone was expertly extracted from each prune before a prune-and-vanilla-flavoured paste was forced into the cavity. The stuffed prunes were dipped into a sugar syrup, which dried to a glossy coating, before being packed for sale.

OPPOSITE, BOTTOM LEFT *Poire William eau-de-vie* is usually associated with Alsace, but we did meet one farmer, Jean Delpont, at Montech near Montauban, who was making this bone-dry and powerful *digestif*. He had cases of William pears stacked in full sun, apparently to develop maximum flavour before proceeding to the distillation process.

the still and then heated so that the vapour is forced off. The vapour travels along an elegant, twisted pipe called a 'swan's neck' that descends into a tank of cold water, where the trapped vapour condenses and the clear alcohol is collected in a container. A lot more technical information was given, but I think I had the gist of it.

Most *eaux-de-vie* are completely clear, but the distinctive amber colour of La Vieille Prune comes from its time in oak barrels. It is a blended product, made by separately distilling different varieties of plum and storing them for one year in 350-litre (77-gallon) barrels. They are then blended by the cellarmaster and stored in 2400-litre (528-gallon) barrels for two years. At some point water is added to achieve a final 42 per cent alcohol.

An even more refined product is La Vieille Prune Réserve Impériale, which spends eight years in oak and has more of the character of an Armagnac than a fruit *eau-de-vie*. Philippe Denoix, our guide for the morning, suggested that the Réserve Impériale be reserved for very good friends at the end of a very good meal.

It is odd that some Anglo-Saxons still find any mention of prunes an excuse for ribald remarks. For the inhabitants of the valley of the Lot the commerce in prunes is of prime importance, be it as liqueurs, creams, tarts, confectionery or dried fruits.

Many recipes from old cookery books suggest soaking prunes overnight. However, the prunes we buy nowadays are soft and do not need soaking. As I have explained on page 148, plums have 80–82 per cent of their moisture extracted during the drying process and in this condition the prunes will last for years. They are dry and chewy and any offered for sale in this condition would definitely need soaking in something before being acceptable in a tart or a stew. Older French recipes suggest soaking them in an infusion of *tilleul* (lime-linden). However, the modern industry rehydrates the thoroughly dried prunes before selling them by adding back a percentage of water, to create the soft product we now buy. These prunes would be in danger of collapse if soaked overnight as many recipes advise.

OPPOSITE We bought this prune jam at a farmers' market and it became a breakfast favourite. Some of us preferred it on bread, other on crunchy toast. The range of preserves offered at the tiny market stalls often surprised me.
OVERLEAF La Vieille Prune, a powerful and wonderful digestif made from distilled, then blended, plum *eaux-de-vie*, is a speciality of Souillac.

la
vieille prune

Souillac

Rabbit with Prunes

Serves 2–3

12 prunes, stoned

3 tablespoons brandy *or* eau-de-vie

125 ml/4½ fl oz red wine

1 × 1.5 kg/3 lb farmed rabbit (minus
the forequarter)

100 g/3½ oz bacon *or* pancetta,
diced

2 tablespoons rabbit fat (rendered
from the kidneys) *or* rendered
duck or pork fat *or* olive oil

500 ml/17½ fl oz chicken stock

2 onions, halved and then quartered
lengthwise *or* 12 small pickling
onions

1 tablespoon plain/all-purpose flour

sea salt

freshly ground black pepper

1 sprig of thyme

I have tasted versions of this dish several times in small country restaurants in both the Dordogne and the Loire Valley (another region noted for its use of prunes in cookery) and decided to test it using my own recipe, which originally appeared in *The Cook's Companion*. I have adjusted the ingredients and timing slightly because when I first wrote the recipe, farmed rabbits were rarely available in Australia. Nowadays they are easy to obtain and tenderness is assured, which in turn has had an effect on cooking times.

In France I made this dish using a farmed rabbit weighing around 1.5 kg (3 lb). Its forequarter and kidneys had already been used for rabbit soup (see page 76); the balance of the carcass weighed about 900 g (2 lb). If the rabbit had been whole the dish would have served four people easily. *Sans* front legs, it was more like a hearty meal for two or, if other courses were to be served, for three.

Soak the prunes in the brandy and wine for 1 hour (alternatively, use prunes already macerated in liqueur). Joint the rabbits, chopping each hind leg into 3 pieces and the saddle into 4 pieces.

Preheat the oven to 180°C/375°F. Choose a heavy-based enamelled casserole big enough to hold the rabbit pieces and other ingredients comfortably. In this pot, sauté the bacon in the rabbit fat until golden, then remove with a slotted spoon and reserve. Brown the rabbit pieces in the fat until well coloured, making sure not to crowd the pot. Remove each piece as it is done and do not hurry this stage. In another pan, heat the chicken stock to hot and set aside until needed.

Sauté the onion in the fat until well coloured. Mix the flour into the onion and stir and scrape until well browned, then add the hot stock, stirring very thoroughly to achieve a smooth sauce. Return the bacon and the rabbit and its juices to the pan. Add salt and pepper to taste and the thyme, then cover with baking paper and cook in the oven for 30 minutes.

Remove the casserole from the oven and stir in the prunes and their soaking juices. Return the pot to the oven for 20 minutes, then test for tenderness. Serve with potatoes cooked with dried *cèpes* (see page 171) or mashed potato. The dish will reheat well the next day, but do so gently.

Eel with Prunes

Eels to be cooked (as opposed to those that have already been hot-smoked) have always been sold live by good fishmongers – they stay alive for a long time out of water and remain shiny due to a protective 'slime'. A dead eel looks unappealing and dull within hours of its death. In Australia the main buyers of live eels are Chinese and northern Europeans, who are accustomed to buying them in this state.

Eels had a special significance during our autumn visit, as related in the 'Autumn Notebooks' chapter (see page 102).

Have your fishmonger kill the eels, gut them and cut them into 6–8 cm/2½–3 in chunks. Put the pieces in a stainless steel bowl with the oil and half the lemon juice and macerate for 2 hours.

Heat the red wine to simmering point with the bouquet garni. Drain the eel pieces and pat dry with a paper towel. In a wide, heavy-based, ovenproof pan with a lid, heat half the butter until it is foaming and sauté the onion, shallot and garlic until softened. Add the eel pieces and turn to stiffen all sides. Tip in the *eau-de-vie* and touch it with a match. Shake until the flames die down, then pour in the red wine and the bouquet garni. Add salt and pepper to taste. Cover with a piece of baking paper and a lid and simmer gently for 15 minutes.

Meanwhile, sauté the mushrooms in a frying pan in the rest of the butter for 5 minutes until just tender, then add the remaining lemon juice. Add the prunes to the eel pot with the mushrooms and all their juices. Simmer for 10 minutes. Work the extra butter to a paste with the flour to make a *beurre manié*.

Lift out the eel, mushrooms and prunes and transfer to a hot serving dish. Increase the heat and boil the sauce to reduce and concentrate the flavour. Add the *beurre manié*, stirring to thicken. Adjust the seasoning. To serve, spoon the sauce over the eels, mushrooms and prunes and sprinkle with the parsley.

Serves 6

2 live eels (total weight approximately 1.5 kg/3 lb)
⅓ cup olive oil
juice of 2 lemons
1 bottle (750 ml/26 fl oz) full-bodied red wine
1 bouquet garni (thyme, bay leaf, parsley stalks)
60 g/2 oz unsalted butter
3 large onions, finely chopped
3 shallots, finely chopped
1 clove garlic, finely chopped
1 tablespoon eau-de-vie de prune (preferably La Vieille Prune)
sea salt
freshly ground black pepper
250 g/9 oz button mushrooms
300 g/10½ oz prunes
extra 2 teaspoons unsalted butter
2 teaspoons plain/all-purpose flour
2 tablespoons freshly chopped young parsley (preferably flat-leaf)

Classic Prune Tart

Throughout the autumn and winter every *pâtisserie* displays glistening, almost black prune tarts. They are delicious and quite chewy. This recipe makes enough pastry for this tart and the Prune and Armagnac Tart on page 160. Freeze for another day the piece you do not intend to use. If you have a second fluted tart tin, you could roll out the extra pastry, line the tin, wrap it in foil and freeze it ready to go for the next time.

If you do not have any Armagnac for the pastry, you can substitute Cognac – but don't tell anyone from the south-west that you have done so. They would defend the character and superiority of Armagnac to the death. I read somewhere and noted down at the time something said by one of my favourite French chefs, Alain Dutournier, who is a Gascon: 'Cognac is dependable, Armagnac is more forceful, more complicated – even excessive at times, and more exciting.'

To make the pastry, put the flour and salt in a food processor and give it a quick burst to blend. Lightly mix the egg and flavourings in a bowl. With the motor running, add the butter to the flour and blend, then add the egg mixture. Process until well combined and the mixture starts to form a ball. Remove the dough from the food processor and give it a few quick kneads, then divide it into 2 pieces and flatten each piece into a disc. Wrap the discs in plastic film and freeze one of them for later use, if desired. Chill the other for 30 minutes before rolling out.

Preheat the oven to 200°C/400°F. For preference use a Teflon pastry sheet; otherwise, dust your workbench with plenty of flour. Roll out the pastry quite thinly, then roll it over the pin and unroll over a 22 cm/8½ in loose-bottomed flan tin. Trim away the excess, reserving the trimmings to decorate the tart. Weight the pastry with foil and beans and bake for 10 minutes. Remove the foil and beans and brush the base with the egg white. Return to the oven and bake for a further 5 minutes. Remove the pastry case from the oven and reset the temperature to 220°C/425°F.

Simmer the prunes for 10 minutes in the water, wine and sugar. Remove the prunes with a slotted spoon and drain over a bowl for 10 minutes. Return any collected liquid to the pan and reduce the syrup by half or until very thick. Arrange the prunes over the base of the tart case in a single layer. Spoon over enough of the wine syrup so that each prune is coated and you can no longer see the pastry. Cut the pastry trimmings into strips and drape in a lattice pattern over the tart, then brush with the egg yolk. Bake for about 20 minutes or until the pastry is golden and the syrup no longer looks runny. Allow to cool completely before eating.

Serves 6–8

40 large prunes, stoned
125 ml/4½ fl oz water
250 ml/9 fl oz red wine
60 g/2 oz sugar
1 egg yolk, lightly beaten

Tart pastry
250 g/9 oz plain/all-purpose flour
tiny pinch of salt
1 egg
1 teaspoon orange-flower water
1 teaspoon Armagnac
150 g/5 oz unsalted butter, diced
1 egg white, lightly beaten

Prune and Armagnac Tart

Serves 8

½ quantity Tart Pastry (page 159)
24 large prunes *or* 24 prunes in alcohol, stoned
4 eggs
100 g/3½ oz castor/superfine sugar
80 g/3 oz ground almonds
125 ml/4½ fl oz whipping cream
1 tablespoon Armagnac (optional)
60 g/2 oz unsalted butter, melted and cooled

Everywhere in the south-west you can buy prunes macerated in *eau-de-vie* or Armagnac. If you are lucky enough to have these, there is no need to add the extra tablespoon of Armagnac listed in the ingredients. To increase the quantities of ingredients for a 28 cm (11 in) flan tin to serve 12, make one and a half times the filling and use extra prunes. The tart, pictured opposite made with prunes in alcohol, is also excellent made with fresh prune-plums.

Preheat the oven to 200°C/400°F. Roll out the pastry to fit a 24 cm/9½ in flan tin as described in the Classic Prune Tart recipe (see page 159) and blind bake for 15 minutes. Remove the pastry case from the oven and reset the temperature to 180°C/375°F.

Position the prunes in the pastry case in such a way that when 8 portions are cut, each will have 3 prunes. (If you are using prunes in alcohol, first strain the fruit over a bowl for 10 minutes and reserve any collected juices.) Mix the remaining ingredients together (if you are using prunes in alcohol, leave out the Armagnac) and pour gently over the prunes, disturbing them as little as possible. Bake until the custard feels firm, about 25 minutes.

Allow the tart to cool before cutting and brush with any reserved juices. Serve warm or cold. The French would not offer additional cream; the English and Australians probably would.

Apéritif Agenais Made with Pruneaux au Monbazillac

Champagne *or* méthode champenoise

Prunes in wine syrup
125 ml/4½ fl oz eau-de-vie de prune (preferably La Vieille Prune)
125 ml/4½ fl oz rum
75 g/2½ oz castor/superfine sugar
700 g/1 lb 9 oz prunes
Monbazillac *or* other sweet white wine

To make the prunes in wine syrup, gently heat the *eau-de-vie*, rum and sugar until the sugar has dissolved. Tip the syrup into a bowl and mix in the prunes. Transfer to a sterilised glass jar and pour in sufficient sweet wine to cover. Seal and then leave for 3 months.

To make the apéritif, put 1 prune in a champagne flute. Cover the prune with some of the liquor and top up with Champagne. Serve with a long spoon in order to retrieve and enjoy the prune.

Mushrooms

I had expected to see an abundance of *cèpes* in the markets during our autumn sojourn, as we had experienced in autumn in Tuscany in 1997. Alas, this was not to be and reinforced better than any book that wild mushrooms are truly 'wild' and cannot be dictated to or counted upon. 'The weather,' said the old-timers and shook their heads. Opinions differed as to the cause of the problem – was it the ferocious storms of winter 1999 or the exceptionally dry summer and early autumn of 2000? – but all agreed it was the fault of the weather. Some rolled their eyes heavenwards, reinforcing that it was quite beyond mortal control.

Bonnie found about four *cèpes* in the chestnut woods near our house but, despite her determined later efforts, it looked like a case of beginner's luck and she found no more. We scoured the marketplace and discovered enough to photograph, but they were not the fine-looking specimens we had used so lavishly in Italy.

Cèpes are the same as what is known as *porcini* in Italian. Their Latin name is *Boletus edulis*. This variety does not exist in Australia to my knowledge, although I have eaten some small mushrooms in Christchurch, New Zealand, that were claimed to be *B. edulis* and certainly had the distinctive swollen stem. They had been gathered beneath century-old oak trees in the Christchurch Botanic Gardens. Various cousins that grow in our forests have been sold as *cèpes*, but they lack the distinguishing stem and, more importantly, the flavour and texture of *B. edulis*. The most common variety found and sold in Australia has a brown, sticky cap and a bright yellow, spongy underside. This mushroom is *B. granulatus* or *Suillus granulatus*, also known as slippery jack or penny bun.

It is common to buy *cèpes* or *porcini* sliced and dried in Italy and Australia, but in France they were not as apparent in this form. Personally, while I quite like the flavour of dried *cèpes*, I find they have little to do with the flavour of the fresh mushroom. Cooks sometimes use the dried product too lavishly and the powerful flavour can overwhelm a dish. (A bit of trivia: I have a colleague, one of Australia's best-known chefs, who sneezes uncontrollably if he comes anywhere near a dried *cèpe*.) We did find excellent frozen *cèpes* in the supermarket at Le Bugue.

Probably the most popular way of enjoying these fresh mushrooms in Tuscany is to brush them with olive oil and grill them over a wood fire, then scatter them with parsley and, sometimes, garlic and serve them. And yet La Mazille is

OPPOSITE *Cèpes* still grow exclusively in the forests. There were very few to be found in 2000 – these four are the only ones we discovered – and local opinion blamed the weather.

adamant that *cèpes* must have a preliminary cooking and declares that without this they are indigestible. I found the Tuscan way quite delectable, although very rich, but I have an open mind, so was interested to read on in La Mazille's book and learn more about how to deal with them in the Périgourdin manner.

La Mazille makes the point that a local child of 8 years old can distinguish between a good and a bad mushroom. The most common varieties found in Périgord are *cèpes, morilles, girolles, oronges* and field mushrooms. She suggests that cooks restrict themselves to those they can identify. Tourists who collect mushrooms during the autumn months can go to the local pharmacist in any French town to have them identified. The pharmacy will have identification posters on display and its staff will be accustomed to pronouncing on specimens brought in.

The *cèpes* are universally regarded as the best of the bunch (La Mazille does not include that other prize fungus, *Tuber melanosporum* – the black truffle – here!). *Morilles* (morels to us) have a distinctive honeycomb structure and are pointed, like a pixie hat. They are a spring mushroom and are also found in Australia. *Oronges* apparently flourish a bit later than *cèpes* and have a bright orange rounded cap and bright yellow gills. La Mazille describes them as looking a little like a poached egg because when they first emerge they are covered with a white membrane. She says that they are as good as – and, for some palates, even better than – *cèpes* in flavour. Apparently they are more delicate in structure than *cèpes* and can therefore be grilled directly without any need of pre-cooking. I do not have any experience of them and would want to have them positively identified before I would consider eating them. There were plenty of mushrooms in the fields around our house at Lavalade, but I have *never* encountered a field mushroom in any French dish or seen them for sale in a French market.

Girolles are now cultivated in France and are therefore seen more frequently in restaurant dishes, but I have never seen any in Australia. The words *chanterelles* and *girolles*, which I had always thought of as different varieties, seem to be used to denote the same mushroom, *Cantharellus cibarius*. They are bright yellow to orange in colour and have an upturned cap with gills, a pleasant smell, a firm texture and a delicious flavour. Some are very tiny, while others are about the size of an average cultivated button mushroom.

Mousserons, or 'fairy-ring mushrooms' (*Marasmius oreades*), are also found in France. These are the small, pointy-capped mushrooms that often appear in a circle on garden lawns after spring rain.

OPPOSITE *Girolle* or *chanterelle* mushrooms are a favourite as they are not only full-flavoured but keep their shape and most of their colour after cooking.

La Mazille on Cèpes and Other Mushrooms

It may be helpful to include a summary of La Mazille's advice for selecting good-quality *cèpes* – visitors to the region may have better luck than I did and see them for sale in the markets. They will be rather expensive. La Mazille says to look for those with a firm cap and a pale colour underneath – a slight greenish or ochre shade is acceptable. Do not buy any mushroom that looks wet or flabby or whose underneath is mushy and dark-greenish. The stem should look firm and not obviously riddled with holes, which might indicate worm infestation.

BASIC PREPARATION

1. Cut the stem across, level with the cap. If it is white and healthy (no worms!), peel it and keep it aside to slice or chop. Cut off and discard the end with the dirt attached.
2. There is no need to peel the cap.
3. Give the mushroom cap a good swish in water and allow it to soak for half an hour. [This seems very strange to me, but I am dutifully translating. Cooks are more usually advised to brush debris from wild mushrooms or, if they are really dirty, to wipe them with a damp cloth. Readers must decide!]
4. If the *cèpe* is a bit tired looking, scrape away the 'mousse' underneath, trim off any dubious bits around the edges and give the mushroom and the stem a quick swish in plenty of water.
5. Drain well, pat dry with a cloth and follow one of the following cooking methods.

COOKING

Opinion is divided even among Périgourdins as to how to commence the cooking. La Mazille herself gives radically different times for sautéing *cèpes* in different sections of her book. In describing making an omelette, she recommends half an hour's cooking, either with or without an initial plunge into lightly salted boiling water for 2 minutes. Later in the book, in the main section discussing *cèpes* and other fungi, she recommends cooking the prepared *cèpes* for 1½–2 hours either in duck fat, half duck fat and half oil, or all oil – a big difference. Half an hour would seem plenty of time to me.

Whichever method is decided on, La Mazille advises to add the chopped stems to the frying pan for the last few minutes together with a bit of chopped garlic and/or shallot mixed with parsley. When the mushrooms are to be served as a dish by themselves, she suggests finishing them in the pan with a quick dash of good wine vinegar or *verjus*.

When discussing the cooking of *morilles* and *girolles*, La Mazille recommends a quick bath in boiling water (this time with some vinegar added), careful draining and drying and then the same sautéing, in this case for a quarter of an hour. She specifically states that a quick sautéing of these mushrooms for 3–4 minutes will almost certainly make the dish indigestible.

I would like to mention once more the wonderful quality of the frozen mushrooms we found in the supermarket at Le Bugue. Whether *cèpes* or *girolles*, the aroma, texture and flavour were outstanding. Given the lack of the fresh product, we were delighted with the substitute. If you are using frozen mushrooms, the packet advises an initial blanching in water for 2–3 minutes and not to thaw the mushrooms first. At the risk of heresy, I would have to say that I have tipped frozen mushrooms directly into a sauté pan and cooked them very gently for no more than 15 minutes and I did not find them indigestible. So, again, the reader will have to decide which method to follow.

LEFT A *cèpe* displaying its distinctive swollen stem. I have never seen the true *cèpe* in Australia, despite marketing claims for *Boletus granulatus* and *Suillus granulatus*.

Lentil and Mushroom Soup

Serves 8

300 g/10½ oz du Puy lentils
water
2 cups chicken stock
sea salt
freshly ground black pepper
Aillade Toulousaine (optional;
   page 205)

Fricassée
6 large wild mushrooms *or* cèpes
2 tablespoons rendered duck fat *or*
   olive oil
1 onion, finely chopped
2 cloves garlic, chopped
1 large potato, peeled and diced
100 g/3½ oz fritons (optional;
   page 309), bought in the market

This soup is my own invention, but I feel sure it would be welcomed by any resident of the south-west. It is lovely just as it is or with a scattering of fresh herbs. The best and most inspired garnish of all, however, is a dollop of *aillade toulousaine* (the walnut paste described on page 205), which I discovered by happy accident when I had some left over from a poached hen.

Rinse the lentils under cold water and drain. Put them in a large pot and add 1.5 litres/2½ pints (6 cups) water. Simmer gently for 20–30 minutes until tender.

Meanwhile, make the fricassée. Chop the mushroom caps and stems into small pieces (if you are using *cèpes*, brush any debris from them before chopping). Heat the duck fat in a wide frying pan and sauté the onion for 3–4 minutes. Add the garlic, potato and mushroom, then cover and sweat for a few minutes. Lift the lid and stir well. Add the *fritons*, if using. Sauté until the potato is tender, the mushrooms have started to colour and there is a bit of a sizzle going on.

When the lentils are tender, tip the fricassée into the lentil pot and add the stock. Bring to a simmer and season to taste. Simmer for 5 minutes, then blend the soup in a food processor. Take care not to overfill the processor as the liquid will be very hot. (If you are using a blender rather than a food processor, do not blend too much at a time as the steam from boiling soup can occasionally dislodge the lid.) The soup will be gloriously shiny and a velvety black or brown colour, depending on the mushrooms used. Reheat and serve very hot, with or without a dollop of *aillade toulousaine*.

Potato with Dried Cèpes

This is great with a moist dish such as Rabbit with Prunes (see page 156) or, if you love potatoes as much as I do, it could be a light meal for three people with a big salad to follow.

If you have access to one, use a lidded, enamelled cast-iron pan 24–26 cm (9½–10 in) in diameter that is not too deep and can be taken directly from the oven to the table, or a lidded, earthenware gratin dish.

Rinse the mushrooms in cold water, then soak them in 500 ml/17½ fl oz hot water for 30 minutes. Meanwhile, parboil the potatoes in lightly salted water for 8 minutes. Drain, then allow to cool for a few minutes before cutting into 1 cm/½ in slices.

Lift the mushrooms from the soaking liquid and pat dry with a paper towel. Strain the soaking liquid and reserve. Roughly chop the mushrooms. Heat the duck fat in your chosen pan and quickly sauté the bacon, then add the garlic, two-thirds of the parsley, and the mushroom. Stir and sauté for 1 minute, then cover the pan and cook for 2–3 minutes. Add the potato and turn to coat well with the mixture. Grind over some pepper. (If you find there is not enough room to mix everything thoroughly, tip the contents into a mixing bowl, turn and toss, and then return to the pan.) Add enough of the reserved soaking liquid to nearly cover the potato. Lay a piece of baking paper on top and put on the lid. Cook slowly for 30 minutes.

Test the potato for tenderness. There should still be a little liquid in the pan. Cook for a further 5 minutes, uncovered, shaking the pan to prevent sticking. Taste to see whether you need salt (the bacon is already salty) and serve at once, sprinkled with the remaining parsley.

Serves 3–4

25 g/1 oz dried cèpes (porcini)
water
500 g/1 lb 2 oz waxy potatoes,
   unpeeled
salt
1 tablespoon rendered duck or
   pork fat or olive oil
40 g/1⅓ oz bacon or pancetta, diced
2 cloves garlic, chopped
3 tablespoons freshly chopped young
   parsley (preferably flat-leaf)
freshly ground black pepper

Potato with Fresh Cèpes or Swiss Brown Mushrooms

In wet weather locals advise to put *cèpes* into a hot oven on a tray for 3–4 minutes before proceeding with any preparation, just in case there are any worms present – they will quickly evacuate!

In Australia I would make this dish using the biggest, fattest flat mushrooms I could find, marketed as Swiss brown or, sometimes, portobello mushrooms. And I might add a small quantity of soaked dried *cèpes* for additional flavour.

Cut the stems from the mushrooms and set aside, then cut the caps into 1 cm/½ in slices. Cut the potatoes into 5 mm/¼ in slices. Do not wash the sliced potato or mushroom. (Additional liquid in the pan will create steam and the mushroom will start to stew. You want the potato and mushroom to soften gently and the flavours to mingle, but without liquid.) Chop the garlic, parsley and mushroom stalks together to a coarse mixture.

Heat the duck fat over moderate heat in a deep frying pan with a lid. Tip in the potato and allow to seal for 1 minute, lifting the slices with a flexible spatula so that most of them have a moment on the bottom of the pan. Add the sliced mushroom caps and turn them carefully for 5 minutes. Add the mixture of stems, garlic and parsley and season to taste. Cover the pan, leaving the lid ajar, and adjust the heat to very low. Cook for 25 minutes, stirring the contents once or twice. The dish is ready when the potato is tender and well coloured. Serve with plainly roasted or grilled meat, *confit* or just a green salad.

Serves 4

2–3 cèpes *or* large, flat Swiss brown
 mushrooms
3 potatoes, peeled
1 large clove garlic
3 tablespoons freshly chopped
 young parsley (preferably flat-leaf)
2 tablespoons rendered duck fat
sea salt
freshly ground black pepper

Omelette aux Mousserons (or Other Wild Mushrooms)

Serves 2

200 g/7 oz mousserons *or* cultivated mushrooms *or* pine forest mushrooms
60 g/2 oz unsalted butter
1 clove garlic, finely chopped
sea salt
freshly ground black pepper
1 tablespoon finely chopped fresh, young parsley (preferably flat-leaf)
6 eggs, lightly beaten

As mentioned on page 169, in October we bought *girolles* from the supermarket deep-freeze – there were no fresh *mousserons* in the market (because it is a spring mushroom) – and I was struck by the intense mushroomy smell that came out of the bag the moment I opened it. At home I would use cultivated mushrooms for this dish, probably Swiss browns for their more 'woodsy' flavour or, in the autumn, thinly sliced pine forest mushrooms (*Lactarius deliciosus*).

If you are using *mousserons*, rinse them and pat dry with a paper towel. If you are using cultivated or pine forest mushrooms, slice or quarter them. Heat 25 g/1 oz of the butter in a frying pan that will hold the mushrooms with a bit of crowding (they will shrink considerably). Add the mushrooms and cook until there is no moisture in the pan. Strain the mushrooms, returning any juices to the pan. Sauté the garlic in the same pan for 30 seconds, then add the mushrooms and toss. Season with salt and pepper and add the parsley. Keep warm.

Lightly whisk the eggs with a little salt and pepper. In a 26 cm/10 in non-stick frying pan, heat all but a teaspoon of the remaining butter over a moderate–brisk heat until foaming. Tip in the egg and immediately tilt the pan so that the egg covers the surface. Tip the pan back flat on the heat and quickly drag the cooked edges to the centre with a wooden spoon, tilting the pan again to allow more uncooked egg to run to the edges. Spoon the mushroom mixture into the centre of the omelette, give it another 30 seconds, then push the pan away from you, causing the far side of the omelette to start to flip. Finish flipping the omelette with a flexible spatula and turn it onto a heated serving dish. The omelette should still be moist in the middle. Skim the browned surface with the remaining butter and divide at the table.

Stuffed Mushrooms

This is a very useful recipe that is as suitable for our large flat mushrooms as it is for *cèpes*. It is worth noting that the *confit* and *cèpe* stuffing in Zuzu's tart (see page 322) would be an excellent alternative stuffing for this recipe.

Cut the stems from the mushrooms. Chop the stems and set them aside for the stuffing. Preheat the oven to 180°C/375°F.

Select a flameproof, ovenproof frying pan or casserole that will hold the mushroom caps neatly. Put the olive oil and garlic halves in the pan and add the mushroom caps. Sauté for a minute or two over moderate heat, turning once or twice, then discard the garlic and set the caps rounded-side down in the pan. Remove from the heat while you make the stuffing.

To make the stuffing, mix the chopped mushroom stems in a bowl with the ham, pork, chopped garlic, parsley, breadcrumbs and egg. Taste for seasoning.

Divide the stuffing between the caps and drizzle with a few drops of walnut oil. Pour the white wine around the caps. Cover with a lid or aluminium foil and bake for approximately 45 minutes. If desired, remove the lid for the last 15 minutes to brown the tops and allow any liquid to evaporate. Serve immediately.

Serves 6 as a first course

12 large flat mushrooms *or* cèpes
1 tablespoon olive oil
1 clove garlic, peeled and cut in half
100 ml/3½ fl oz dry white wine
walnut oil

Stuffing
reserved stems from the mushrooms, chopped
100 g/3½ oz cooked ham, minced
100 g/3½ oz minced pork *or* rillettes
1 garlic clove, finely chopped
1 tablespoon freshly chopped young parsley (preferably flat-leaf)
2 tablespoons fine breadcrumbs
1 egg
sea salt
freshly ground black pepper

OVERLEAF These chickens near Lavalade seemed to be living in paradise: they had plenty to eat, shelter when they wanted it and could roam outside their enclosure all day long. Every farmyard we looked into had its own chickens.

Salad of Cockscombs and Mushrooms

Serves 2

4 cockscombs *or* 2 pig's ears
  or 1 pig's trotter/foot
salt
1.5 litres/2½ pints chicken stock
several sprigs of thyme
2 bay leaves
5 cloves garlic, peeled
2 handfuls small salad leaves
2 tablespoons olive oil
1 tablespoon unsalted butter
4 large wild mushrooms *or*
  flat cultivated mushrooms
½ cup strong veal stock
1 teaspoon sherry vinegar
1 medium-sized tomato, diced
freshly ground black pepper

Vinaigrette
1 teaspoon sherry vinegar
1 teaspoon walnut oil
1 tablespoon extra-virgin olive oil
sea salt
freshly ground black pepper

I ate this on day one of the autumn trip in 2000. A fast drive from Toulouse airport brought us to the peaceful and beautiful Restaurant Les Jardins de l'Opéra with its internal wintergarden, just a few metres from the hubbub of the city's main square, Place du Capitole. No time for jet lag! It was straight into an exciting lunch, with this dish from chef Dominique Toulousy being the highlight for me.

This salad is for the adventurous cook. First you need to obtain your cockscombs (no easy task – they may only be obtainable if you live on a farm), which should be from a rooster, not a hen, as those from hens are very small. Cockscombs are texture food, being rather crunchy and gelatinous, which is why I have suggested pig's ears or a pig's trotter as a substitute.

Put the cockscombs on a tray and prick them all over with a needle. Scatter generously with salt, cover and refrigerate overnight (if you are using pig's ears or a pig's trotter, there is no need to do this). Next day, rub the cockscombs with a cloth to take off the skin. Put the cockscombs in the chicken stock with the thyme, the bay leaves and 4 of the garlic cloves. Simmer for about 2½ hours until tender. Allow to cool in the broth. (Pig's ears will take somewhat less time; trotters probably the same time as the cockscombs. Lift out the pig's ears or trotter when they are cool enough to handle. Slice the pig's ears, or bone and then slice the trotter.)

To make the vinaigrette, mix all the ingredients. When ready to serve, toss the salad leaves in a small quantity of the vinaigrette and arrange them in a little heap on each warmed plate. Slice the remaining garlic clove. Heat the olive oil and butter in a pan and sauté the mushrooms (whole or sliced as you wish) with the garlic. Add the cockscombs (or ears or trotter), reserving the broth for another use (see below), and toss to mix. Pour in the veal stock and vinegar, then add the tomato. Swirl so that everything is well coated and bubbling and then spoon onto the salad leaves. Grind over some pepper and serve.

Using the broth
The broth will be deliciously flavoured and will probably set quite firmly. Use it to set a small bowl of assorted potted meats, such as ham, tongue and chicken breast. Toss your chosen meats with plenty of freshly chopped parsley and a little chopped garlic and season to taste. Pack into a ceramic bowl. Melt the jellied broth and pour over the meats. When it has set, turn out and slice. Serve with a green salad and mustard or with mayonnaise made using French walnut oil.

Rabbit with Cèpes from Le Centenaire

Serves 2

1 × 1.5 kg/3 lb farmed rabbit
extra-virgin olive oil
2 cups well-flavoured chicken stock
sea salt
freshly ground black pepper
2 medium-sized waxy potatoes
   (such as Desiree), peeled
2 tablespoons rendered goose fat
2 large, full-flavoured mushrooms
   (such as Swiss brown)
25 g/1 oz dried cèpes (porcini)
3 tablespoons clarified butter

Mushroom custards
2 large, full-flavoured mushrooms
   (such as Swiss brown), sliced
extra-virgin olive oil
½ cup whipping cream
2 egg yolks, lightly beaten
sea salt
freshly ground black pepper
unsalted butter

This special dish was one I ate at Le Centenaire restaurant at Les Eyzies de Tayac during the autumn trip (see page 348). Chef Roland Mazère generously shared the recipe with me. It is always a bit of a challenge asking a chef for a recipe because often the dish is so familiar to him or her that it is transmitted in a kind of 'cook's shorthand'. You have to read behind the words and sometimes even improvise or invent. In this case, the translation and interpretation are mine and I hope it will be as delicious as the original was.

I do wonder what happens to the rabbit's forelegs after they have given their flavours to the braising pan, and also whether there might have been some fresh herbs added to the pan for the initial braise – a bay leaf, maybe a good sprig of thyme and some garlic? Chef Mazère included the rabbit's kidney, sautéed, and added a cornmeal fritter to his presentation, as pictured opposite.

To make the mushroom custard, preheat the oven to 90°C/200°F. Sauté the mushroom briskly in a frying pan in a little olive oil, stirring or shaking until it is tender. Pour on the cream to warm through. Transfer the contents of the pan to a food processor and purée. With the motor running, add the egg yolks. Season with salt and pepper. Butter 5 or 6 small moulds of 50–60 ml/1¾–2 fl oz capacity. Fill the moulds with the custard mixture and cook in the oven for 1 hour until just set. (Note that these custards are *not* cooked in a water bath – the very low oven temperature removes the need for this.) Take out of the oven and keep in a warm place (in a pan of hot water, for instance) until ready to serve.

Remove the forelegs and shoulder section and the hind legs from the rabbit. Split the rest of the rabbit down the backbone using sharp poultry scissors, then separate each half into the rack and meaty loin section. Season the shoulder and foreleg portion and the hind legs, then brown these pieces in 1 tablespoon olive oil in a frying pan deep enough to hold the stock. Pour over sufficient chicken stock to just cover and bring to simmering point. Cover and cook gently for 20–25 minutes until tender. Strain the juices, pressing hard on the solids. Set the juices aside until needed.

Meanwhile, trim the racks so that each rib bone is exposed, as for a rack of lamb. Neaten the loin portions. Season the racks and loins with salt and pepper and quickly brown them in 1 tablespoon olive oil. They should be quite rare at this stage. Set aside until needed.

Trim the potatoes to an even barrel shape and cut each one across into 4 thick slices. Cook the potato in half the goose fat over moderate heat for about

10 minutes until tender, then transfer to a plate. Cut the mushrooms into pieces and sauté briskly in the same pan in the rest of the goose fat. Line a small baking dish or ovenproof frying pan with baking paper and assemble on it the potato and mushroom into 4 stacks, in alternating layers of potato and mushroom. Set aside until you are ready to finish the dish. Also set aside for later deglazing the pan in which you cooked the vegetables.

When you are ready to serve, preheat the oven to 225°C/425°F. Grind the dried mushrooms to a powder in a spice grinder (do not soak them first) and mix with the clarified butter. Put the rabbit racks, loins and hind legs on an oven tray and brush generously with the butter/mushroom mixture, using it all up. Transfer the oven tray and the pan with the potato-and-mushroom stacks to the oven and bake for 5 minutes. Remove from the oven and divide the meat and vegetables between 2 heated plates. Unmould a mushroom custard onto each plate.

Quickly deglaze both the oven tray and the mushroom/potato pan with some of the reserved rabbit juices and spoon around the pieces of rabbit on the plates. Serve immediately.

Walnuts & Chestnuts

$\mathcal{E}$nglishman Philip Oyler wrote three classic books, *The Generous Earth*, *Sons of the Generous Earth* and *Feeding Ourselves*, describing rural life in the south-west of France directly after the Second World War. He was an estate manager employed in both England and France to restore productivity to estates and farms that had fallen into disrepair due to the lack of manpower during and after the two world wars. *The Generous Earth* is set in the Dordogne Valley and is full of anecdotes, observations and character portraits. Oyler was concerned to point out to English farmers the error of their ways. He saw in France a rural population that was living a satisfying and full life, utilising natural resources and growing and harvesting using methods that maximised the potential of their land and their quality of life. He contrasted this with what he saw as wasteful and foolish farming practices in England, blaming the effects of the industrial revolution for many of the worst examples.

There is little doubt that Oyler was presenting a somewhat idealised picture of the life of the French peasant, almost as if he were describing life on Walden Pond according to Henry David Thoreau. But 50 years after Oyler wrote, there is much that is still recognisable, even if the teams of oxen about which he was so enthusiastic have been replaced by tractors, which he found intrusive, insensitive and environmentally barbaric. Walnut cultivation, for example, is one part of agricultural life in the south-west that has not changed greatly since Oyler's time.

Walnuts

OPPOSITE Walnut oil purchased from the Moulin de la Tour at Sainte-Nathalène (see page 191), where we made many purchases. We were told that the opened oil would still taste wonderful in two years' time as long as it was stored in the refrigerator.

Oyler claimed that for many peasant families the walnut crop was one of the most important: it could be relied upon to pay the rates and taxes, whereas other crops might be less dependable. In south-west France every house has its walnut tree and when we were there in autumn we drove past grove after grove of well-tended trees. Like the plum trees, these were well spaced so that the sun and light could get to them and the centres were pruned to maximise access to light. Families were gathering the nuts in their groves alongside the road to the nearest good-sized market town to Lavalade, Le Bugue. Here I visited the early-morning wholesale

market of walnuts and chestnuts, where sacks and sacks of the valuable crops were being sold in a friendly and leisurely manner. There was a separate section for the selling of the nuts in wholesale quantities. A massive set of scales with weights was on hand to weigh the 50 kg (110 lb) sacks brought by the farmers. It seemed to be a social occasion as well as business, with the men standing around chatting and smoking long after the transactions were complete and the sacks had been bundled into vans.

Apart from groves of walnuts, you still see walnut trees on the roadside verges. Oyler said that every tree belonged to someone and that, while no-one begrudged a passer-by a few nuts, it would have been considered improper for passers-by to gather fallen nuts seriously. Then he continued by saying, somewhat contradictorily, that if the nuts were gathered into sacks, the owner of the tree would share the crop with the gatherer. The owner profited by someone else's labour; the labourer was rewarded with nuts he or she could sell.

Henriette Deroeux told me that walnuts must be allowed to fall naturally – they are still immature on the tree and if picked in this state will shrivel to nothing. Even when they are allowed to fall, it is important that they be thoroughly dried before being bagged for sale, as damp walnuts will become black. Walnuts are much loved by rats and mice and in old farmhouses were spread on racks in a high, warm and airy spot that was inaccessible to foraging rodents.

Once dried, the nuts are cracked and eaten, or sold into commerce or sent to the walnut mill to be converted into the lovely oil that gives such a delicious character to many local dishes. Nothing is wasted. The wood from the walnut tree is highly sought after for furniture making, and we saw many religious statues carved from walnut wood. The shells were formerly ground finely and used to dust the floor of the old brick bread ovens. At the walnut mill we visited at Sainte-Nathalène (see page 191), the crushed shells were strewn over the muddy path between the mill and the shop that sold the products, while the residue from the crushing of the nuts for oil was given to the cows. And the region is famous for several liqueurs made from either the leaves or the husks of green walnuts (pages 196–8).

Oyler described the evenings spent around the open hearth cracking walnuts from the harvest and I later heard a similar story from our guide at the walnut mill. This young man was in his mid-twenties and was relating an activity he had actually participated in, so there *are* families that continue the tradition. His eyes lit up as he told us of the many evenings he had spent listening to his grand-father while his own hands were kept busy with the mallet and little board held between his knees. It was the women who were the experts and they used a small wooden mallet and a smooth slab of the *lauze* roofing stone. Apparently a good 'cracker' could crack five nuts per minute. Only perfectly cracked walnuts were suitable for sale.

OPPOSITE Grilled bread with Roquefort and fresh walnuts – one of the truly great food combinations.

Every account I have read or heard of these evenings tells of friendly banter interspersed with the regular tapping of the mallets, and it is always recounted with great warmth. The activity of shelling the nuts (*l'énoisement*) brought a number of families together to share the work (and the fun), much as they would have done earlier in the autumn to strip the corn of its husks or to shell and roast chestnuts. These evenings of shared labour and storytelling were known as *les veillées d'hiver*. La Mazille is one writer who describes them; here is my translation of her words: 'No sooner has one finished gathering the chestnuts, and stoked the fire with the first corn cobs of the year, than it is time to think of the new task, one that makes the time pass happily. One is invited to come and shell walnuts as for *"une petite fête"*. On the appointed evening everybody comes to the home of the one who is about to press his walnut oil. Several lamps are lit. We open the sacks and bring out the mallets . . . We chat, we laugh, we talk about nothing at all. We eat and we drink. The young start to sing, matching the rhythm of the song to the blows of the mallet . . .'

In reading about cracking walnuts, I found one authority who said that walnut shells are excellent as fuel in the fire. Another said, 'Do not put walnut shells on the fire as they will explode.' I take this contradictory advice to mean: 'Don't put the shells on a fire indoors, and do it with care outside'!

THE OLD MILL

With all this background in my head, I was eager to visit a mill where walnuts are still crushed in the old way. The 16th-century walnut-oil mill at Sainte-Nathalène, Moulin de la Tour, is one of only 15 such mills left in all of France, and one of only four that are open to the public. It was dark and crowded inside and, at first, difficult to see what was happening. There were two or three shadowy workers concentrating on their task, and some interested bystanders who were presented to me as the owners of the nuts being processed, come to collect their oil.

Our guide spoke excellent English and made sure that we appreciated every detail. The machinery is 150 years old and the mill is powered by water. The mill-wheel is made of oak that has gradually become calcified by a limestone deposit in the water over the centuries, thus protecting it from being worn away by this same water.

We were told that the annual walnut harvest in Périgord is around 15 000 tonnes (14 750 tons), of which 90 per cent are still cracked by hand. The production of the rich, flavoursome oil is remarkably fast compared with the slower stream I have seen extracted from olives using a comparable small press. Each batch uses 30 kg (66 lb) of shelled kernels and in two and a half hours this quantity yields around 15–20 litres (3–4½ gallons) of oil. The kernels are crushed and then a litre (2½ pints) of water is added. The resultant paste is cooked in a cauldron for 45 minutes to a temperature of 50°C (125°F), filling the air with its lovely toasty aroma. There is no thermostat – experience alone is used to judge the correct moment to pour the paste into the press.

The press is lined with a nylon filter, a modern advance (it was once lined with sheepskin or goatskin). Twenty tonnes of pressure is applied by ancient blocks of wood that sink into the paste and the thick oil starts to ooze immediately. The full pressing takes 45 minutes. Local people like to add a little salt to the walnut paste, believing that this will delay oxidation of the oil. Hazelnuts and almonds are treated in the same manner, but yield less oil than walnuts (30 per cent recovery versus 50 per cent for walnuts).

At the end of the pressing process a compacted mass of walnut debris is left. These walnut 'casts' or cakes become the final casing around the pressing block. They contain protein, fibre and vitamins and are later broken up and sold as animal food or even as bait to be used in the catching of freshwater fish, just as Oyler described several decades ago. In Christchurch, New Zealand, at a food gathering in May 2001 called 'Savour New Zealand', I listened to the experiences of Malcolm and Jenny Lawrence, the first producers of cold-pressed walnut oil in that country. They use similar methods to the ones I observed in France and presented for sampling a pleasant savoury biscuit made using some of the debris from the press.

A tasting was the reward for our patience and attention to the process at Sainte-Nathalène. What depth of flavour, what freshness! Nut oils are quite fragile

OPPOSITE A wooden mallet and grooved board (left) were used for gently cracking walnuts. This activity has entered the local folklore and there are many accounts of families gathering around the fire in the evenings and telling stories while their hands were busy with these little mallets. Our guide at the walnut mill (right) told us such a story. Here, he is scooping crushed and toasted walnut paste into the walnut-oil press during our tour.

OVERLEAF The interior of the walnut-oil mill at Sainte-Nathalène, showing the nuts being crushed by the millwheel on the left of the picture and then the crush being toasted and stirred in the hot vat on the right, before being pressed.

and very susceptible to rancidity if exposed to oxygen. The advice given to us was to use the oil, once opened, within two months if it was to be stored on a shelf, or two years if stored in the refrigerator. I remain to be convinced that an opened can of walnut or hazelnut oil would have this powerful richness after two years. (However, one year after my visit I still had opened cans of both walnut oil and hazelnut oil in my refrigerator, and both still tasted magnificent.)

As all cooks know, these roasted-nut oils are too powerful to be used on their own in large quantities – which is not a bad thing, as true cold-pressed nut oils are expensive. You should never use them for frying; the high heat means that the flavour disappears. I found the following jottings in a margin of my autumn notebook, a reminder of some of the ways in which we used the local oils:

- a drizzle of walnut oil on white beans
- *brandade* made with a percentage of walnut oil
- potato salad dressed with a little walnut oil
- green salad made with a drop or two of walnut oil with maybe a few freshly cracked walnut kernels, some tomatoes and a few slivers of Roquefort
- a light touch with either hazelnut or almond oil over cooked green vegetables
- a few drops of hazelnut oil as a final touch on an escalope of *foie gras*
- mayonnaise with some walnut oil to accompany a poached fish
- grilled trout drizzled with a few drops of roasted almond oil.

Needless to say, we bought lots of oils during our stay and I also bought two packets of another delectable Périgourdin speciality, *les arlequins* – toasted walnut halves dipped into best-quality dark chocolate and then thickly sprinkled with cocoa. I shared one packet at the time and took one home with me. As I unpacked my suitcase I laid the packet on a low table for just a minute. When I went to move it a little later it had disappeared. I found my poodle, Rosie, outside in the garden, quietly groaning, her muzzle covered in chocolate. I was very angry and almost pleased to see her distress. She took a day or so to recover.

OPPOSITE This colourful salad was made using some of the season's freshest walnuts, a little Roquefort, some tomatoes and green leaves from the market, and a few drops of walnut oil.

Walnut Liqueurs

It is probable that every local in the south-west once made his or her own walnut-based liqueur. The boutiques of today sell versions of these liqueurs, variously named. I have included two recipes told to Philip Oyler by Clélie, a friendly innkeeper: walnut quinquina (see below), made from newly opened green leaves, and *crème de noix*, or *brou de noix*, made from the husks of immature nuts (page 198). There is also a slightly different version of *brou de noix* from La Mazille's book; her recipe for *vin de noyer*, and André Deroeux's *vin de noix* recipe, carefully written down for me by Henriette.

Henriette answered my question as to why some liqueur recipes specify *eau-de-vie* and others specify alcohol. In former times, she said, each household would have made its own *eau-de-vie* from fruit grown on the property, and this *eau-de-vie* would have been the spirit used to make special liqueurs because it was readily available. Such *eau-de-vie* would always retain the perfume and essence of the fruit used in the distillation. Nowadays the manufacture of *eau-de-vie* is strictly controlled and it is mostly available from specialist stores and is very expensive. On the other hand, inexpensive pure alcohol is sold at the local pharmacy. It is 90 per cent proof and can be broken down with equal parts of distilled water to achieve a final proof of 45 per cent – more or less the strength of commercial *eau-de-vie*.

Professional cooks' suppliers sell an *eau-de-vie* that is 50 per cent proof and intended solely for culinary purposes. This can be used in the recipes that follow, but it is stronger than the *eau-de-vie* of 42 per cent normally sold in the south-west. Vodka can be substituted, or the quantity of *eau-de-vie* used can be reduced by one-quarter and the volume made up with distilled water.

Clélie's Walnut Quinquina

This liqueur is described rather loosely by Oyler in The Generous Earth *and I have paraphrased his words.*

On midsummer's day, pick some newly opened green leaves from a walnut tree. Dry them briefly in the sun and then continue the drying indoors to retain their colour. Several days later, when the leaves are brittle, rub them into small pieces and put into clean wine bottles to fill the bottles by one-third. Pour in a generous quantity of *eau-de-vie* to cover the leaves well, then put the bottles into a cellar and leave for a fortnight. Strain the liquid through fine muslin and return it to the bottles. Fill with sweetened red wine (red wine heated with sugar lumps – Oyler gives no quantities).

Vin de noyer

This is a similar liqueur to quinquina, from La Mazille.

Macerate the leaves in the *eau-de-vie* for 48 hours in an earthenware pot or similar, covered. Add the wine and leave for a fortnight. Strain the liquid through muslin and add the sugar, stirring until it dissolves. Bottle the liqueur and let it rest for several days before drinking.

75 g/2½ oz walnut leaves, central ribs removed
1 litre/1¾ pints eau-de-vie
3 litres/5¼ pints matured red wine
1 kg/2 lb castor sugar

André's Vin de Noix

Cut each walnut into 4 pieces. Place everything in a stainless steel or glass container (or a glazed earthenware crock, as André prefers), cover and leave for 2 months, mixing well once a week. Strain into sterilised bottles. Although there were no specific instructions to be patient before tasting, I imagine the liqueur would improve with a few weeks' maturing in the bottle.

Makes approximately
  3 × 750 ml/26 fl oz bottles

10–12 green walnuts, picked
  when soft enough to be pierced
  by a needle
2 litres/3½ pints red wine
  at 12 per cent alcohol by volume
500 ml/17½ fl oz alcohol
  at 45 per cent proof
625 g/22 oz sugar
several green walnut leaves
1 cinnamon stick (optional)

LEFT A colourful sign outside a boutique specialising in walnut products.

Clélie's Crème de Noix

This liqueur, made with the green husks of soft walnuts, is described by Oyler in The Generous Earth. *The walnuts are ready when a needle can be easily pushed through the whole nut – exactly the same method as is used to test for the moment to pick green walnuts for pickling. In France this is at the beginning of July; in Australia it is usually just before Christmas Day. The date will vary with the region and the needle test is the only way to be sure.*

Take a quantity of green walnut husks and pound them to a pulp using a mortar and pestle. Transfer the paste to an earthenware jar until the jar is nearly full. Cover with *eau-de-vie* and leave for a fortnight. Strain through muslin – the liquid will be jet black – and fill wine bottles to three-quarters with the liquid. In a small saucepan over a low heat, dissolve some sugar and a little honey in *eau-de-vie*. Cool this syrup and then top up the bottles with it. Seal the bottles and store them in the cellar. The liqueur can be drunk at once but is even better if left for a few years.

La Liqueur de brou de noix

20 young walnuts
1 clove
zest of 1 lemon or 1 cinnamon stick
2 litres/3½ pints eau-de-vie
lump sugar

This recipe is from La Mazille. She specifies eau-de-vie *at 65 per cent! For this recipe I would use* eau-de-vie *at 50 per cent undiluted, as described on page 196. When you can pierce the young nuts with a needle or fine skewer, it is the moment to proceed.*

Grate the walnut husks into a bowl, wearing gloves to protect your hands from the stain, which is very hard to remove. You can just crumble the walnuts without grating the husk, but the grated husks give more flavour. Some cooks only use the grated husks and throw away the young walnuts.

Crush the walnuts in a mortar. Put the crushed walnuts and grated husks into a glass jar with the flavourings and add the *eau-de-vie*. Leave for 2 months in a warm and sunny spot. At the end of this time, strain the mixture and add finely crushed sugar lumps in the ratio of 200 g/7 oz sugar to 1 litre/1¾ pints strained liquid. Leave for a further 2–3 weeks and then strain through muslin and bottle.

OPPOSITE The walnut liqueur most commonly sold and tasted is syrupy and almost black in colour. I have put all the ingredients together for André's own recipe (see page 197) and now must wait and see. For this photograph I cheated and poured two shot glasses of some liqueur we purchased in the boutique attached to the Moulin de la Tour, so that readers could see the colour. In the foreground is Henriette's handwritten recipe.

Chestnuts

In contrast to the groves of walnut trees in the south-west, there are no chestnut 'groves' as such – the trees grow wild in the forests. The large majority of them are *châtaigniers* (*Castanea sativa*) that produce two or three nuts to a shell. Grafted trees are considered superior and produce *marrons*, which have one large nut to a shell. (Interestingly, in older books such as those by Philip Oyler and La Mazille, *marronniers* are said to yield two nuts to the shell. Modern authorities claim there is only one.)

Oyler stated that someone owned every chestnut tree as well as every walnut tree. I cannot say if this is so nowadays. Certainly our autumn household gathered many chestnuts from the roadside and the forest, adding them to stuffed cabbage and roasting quite a few in a long-handled chestnut-roasting pan over our outside barbecue fire.

Although chestnuts look so well protected in their prickly outer coats and smooth brown shells, like walnuts they quickly rot after gathering unless they are thoroughly dried. Chestnuts mature during the heat of September and the practice used to be to strip off the prickly husks and plunge the nuts into cold water and keep them there for 48 hours before they were spread out to dry. Even dried, their shelf-life is not long and it is not unusual for cooks to find that some of their chestnuts have gone bad. Householders should buy smallish quantities, store them in an airtight container in the refrigerator and use them within a few weeks.

In my home state of Victoria, entrepreneurial producers Jane and Brian Casey of the Australian Chestnut Company in Myrtleford have developed Cheznutz, a business specialising in peeled whole chestnuts, and Jane informs me that techniques have not changed much in the intervening generations. Small growers such as the Caseys harvest their nuts and immediately plunge them into water at 0ºC (32ºF), then store them in a high-humidity coolroom. Larger growers follow much the same principle but on a bigger scale and plunge the nuts twice, with the initial cold bath serving to collect suspect nuts, which float to the top. The good ones are transferred to a vat of water at 0ºC for 20 minutes before being moved to a high-humidity coolroom, which is also at 0ºC.

The high starch content of the chestnut means that until relatively recently in many poor communities, and in times of famine, it was used to make flour and consumed as a basic food. Because of this, chestnuts are still associated with poverty by some European country people whereas Australians might be more accustomed to thinking of chestnuts as a luxury garnish or the exquisite sweetmeat *marrons glacés*. Nowadays chestnuts feature in many Christmas dishes in France, whole or chopped as stuffing or garnish for the Christmas turkey, and as a sweetened puréed

OPPOSITE Chestnuts fresh from the tree, with their prickly husks (or 'burrs'). Edible chestnuts (*Castanea sativa*) should not be confused with the semi-poisonous nuts of the ornamental flowering horse-chestnut tree. These nuts, known as conkers, have a flattened, smooth top, while edible chestnuts have a distinctive pointed top.

filling for the Yuletide log cake. The plentiful supply of chestnut trees in the forests means that chestnut honey is readily available for sale. This dark honey is distinctively flavoured and combines well with walnuts to make a very special tart (see page 214). Some of the nuts are fed (or used to be fed) to the pigs. And as with walnuts, the timber of the chestnut tree is used for building and for furniture making.

La Mazille goes into considerable detail on how to peel the difficult inner skin from chestnuts, and gives several cooking methods, including wrapping the chestnuts in cabbage leaves and steaming the parcels with a small quantity of water in a pot with a tight-fitting lid, or on a bed of sliced potato. She also says that locals liked their chestnuts cooked in sweet wine, or crushed with unsalted butter, or simmered in sweetened milk. Well-off families, she says, had specially shaped, curved silver knives, designed both to lift the inner skin and to enable them to stuff the nut with butter. I love the flavour and texture of chestnuts and find this idea of chestnuts and butter very appealing. I think I would add a tiny bit of sea salt.

ADVICE ON DEALING WITH CHESTNUTS

In *The Cook's Companion* I have written in detail about the problem (and it is a problem) of removing the inner skin of chestnuts. I quote myself: 'Whatever method is planned to remove the outer and inner skins of a fresh chestnut, the outer skin or shell must be pierced to relieve the heat and pressure that builds up during cooking. If the shell is not cut, the chestnut may explode. The best implement for slitting chestnuts is the extremely sharp Stanley knife, available at craft and hardware stores. Hold the nut down flat on a board to score it. If you need whole chestnuts, you can boil, roast, deep-fry or microwave slit nuts before removing the outer and inner skins. If the flesh is to be used for soup or a purée, where looks do not matter, process the nut by boiling, roasting, frying or microwaving it, and then cut it in half and scoop out the flesh with a small, sharp spoon.'

As mentioned on page 200, we are fortunate in now being able to buy perfectly peeled whole chestnuts, which makes what was once one of the most labour-intensive tasks a breeze. La Mazille refers to what sounds like a most helpful gadget called *un déboiradour*, used to assist in loosening the inner skins of chestnuts. Apparently it had two serrated pieces of wood joined in the middle, which were agitated a bit like scissors in the pot of hot water where the nuts had simmered after they had been fairly readily relieved of their outer coat. The obvious question is: How do you find such a gadget?

OPPOSITE Chestnut vendors are still a common sight in French country markets. The smell of the roasting nuts on the cold autumn air is most enticing.

Aillade toulousaine

This versatile sauce is great with cold meats and I mention it when writing about *la poule avec sa mique* (see page 354) and grilled *magret* (page 48). It is also special with cold poached fish or vegetables or spread onto hot toast and served with an apéritif. This recipe is reprinted with minor variations from *Stephanie's Feasts and Stories*.

The photograph opposite features a worn alabaster mortar and wooden pestle that I found in an antique shop near Toulouse. During the autumn trip I used the mortar and pestle over and over again, including to pound walnuts for *aillade toulousaine*, as shown here.

Crush the garlic to a paste with ¼ teaspoon salt. Put the paste in a food processor with the walnut pieces and blend until the nuts are finely ground. With the motor running, gradually add the oil and then the cream. Stop the machine once to scrape the sides and ensure that a layer of nuts has not stuck to the bottom of the bowl. When the sauce is thick and smooth, transfer it to a clean bowl, stir in the parsley and season to taste with salt and pepper.

Makes 1 cup

1 clove garlic
sea salt
100 g/3½ oz best-quality walnut pieces
30 ml/1 fl oz walnut oil
60 ml/2 fl oz whipping cream
2 tablespoons finely chopped fresh, young parsley (preferably flat-leaf)
freshly ground black pepper

Walnut-oil Sauce for Grilled Fish

This recipe is based on one given in La Mazille's book, where it is attributed to a cook named Victorine. La Mazille's recipes for grilled fish all assume that you have a fiercely hot bed of coals.

Quatre-épices, which means 'four spices', is a frequently specified ingredient in French recipes. The combination of spices may vary, but I use 3 parts freshly ground peppercorns to 1 part freshly grated nutmeg, 1 part powdered ginger and ½ part ground cloves, mixed well. I only ever make up a small quantity to ensure it always tastes fragrant and fresh.

Tie the bay leaf, parsley sprig and basil leaf together with string. Put everything except the chopped parsley and salt into a small heavy-based pan and reduce by three-quarters over moderate heat for 15–20 minutes. It should simmer, not boil. Add the chopped parsley and taste for salt. Spoon over crispy grilled fish. One tablespoon per person will be sufficient as the sauce is rich and intensely flavoured.

Sufficient for 2 fish

1 bay leaf
1 sprig of fresh, young parsley (preferably flat-leaf)
1 basil leaf
50 ml/1¾ fl oz walnut oil
50 ml/1¾ fl oz water
100 ml/3½ fl oz dry white wine
1 sprig of thyme
tiny pinch of quatre-épices
3 turns of the pepper mill
1 tablespoon freshly chopped young parsley (preferably flat-leaf)
sea salt

Walnut Mayonnaise from La Mazille

I have translated this recipe just as it is written to show the charm of La Mazille's work. Modern cooks may need a bit more advice as to quantities: try ½ cup walnut oil to 1 egg yolk. Your taste buds will have to guide you when adding the 'nothing' of mustard and the 'idea' of vinegar.

You carefully crush raw garlic to which you add one very fresh egg yolk, salt, pepper and a nothing [*un rien*] of mustard. You work with a fork, without hurrying, adding the walnut oil, little by little. When the mayonnaise is thick enough, you finish it with an idea [*une idée*] of vinegar and some freshly chopped herbs. This mayonnaise goes well with cold lamb. One way not to fail with this sauce is to let a little of the egg white remain with the yolk before starting to add the oil. This is one of the most infallible methods.

Potato and Walnut Cakes

Makes 4

300 g/10½ oz potatoes, peeled
2 cloves garlic, peeled
30 g/1 oz walnuts, finely chopped
1 tablespoon freshly chopped young
   parsley (preferably flat-leaf)
1 teaspoon freshly snipped chives
1 tablespoon melted unsalted butter
1 egg, separated
sea salt
freshly ground black pepper
1 tablespoon plain/all-purpose flour
2 tablespoons rendered duck *or*
   pork fat

This is a dish to make with sweet and crunchy new season's nuts. Nothing could be worse than using walnuts that are in any way stale or rancid.

Simmer the potatoes and 1 garlic clove until tender. Drain and mash. Chop the remaining garlic clove and stir it into the mash with the walnuts, herbs, melted butter and egg yolk. Whisk the egg white until it holds soft peaks and fold it into the mash, which will be an interesting beige colour. Taste for seasoning.

Divide the mash into 4 and shape into cakes, then dip into the flour. Heat the duck fat in a frying pan and gently fry the cakes on each side until golden brown and crusty. Enjoy with a salad as a lunch dish for 2 people, or serve as an excellent garnish for grilled sausages or a grilled or roasted quail, or alongside some crisp *confit*.

Variation
Cooked chestnuts can be used instead of walnuts.

Chestnut Soup

This most elegant soup, based on my recipe in *The Cook's Companion*, is most definitely *un potage*, not *une soupe* (see page 65). It is a smooth taupe cream with the distinctive faint sweetness of chestnuts.

In a heavy-based stockpot, sweat the potato, celery, onion and garlic in the butter over gentle heat for 5 minutes. Add the chestnuts and stock and simmer, covered, for 25 minutes until the nuts and vegetables are quite tender.

    Strain through a colander into a bowl and purée the solids in a food processor. Return the liquid to the solids (holding back about 1 cup in case the soup is too liquid for your taste), then strain back into the pot. Add the cream (or crème fraîche for extra tang) and simmer the soup for 15 minutes to allow it to reduce slightly. Season to taste. Before serving, add the alcohol to the hot soup. Garnish with chopped parsley.

Variation

A cupful of shredded duck *confit* could be warmed in the alcohol and divided between the bowls at the moment of serving.

Serves 6–8

1 potato, diced
1 stick celery, finely sliced
1 onion, finely chopped
2 cloves garlic, sliced
40 g/1 ⅓ oz unsalted butter
1 kg/2 lb chestnuts, peeled (to yield 500 g/1 lb 2 oz) or 500 g/1 lb 2 oz peeled chestnuts
1 litre/1 ¾ pints chicken stock *or* water
100 ml/3 ½ fl oz whipping cream *or* crème fraîche
sea salt
freshly ground black pepper
1 tablespoon Armagnac or amontillado sherry
freshly chopped young parsley (preferably flat-leaf)

Crunchy Lamb with Walnut Oil and Mustard

ÉPIGRAMMES D'AGNEAU

Makes 10–12

2 tablespoons walnut oil
2 tablespoons mustard of your
  choice
sea salt
freshly ground black pepper
2 eggs
2 cups coarse breadcrumbs
olive oil

Broth

1 onion, sliced
1 stick celery, sliced
1 carrot, sliced
1 bouquet garni (thyme, bay leaf,
  parsley stalks)
2 cloves garlic, peeled
6 peppercorns
1 cup dry white wine
1 litre/1¾ pints cold water
1 × 500–700 g/18–25 oz lamb
  breast, bones in

The French name for this dish, *épigrammes d'agneau*, presumably refers to the clever transformation of a rather fatty, forgettable and insipid cut of meat into something piquant, spicy and memorable. 'Witty lamb' is a possible English translation!

These crispy golden morsels make delicious hand-around party food. Served with a salad, as pictured opposite, they could just as easily be a simple lunch. At Lavalade we used *moutarde violette*, a mustard made with grape must (the lees left after the grapes have been crushed for wine) that becomes a startling purple in colour and is a speciality of the town of Brive-la-Gaillarde in Périgord.

To make the broth, put all the ingredients except the lamb into a pot, then bring to a simmer and skim. Add the lamb and simmer very gently for about 2 hours until a skewer slips through the meat without resistance.

Lift the meat out of the broth with a slotted spoon and drain on a rack over a plate (return any drained liquid to the pot). Slip out the rib bones and cut away the bones that run diagonally. Slice off any fat deposits. Strain the broth and use it later to cook some dried beans, or as the base of a soup.

Mix the walnut oil with the mustard and generously paint both sides of the cooked lamb with about two-thirds of this mixture. Season with salt and pepper. Cover with a sheet of baking paper and press with a heavy weight such as a large, unopened olive-oil tin placed on its side. Refrigerate for several hours.

Remove the weight and paper and brush the lamb again with the remains of the walnut-oil mixture. Cut into serving pieces (fingers, triangles or squares). Whisk the eggs in a shallow dish and grind in some pepper. Dip the lamb pieces in the egg mixture and press a good coating of breadcrumbs onto each side of the meat.

In a frying pan, heat olive oil to a depth of about 5 mm/¼ in and sauté the meat, turning it carefully so that all sides become crisp and golden. Drain on kitchen paper. Serve as a hand-around hot savoury, or with a green salad and either a mayonnaise made using a percentage of walnut oil, a rich tomato sauce, more of the mustard or *aillade toulousaine* (see page 205).

Walnut and Rum Tart

This recipe appears in a slightly different form in *Stephanie's Feasts and Stories.*

Make and chill the pastry as described, then roll it out and line a 28 cm/11 in loose-bottomed flan tin. Chill for 20 minutes. Preheat the oven to 200°C/400°F.

Line the pastry case with aluminium foil and fill it with baking weights or dried beans. Bake for 10 minutes. Remove from the oven, remove the weights and foil and brush the base of the tart with the apricot jam. Reset the oven temperature to 180°C/375°F.

To make the filling, grind the walnuts in a food processor until quite fine. Beat the castor sugar and egg yolks in an electric mixer until thick and very pale, then add the ground walnuts, butter, cream and rum. Whisk the egg whites until soft peaks form, then gently fold into the nut mixture.

Pour the filling into the tart shell. Bake for 45 minutes until the filling is golden and feels springy when touched lightly with the palm of your hand. Remove the tart from the oven and leave to get quite cold before icing. Lightly toast the walnut halves on a baking tray in the turned-off oven.

To make the icing, melt the chocolate with the butter in a bowl over a saucepan of hot water. Stir until smooth, then pour over the cold tart, tilting it so that the icing flows smoothly and evenly. Mark each portion with a toasted walnut half and allow the icing to set before slicing.

Serves 10

1 quantity Damien's Pâte Brisée
   (page 132)
½ cup smooth apricot jam, warmed
10 perfect walnut halves

Filling
250 g/9 oz freshly shelled walnuts
250 g/9 oz castor/superfine sugar
4 eggs, separated
100 g/3½ oz softened unsalted butter
2 tablespoons whipping cream
100 ml/3½ fl oz rum

Icing
100 g/3½ oz dark couverture
   chocolate
30 g/1 oz unsalted butter

PAGES 210–11 This beautiful house in Sarlat is situated near the cathedral and is in the style of a house in the country rather than the more usual townhouses in the surrounding streets.
OPPOSITE The enticing small tarts on sale in the markets included walnut and rum tartlets with chocolate icing (left) and walnut and honey tartlets. I have opted to give recipes for large versions of these (this page and page 214), which have the added advantage of maximum delicious filling and minimum pastry.

Crunchy Walnut Tart with Chestnut Honey

½ quantity Damien's Pâte Brisée
(page 132)
120 g/4 oz unsalted butter, melted
and cooled
150 g/5 oz chestnut honey *or*
other variety of honey
100 ml/3½ fl oz double/heavy cream
2 tablespoons rum
300 g/10½ oz walnut pieces, broken
150 g/5 oz sugar
5 egg yolks

This recipe produces a tart such as those seen in all the village *pâtisseries* throughout the autumn months. It is crunchy and memorable and a total contrast to the preceding recipe. It is also a very good way of showcasing a special variety of honey.

Make and chill the pastry as instructed, then roll it out and line a 24 cm/9½ in loose-bottomed flan tin. Chill for 20 minutes. Preheat the oven to 200°C/400°F. Blind bake the pastry case for 20 minutes, then remove from the oven and reduce the oven temperature to 190°C/375°F.

Warm the butter, honey, cream and rum together. Mix the walnut pieces and sugar in a bowl. Lightly whisk the egg yolks, then whisk them into the honey mixture and pour over the nuts and sugar. Stir until well mixed, then pour into the pastry case. Bake for 40 minutes until the tart looks well caramelised. Be careful as you remove the tart – any dribble of filling that falls onto your skin will stick and burn like caramel. Allow to cool before cutting with a sharp knife.

Walnut honey biscuits

I had a small quantity of filling remaining and some pastry trimmings. A few days later I re-rolled the pastry to a rough circle, put it on a pizza tray and spread a very thin layer of the filling on it. It cooked in about 15 minutes to a crisp biscuit with a bubbly crust. When it was cold I cut it into pieces and it was much admired served with coffee at the end of a simple dinner.

Markets

When asked to explain my passion for France, I think immediately of the markets. There are markets of all sizes, in covered halls, arcades, small streets and large squares, markets that trail through entire towns, markets that specialise in one thing – truffles, for example (I describe on page 272 the first truffle market of the 1999–2000 season held at Excideuil), or walnuts – and markets that combine produce with baubles for tourists.

As you approach a town or village on market day the traffic is three times as heavy as usual and you are prohibited from approaching the centre of town. Finding a parking space can be devilishly difficult but, once this is achieved, you will never be in doubt as to where the market is: you have only to follow the stream of people carrying baskets or pushing trolleys, either returning to their cars with bulging bags or heading off to shop. Markets are not restricted to remote villages and small provincial towns: I have shopped in several street markets in Paris and experienced the same joy. If you are a food lover your pulse will quicken at the sense of excitement in the air and you will be left in little doubt that the market is of prime importance to the local community.

The significance of these markets for me is not just that they are beautiful and smell good and are piled with the freshest, most colourful fruits and vegetables; it is that they are ongoing proof that the French (of both sexes and a fair sprinkling of ages – although there are fewer people under 30 at markets, it must be said) *care* about their daily food. They want to sniff the plums; they need to closely inspect a fish before buying it; they want the butcher to trim the piece of pork just so; they want their *cabécou* in a certain condition. All of these requests are considered absolutely appropriate and usual by the stall-holders. It is a serious matter, buying food, worthy of people's full concentration. It is also a joyful and social occasion and there is a good deal of banter between shoppers and stall-holders and an exchange of ideas about how best to cook the produce being purchased.

The attention extends to the wrapping, the careful placing in the bag and the essential courtesies with which everyone greets everyone else. These greetings and farewells – '*Bonjour, Madame*' and 'Have a lovely afternoon' – are considered basic good manners, whether at the market or in local shops. No matter how small your purchase, it is important to acknowledge the shopkeeper politely on entering and to farewell him or her as you leave.

OPPOSITE The serious shoppers arrive early to market, such as here at Périgueux. They are well wrapped against the chill of the morning and far too intent on their business to notice the glorious pale sunshine washing the surrounding buildings.

I am not saying that we must all live like French farmers. Nor am I saying that France is still a land of peasant farmers and that there will be brilliant food wherever you turn. But it is balm to my foodie soul to travel in rural France. We may have a few farmers' markets in Australia (and I do all I can to encourage them), but let us not fool ourselves that they are of major importance to the majority of shoppers, as they are in France.

In addition to the regular markets held in every town and most villages, there are now specialist markets known as *marchés des producteurs de pays* (which we would call 'farmers' markets'), where the goods sold have been exclusively produced by the stall-holders. They bring to market whatever surplus they have and the buyer can be assured of freshness and of tender loving care.

It is worth passing on a good tip for travellers in country France: do all your food shopping before 12 noon – or you risk going without – then dawdle before leaving the town. The French hit the roads at five past twelve and drive with incredible ferocity to get home for lunch. From 12.20 to about 1.45 you will probably have the roads to yourself to amble along and choose a good spot for a picnic.

During the house party at Lavalade, marketing was a daily necessity with 10 people to feed, not to mention the extra dishes to be cooked and photographed for this book. Going to the market was probably one of the most enjoyable chores and guests fought to join these expeditions. We had a very small, very local market at Sainte Alvère on Monday, a comprehensive market at Le Bugue on Tuesday and Saturday, and on Wednesday we could choose between Périgueux (taking in a tour of the city as well) and Montignac.

An advantage of visiting the region in autumn was the lack of visitors. In the summer, market days inevitably meant chaotic traffic snarls as locals and visitors jostled to find a park. Julie and I visited the Sarlat market twice on Saturday mornings in summer. Our first visit, on 3 July, was memorable (see page 223), but when we went again one week later, Sarlat was transformed. Instead of a bustling market centre, we found a nightmarish bottleneck, with cars banked up for more than a kilometre in and out of the town. The car park had disappeared under a multi-coloured mountain of T-shirts and plastic toys. We took the first minor road we could find and went elsewhere. Sarlat is a special place, one of the loveliest towns in France – but, if you can, you should make every effort to visit outside the holiday season.

Another advantage of autumn is that there are many special fêtes celebrating particular ingredients. I noticed *la fête des châtaignes, la foire aux cèpes, la fête des vendanges* (grape harvest festival) and *la fête des fruits oubliés* (festival of forgotten fruits). All of these were to be held in the month of October in various towns and all were advertised at the local tourist office.

OPPOSITE Wild strawberries or *fraises des bois* (which, despite their name, are now widely cultivated) taste sublime and the scent is quite wonderful. They are highly perishable and should be eaten without delay after purchasing.

JAUBERTIE
24380 Sᵗ MAYME de PEREYRO
Tel: 05 53 54 91 70
Fax: 05 53 54 70 69
POIDS NET: 125g

Sarlat-la-Canéda

Sarlat-la-Canéda is perhaps the best-known town in the Dordogne region. Its medieval heart is treasured and well preserved, and around every curve of the twisting, narrow streets is glimpsed yet another interesting building or a different angle of the impressive cathedral. The guidebook warned us that parking on a Saturday morning would be hell. We managed without too much trouble but would advise other visitors to drive right through the town to the much larger car park on the road to Brive than to use the one designated for '*Parking Tourisme*'. From the larger car park you will be approximately 15 minutes' walk from the market.

And what a lovely market it is, in this most beautiful town. The stalls wend their way through various side streets as well as occupying the central Place de la Liberté. When Julie and I visited there was plenty of business going on, all conducted in a calm and courteous manner with no shouting or spruiking.

As might be expected, stalls selling *foie gras* and *confit* were everywhere (I have written in more detail about these in the 'Foie Gras & Confit' chapter). If there were poultry stalls in profusion, so were there peach sellers. Such peaches! Small, with velvety, deep purple–pink skins, their flesh was purple bleeding to white and their flavour sweet and fragrant. These were the very special and rarely seen *pêches de vigne*. Then there were larger ones with creamy-white, fine flesh, or with juicy yellow flesh that was crimson next to the stone.

And the apricots – we nearly ended our friendship over these the first time we went to Sarlat. One woman at a stall right at the beginning of the market had baskets of large, ripe, rose-blushed fruit. Julie wanted to buy some but I demurred, fearing they would squash in the basket, and suggested they should be our last purchase. Of course, there were none left when we passed by again. We resolved to pounce next time and compensated with a tub of strawberries, admiring the wares on another stall of red gooseberries, blackcurrants, red and white currants, loganberries and raspberries. There were many stalls like this one, where the produce came from a particular farm.

We bought fine walnut oil, and pork sausages for slicing (including one as round and grey as a stone called a *galet du Périgord*), and olives (wrinkled black and split green), and beans and potatoes, and shallots labelled as *cuisses de poulet* ('chicken-thigh' shallots), and enormous leafy salads that had been pulled from real garden beds, in contrast to the hydroponically grown, 'designer'- sized salad greens that are increasingly saturating our markets at home in Australia. What a relief these French salads were. We also bought a small *croustade aux pommes* or apple tart. These tarts, variously called *croustades*, *tourtières* and *pastis*, come in various sizes and are popular throughout the south-west. '*Pastis*' seems to refer more specifically to the pastry itself, which is a work of art and resembles filo. It is stretched by hand

OPPOSITE, TOP If you visit Sarlat market on a Saturday morning, go very early. My advice would be to avoid it during summer after 14 July and look for a quieter market further afield.
OPPOSITE, BOTTOM LEFT Market stalls offer a seemingly infinite range of *saucissons* for slicing at apéritif time.
OPPOSITE, BOTTOM RIGHT Apricots are one of the attractions at a summer market. If you see some, buy them straight away or you might miss out, as Julie and I did.
OVERLEAF I always love seeing the mix of generations and sexes at popular market stalls in France. Here is an excellent example, at Sarlat on a Saturday morning. Even though the sky was grey, the colourful umbrellas and rain jackets made the scene a lively one.

and allowed to crumple and fold on the top of the pie into airy veils (see page 252). The tart we bought was filled with an almond frangipane mixed with a purée of apples and a liberal lacing of *eau-de-vie*.

Our autumn expedition to the market at Sarlat was on a rainy Saturday. Several in the group bought smart berets; others went for the less chic but more practical plastic rain bonnets that were the choice of many of the locals. An unforgettable feature of a French autumn market are the game birds hanging in full plumage – pheasant, partridge, pigeon – and wild rabbits still in their fur. Maggie bought a wild partridge and I bought two large rabbits and we looked forward to tasting them both. Everyone made at least one purchase at the copper cookware stall of Gérard Leclerc from nearby Pinsac. One pan came back to the house with us and was christened with some tiny and sweet *moules de bouchot* (cultivated mussels; see page 245) I bought at the fish stall. The queue was very long. The man in front of me ordered 5 kg (11 lb) of the mussels and for one moment I thought I was going to miss out. My order finished the tub for the day.

We had to be decisive at another stall also, where I spied several punnets of wild strawberries. I bought two, and one of super-sized raspberries, and paused to note the method used to make a jar of wild strawberry and raspberry jam. I rushed to tell the others of my find and when they crowded around to buy more, maybe 15 minutes later, the *fraises des bois* were all gone. We did buy several punnets of the small, sweet and highly perfumed local strawberries, and later Maggie made some delightful jam that reminded me of a similar recipe immortalised in my grandmother's book of recipes and reprinted in *The Cook's Companion*.

The salads were being sold at an average of three for 10 francs (about A$3). No all-of-a-kind trays of hydroponic salads here, just freshly picked leaves, frilly or crispy or floppy depending on the variety. I chose frilly oakleaf, crispy escarole and a floppy butter lettuce. The tomatoes were bumpy and spotty and, once again, grown by the stall-holder. They tasted magnificent.

Of course, not all our market purchases were food. *Brocante* markets also abound in the south-west and Sarlat had a good one while we were there in mid-October. These second-hand markets usually include valuable pieces as well as flea-market trash and treasure. They are very seductive. Maggie once bought a pair of carved wooden doors at one and then had to face the logistics of transporting them to Australia. She did it and they now look extremely handsome in her home. We were not really looking for doors, but there was lots of excitement about old silver spoons and forks, heavy-bottomed faceted wine glasses, faded faïence plates, copper pots with the patina of long usage, and one of the true treasures of almost all *brocante* markets: old linen. There were embroidered tablecloths, napkins, bed-sheets and towels. I found a wooden mandoline (a device for slicing vegetables) that was more than 1 metre in length and could only wonder at who had needed such an implement. A hotel kitchen, perhaps?

OPPOSITE, TOP LEFT Some in our group purchased berets at the market. I bought two to send home, but the parcel was lost in transit. Also in it were the wonderful old copper saucepans immortalised on the cover of this book, and a few other inexpensive but treasured bits of *brocante*.

OPPOSITE, TOP RIGHT The major part of the garlic crop is picked at the end of summer and hung to dry thoroughly until the tops have completely withered. This dried garlic, which can be either the pink or white variety, is then braided for sale, as you see here. Some garlic is harvested in early summer and sold fresh, still with a bit of green stem attached. The heads feel firm and the skin is thick and almost damp. The cloves within are particularly juicy, but do not keep for long.

OPPOSITE, BOTTOM LEFT I think I was overwhelmed by the difficulty of getting this giant mandoline home – otherwise, why didn't I buy it?

OPPOSITE, BOTTOM RIGHT Dahlias are Anna's favourite flower and were everywhere in the markets in October. I cannot say I warm to their stiff shapes and unsubtle colours, but everyone else disagreed with me.

Lauzerte

Another day, another outing and another market. On our way north from an excursion to prune country on the summer trip we happened on Lauzerte, an attractive *bastide* town. The weather was very moody, with dramatic clouds. We parked the car without any trouble at all and enjoyed a much smaller market experience than we had had at Sarlat. Here the 14th- and 15th-century houses were built using the white limestone of Quercy, an altogether different look from the honey-coloured stone of the Dordogne.

On one stall were a few of the frilly tarts we now knew as *croustades*. I asked the woman at the stall if she had made them. She said, 'I didn't – he did', indicating the man at her side. Abashed, I asked him about the technique of making the dough. He was pleased to describe how it had to be stretched finer and finer over the backs of the hands, and said that such pastries are known as *tourtières* here in Quercy and *croustades* in the Dordogne – a distance of maybe 50 km (30 miles). I bought the smallest one for our picnic. I should report that although the apple slices inside were golden and delicious and absolutely drenched with *eau-de-vie*, the pastry itself smelled and tasted stale. With subsequent knowledge I now wonder if what I had registered as stale butter was in fact pastry made from pork fat, which is the traditional method. Modern pastry shops have all switched to butter, but it seems possible that the man made his *tourtière* as he was taught by his mother or grandmother.

At the market everyone was cheerful and seemed to have all day to negotiate a purchase. Many of the men wore berets. We bought black cherries, huge apricots (at last!), tomatoes, crinkly green cabbage and strawberries, and some farm-made sausage and bread and *cabécous* from a sweet, smiling girl. The cheeses were 10 for 30 francs (about A$8.50), and we could choose between three days old, one week old, and much older and harder. We had everything we needed for a simple lunch somewhere in the glorious countryside.

Le Bugue

One day in summer we visited friends Wendely Harvey and Robert Cave-Rogers, who were putting the finishing touches to a mammoth project of converting a stone house into a cooking school with accommodation for eight. They were situated just beyond Les Eyzies at Le Combe and their nearest market was at Le Bugue, on the Vézère River. Part of the cooking course would be aimed at showing the students the best of the artisanal produce in the region, and where better to do this than at the local market? We went along to meet their contacts.

OPPOSITE These airy apple tarts, known as *croustades*, *tourtières* or *pastis* depending on which part of the south-west you are in, were displayed with a card telling the purchaser that they were a regional speciality of the *départements* of Lot and Lot-et-Garonne and were made by the vendor, not brought in from a factory. How on earth do you eat such a tart, you might wonder. The answer is simply to cut it into wedges – but expect to be showered with sticky fragments of pastry in the process.

59ᶠ

Tourtière aux.Pommes.

Patisserie Regionale
Specialité du lot et garonne
et lot

Fabrication Maison

FINSTER.BACH - GAVAUDUN 47150.

I spoke with a rather disgruntled goat's cheese farmer who, in reply to a query as to whether he would be able to receive a group interested in cheese-making, said he could not possibly allow anyone to visit his farm because he was far too busy: 'Maybe in October.' He told me that the future for handmade cheese was doubtful, that the big factories, producers of industrial cheese, were competing with the small artisans and that taxes and production costs were constantly rising. All in all he did not know how long he could hold out. When I suggested this was a tragic scenario, he snapped that it was tragic for me but not for him. He, after all, had many other strings to his bow! I left him feeling unsure what to think.

In contrast, the man selling Cantal cheese was in high spirits. He had travelled for three hours from his home town, Laguiole, in the Auvergne (the same place as makes the French version of the Swiss army knife, an elegant, wickedly sharp folding dagger knife with the motif of a fly, called after the town), to attend the market and was pleased to chat. He saw nothing grim about the future for his cheese.

I bought organically grown raspberries and homemade strawberry jam and wished I could take some of the chestnut honey home to Australia. An old lady showed me her son's speciality – something I had not seen before – of a cured *magret de canard* rolled in pepper and stuffed with *foie gras*, intended to be cut into thin slices to enjoy with an apéritif. We bought mussels and hurried home to cook them, taking one wrong turn that deposited us right at the foot of spectacular Beynac Castle.

In autumn, Le Bugue was the nearest good-sized market to our rented house and we got to know it well. On one occasion I wanted to buy a special piece of pork in order to make *l'enchaud de porc truffé* (truffled loin of pork), a splendid dish and an appropriate way of utilising the canned truffle I had been given by André (see page 67). I asked at one of the cheese stalls for advice and was directed to the shop of M. Bounichou, a high-quality butcher. I enjoyed describing the dish I wanted to make. Both the butcher and I thought the piece of pork loin he had on display in the shop was too small to feed 12 people, so out came a huge side of pork, far larger than any I had seen in Australia, and a bigger piece was cut. The meat was then boned and I requested extra fat to 'bard' the joint (to protect it from drying out during cooking) and asked the butcher to please wrap up the bones as well. The barding fat was cut from a roll of thinly sliced pork fat that was stored rolled with parchment paper so the buyer could indicate exactly how much was needed. What a wonderful resource! I was very taken with this butcher and ordered some massive *entrecôte* steaks for our barbecue that night. He told me with such reverence in his voice that it was Limousin beef that I understood it was very special. Once again the meat was cut with great care and after consultation as to thickness. I felt I was in the hands of an expert. Jonathan Gianfreda, my butcher in Melbourne, later told me that Limousin beef

OPPOSITE We bought outstanding meat at M. Bounichou's wonderful butcher's shop at Le Bugue. The blackboard outside listed his daily cooked 'specials' – that day he had guinea fowl with prunes and quail with grapes. The butcher wore a one-shouldered apron, like Henriette. This design seemed to hold the apron securely in place and offer maximum protection while leaving the arms unrestricted (as opposed to a white coat, for example).

is cut from a giant 300 kg (660 lb) animal, whereas the largest beef available to an Australian customer would be from an animal weighing 180–200 kg (395–440 lb). I should perhaps add that 'mad cow disease' in French animals was first mentioned after our trip.

Sainte Alvère

One rainy autumn Monday I went with Angie Clemens to our nearest small market, at Sainte Alvère. There were probably only five or six stalls and I made the mistake of asking a man from whom I had just purchased some new season's pink garlic and organic yellow and red tomatoes if he had a lemon. He looked at me with a puzzled air and said, 'I don't grow lemons.' I had foolishly failed to realise that he was a *producteur* (grower) and on intimate terms with every tomato and onion at his stall.

Sainte Alvère, like every market we visited, was a treasure trove of culinary knowledge. It would soon be Halloween and I admired a towering display of brilliant pumpkins whose flesh was an astonishing orange colour. The stall-holder warmed to my interest and described her pumpkin soup/gratin, in which she layers pumpkin, ham, day-old bread and Comté cheese with cream and milk and slowly bakes it until it puffs (see page 238). I wanted to rush home and try that one immediately. 'Or,' she said, 'cook the pumpkin in milk, add some eggs, sugar and flour [she was vague as to quantities] and a little *eau-de-vie*, bake as for a *clafoutis* and eat it warm.'

Le Marché au Gras

While *confit* products are available everywhere every day of the year, you must visit in the wintertime if you want to see the birds actually opened out to display their raw livers, which happens at *le marché au gras* (literally, 'fat market'), held in various south-western towns. I was fortunate to visit *le marché au gras* at Périgueux and also at Excideuil on the same day as attending the first truffle market of the season in the last days of November. (There are more details about *les marchés au gras* in the 'Foie Gras & Confit' chapter.)

Money may sometimes be scarce in the country and neither duck breasts nor *foie gras* could be regarded as everyday fare, but the local people's enthusiasm for their own produce still seemed to be very high at the market. Those I talked to in Périgueux were without exception cheerful, practical and delighted to pass on their favourite recipes.

As well as duck and goose products, I saw in this winter market *crosnes*, a little-known vegetable (*Stachys affinis*) usually translated as a Chinese or Japanese artichoke. They are shaped a bit like a corkscrew or a string of knobbly beads and are quite small. They have a flavour not dissimilar to salsify, the old man at the stall said. He advised to rub them with a cloth and some coarse salt to get rid of the skins.

And there were medlars, properly squishy and ready for Christmas, and cardoons, another Christmas treat, and bundles of beef short ribs neatly tied for use in a pot-au-feu, and a small mountain of *hachis*: minced pork fat, green with chopped parsley and aromatic with garlic, for enriching a bean soup or a simmering casserole. The man at this stall advised me to fry the *hachis* quickly before adding it to a stew. He also passed on the advice that if you want to chop pork fat it is a good idea to heat the chopper first. All these comments and advice seemed to be a natural part of every market experience.

RECIPES FROM THE MARKET WOMEN AT EXCIDEUIL

I was surprised to see the rows and rows of stripped duck carcasses for sale at Excideuil. They were called *les demoiselles* (young ladies). In turn, the market women were surprised at my ignorance and only too happy to share certain favourite ways of using this by-product of the fattened-duck industry, including

SALSIFY AND SCORZONERA
Salsify is an ingredient that is not often seen in Australia. It and its near relative scorzonera are root vegetables that belong to the daisy family. Salsify looks like a long, tapered carrot with a rough brown skin, while scorzonera has a black skin. They are both popular in the south-west and are in season during autumn and winter. They have a delicate flavour, somewhat reminiscent of parsnip. It is said that salsify tastes a bit fishy and it is sometimes known as the oyster plant. I don't think it tastes anything like an oyster! Both vegetables discolour after peeling, so you need to have a bowl of acidulated water ready. They roast and braise beautifully, just like parsnips do.

LEFT *Crosnes*, or Chinese artichokes, are said to taste somewhat like salsify, which is the vegetable you can see at the top left of the picture. To Australians, *crosnes* look remarkably like the well-known indigenous food witchetty grubs.

a recipe using the duck's blood. I am passing on these recipes for interest and authenticity, knowing that the reader will have to be in the south-west before he or she can try these specialities.

Roasted duck carcass

Put a duck carcass over a fire of burned-down coals and turn it until it is an appetising brown all over. Remove the *aiguillettes* (underfillets) with a sharp knife (probably a Laguiole; see page 231) and enjoy with a slice of country bread and a sprinkling of salt and pepper.

Sanguette

Mix finely chopped garlic and plenty of salt and pepper in a deep plate. Hold a freshly killed duck over the plate and allow the blood to drain onto it. Stir the blood and allow it to coagulate, then tip the seasoned blood into a deep pan of simmering, salted water and simmer for 15 minutes. Remove the blood cake with a fish lifter or similar and drain well. This delicacy is eaten as it is or fried and put on toast, or with a sauce of well-cooked puréed onion and plenty of country bread.

Ragoût of duck carcass

In a deep pot, fry 2 duck carcasses in a little duck fat until well browned. Pour over 1 cup water and let it bubble and reduce almost completely. Peel and roughly chop 2 onions, 2 carrots, 2 stalks of salsify and 4 potatoes, and chop 2 sticks of celery. Tuck the vegetables inside each carcass, then half-cover the carcasses with water. Cover with a tight lid and simmer for 1 hour, checking the water level once or twice during cooking. This quantity serves 2 people. To eat, suck at the bones and enjoy the broth and vegetables with plenty of country bread. The women in the market laughed at me when I asked if one should eat the bones. 'If you want to,' they said.

Papillote of duck carcass

Plenty of chopped garlic and parsley were added to the same ingredients used in the ragoût above to make another simple dish. This time the carcass and vegetables were wrapped in baking paper and roasted in the oven for 1 hour at 180°C/375°F.

OPPOSITE, TOP At this stall the vendor displayed *confit* duck legs alongside a portion of *hachis* – pork fat mixed with minced garlic and parsley, used to add richness and savour to slow-cooked dishes and stuffings.

OPPOSITE, BOTTOM LEFT The market women at Excideuil gave me some ideas on how to use these duck carcasses, sold with their breast underfillets still attached (see recipes on this page).

OPPOSITE, BOTTOM RIGHT It was remarkable to see the fattened ducks on display at *le marché au gras* at Excideuil. The vendors willingly answered my questions about their products.

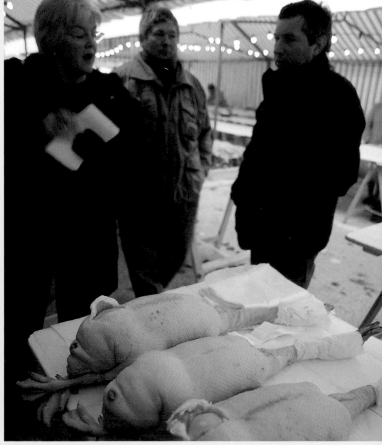

Pumpkin Soup Gratiné with Comté Gruyère Cheese and Bayonne Ham

Serves 6

800 g/1 lb 12 oz pumpkin, seeded
    and peeled to yield 500 g/1 lb 2 oz
4 large slices country-style bread,
    crusts removed
30 g/1 oz unsalted butter
2 slices raw ham (approximately
    60 g/2 oz), cut into small pieces
125 g/4½ oz Comté Gruyère or
    similar melting-type cheese,
    finely sliced
freshly ground black pepper
freshly grated nutmeg
sea salt
2 cups chicken stock
1 cup whipping cream

Comté Gruyère is made from cow's milk and comes from the Auvergne. The raw ham we bought locally was sold as *jambon de Bayonne*, but I do not know whether it actually came from Bayonne. I do know that the pumpkins came from our neighbour's garden, where they lolled among the leaves looking a little like decorative garden ornaments – a flash of brilliance against the dark soil and the darkening autumn landscape.

Preheat the oven to 180°C/375°F. Cut the pumpkin into 5 mm/¼ in slices and then cut the slices into large pieces. Cut the bread into 4 cm/1½ in squares.

Using one-third of the butter, grease a 1.5 litre/2½ pint ovenproof dish. Layer a third each of the pumpkin, bread, ham and cheese in the dish, seasoning as you go with pepper and nutmeg and a little salt. Repeat the layers twice, finishing with cheese. Mix the stock and cream and gently pour over. Dot with the remainder of the butter. Cover with a lid or with lightly buttered aluminium foil and stand the dish in a pan with water to come two-thirds up the sides. Transfer to the oven and cook for approximately 1 hour.

Remove the dish from the water bath, take off the lid and test to see if the pumpkin is tender. If not, cover and return to the oven for an extra 15 minutes. When the pumpkin is tender, uncover the pot and return it once more to the oven until the top has browned. Serve at once. The gratin should look lightly puffed and have an appetising crust.

Variation

Once the pumpkin is tender, ladle the soup into individual gratin dishes. Twenty minutes before serving, return the dishes to the oven and bake until golden and lightly puffed. Warn your guests that the dishes will be very hot.

PREVIOUS PAGES At this market cheese stall the cut cheeses were protected by plastic bags – a new phenomenon in my experience. Most of those displayed here are made with unpasteurised cow's milk and are hard-style cheeses, including Cantal, at different stages of maturity.
OPPOSITE There were pumpkins of every shape and colour at the markets, including the variety Australians know as butternuts. Here you can see the brilliant colour of the flesh of one of the most popular local varieties.

Green Beans in the Manner of Quercy

Serves 4

400 g/14 oz young green beans, trimmed
2 eggs
1 tablespoon red-wine vinegar
1 shallot, finely chopped
1 tablespoon freshly chopped young parsley (preferably flat-leaf)
sea salt
freshly ground black pepper

This is a superb way of serving best-quality beans. In 'our' markets in France the beans were locally grown and proudly labelled. Each one was no bigger than my little finger and half the thickness. They were so exquisite that on one occasion we had for lunch beans prepared as in this recipe and small, newly dug potatoes and nothing else. The sauce works just as well for new season's carrots or broad beans.

Timing is everything – the idea is to make a creamy sauce, not scrambled eggs. The vegetable serving dish must be beside the cook and the cooking pot must be large enough for the vegetables to be given a quick toss.

Have ready next to the stove a warmed serving dish. Cook the beans in plenty of boiling water until just tender. Meanwhile, whisk together the eggs and vinegar. When the beans are cooked, remove 1 tablespoon of the cooking liquid and whisk it into the egg mixture. Quickly drain the beans and put them into the warmed serving dish. Put the empty pan back over a low heat and tip in the egg mixture. Stir with a wooden spoon and in a minute or so you will have a creamy sauce. Remove the pan from the heat and add the beans, shallot and parsley. Shake together so the beans are well covered with sauce. Season to taste, then return the beans and sauce to the warmed dish and serve.

Maggie's Artichokes, Onions and Potatoes Stewed in Verjus with Mushrooms

In France we bought large artichokes that, when stripped to the heart, were exceptionally meaty. Each heart was 8 cm (3 in) in diameter. In Australia you should allow 2 artichokes per person. The potatoes we chose were no larger than my thumb. They were called Roseval and had red skins and creamy flesh. Any small waxy potato would do – kipflers or patrones would be perfect in Australia. And we used the small, yellow, upturned *girolle* mushrooms.

The use of *verjus* was typical in medieval times and seems to be experiencing a bit of a revival, although the *verjus* on sale in France is much sharper than that made by my good friend Maggie Beer. Maggie's verjuice, which is widely available in Australia and is also sold in Britain, relies on cold stabilisation to prevent fermentation, as is done in fine winemaking. In consequence, her verjuice exhibits noticeable bottle development. The French product is pasteurised to prevent fermentation, which I feel dulls the flavour.

To prepare the artichokes, pour the *verjus* into a small bowl. Wearing disposable gloves, take an artichoke and tear off the outside leaves until the heart is reached. Cut off the top half of the artichoke and hollow out the heart using a sharp teaspoon, disposing of all of the hairy choke. Trim the outside of the exposed heart so that all the leaf attachments are removed. Cut the stem close to the heart. Halve the heart and quickly roll it in the *verjus*. Thickly peel the trimmed stem and moisten it with *verjus* also. Continue until all the artichokes and stems are trimmed and waiting in the *verjus*.

Select a lidded ovenproof pan in which the artichoke hearts and other vegetables will fit tightly in 1 layer. Drain the artichokes and their stems, reserving the *verjus*. Heat one-third of the olive oil in the pan and seal all the artichokes and stems over high heat. Add the garlic, onions and potatoes. Seal and toss quickly. Add the bay leaf and thyme, the strained *verjus* and the rest of the olive oil. Grind over some pepper. Cover with baking paper and a lid, lower the heat and braise gently on top of the stove or in the oven at 180°C/375°F for about 1½ hours until the vegetables are tender and the juices have emulsified and reduced.

Fifteen minutes before serving, sauté the mushrooms in the butter and add to the pan. Stir. Adjust the seasoning and sprinkle with the parsley. Spoon the juices over and make sure there is good bread for mopping. You could add a few leaves of lamb's lettuce (*mâche*), if desired.

Serves 4

375 ml/13 fl oz verjus
4 large *or* 8 small artichokes
200 ml/7 fl oz extra-virgin olive oil
8 fat garlic cloves, peeled
8 small onions, peeled
8 tiny waxy potatoes
1 bay leaf
several sprigs of thyme
freshly ground black pepper
8 small Swiss brown mushrooms
2 tablespoons unsalted butter
sea salt
2 tablespoons freshly chopped young parsley (preferably flat-leaf)

Mussels Cooked in My New Copper Pan

Moules de bouchot are cultivated on ropes and are usually sand-free. They are tiny – each no bigger than an almond – yet the shells are full of sweet mussel meat.

This is the simplest method of cooking mussels. You can add diced tomato and/or freshly chopped chilli and add a different herb at the end. The straining of the juices is optional. If you prefer the crunch of the shallot and celery, don't strain the sauce and accept that an occasional grain of sand is part of the experience.

Wash the mussels in plenty of cold water. Scrub the biggest barnacles from the shells with a hard brush and pull off the beards using a sharp, downward tugging movement. Discard any mussel that is broken or gaping open.

Have at the ready a hot serving dish and, if you wish to strain the sauce, a small bowl with a fine-meshed strainer resting in it. Scatter the shallot and celery in a pan that will hold the mussels in 1 or 2 fairly even layers. Put the mussels on top, then pour over the wine and add the bay leaf. Cover tightly with either the lid of the pan, a sheet of aluminium foil or another, upturned pan. Turn the heat to full. After 3–5 minutes the steam will gush and force up the cover and the mussels will all have opened. Remove them with a slotted spoon to the hot dish.

Add the butter and parsley to the original pan and bring to a rapid boil. (If desired, first pour the mussel juices through the fine sieve to collect any sand. Rinse out the frying pan quickly, then return the juices to the pan and add the butter and parsley.) Grind in some pepper and then pour the sauce over the mussels (or return the mussels to the sauce in the pan, if the pan is to be the serving dish). Serve with plenty of bread for mopping.

Serves 2–3

1 kg/2 lb mussels
3 shallots, finely chopped
1 stick celery, finely chopped
½ bottle (375 ml/13 fl oz) dry white wine
1 bay leaf
1 tablespoon unsalted butter
1 tablespoon freshly chopped young parsley (preferably flat-leaf)
freshly ground black pepper

Rabbit with Mustard and Verjus

Serves 3–4

1 × 1.5 kg/3 lb 4 oz farmed rabbit,
  cut into pieces *or* 1 kg/2 lb rabbit
  pieces on the bone
2 tablespoons rendered duck fat
freshly ground black pepper
1 tablespoon mustard of your choice
2 cloves garlic, chopped
100 ml/3½ fl oz verjus
200 ml/7 fl oz chicken stock
1 cup seeded grapes (optional)
sea salt
2 tablespoons freshly chopped young
  parsley (preferably flat-leaf)

For this dish I used a pot of mustard bought at Brive, which was violet in colour from having been made with *moût de raisin* (grape lees). Use your favourite variety, although powdered mustard is not recommended. Unable to resist them at the market, I also added some tiny new potatoes at the same time as the stock. This is entirely optional.

As with so much of the cooking in the region, the ideal pot for this rabbit dish is one that is wide enough to accommodate all the pieces for the initial browning and that can then go into the oven or be used on top of the stove. Attractive, colourful pots such as the one pictured opposite are on sale at the markets and have the added advantage that they can be presented at the table straight from the stove, still bubbling hot and intact. If you buy a pot from the market, follow the instructions to soak it overnight first and do not heat it empty.

Trim the rabbit pieces neatly, reserving the belly flaps and the bony tail end of the saddle for another use (label and freeze them and use when making stock or soup). Heat the duck fat in your chosen pot and thoroughly brown the rabbit pieces. Pour off the excess fat and grind quite a bit of pepper over the meat. Stir in the mustard over a high heat. After a few minutes, add the garlic. Stir until the garlic smells wonderful – it must not brown, however – and then trickle in the *verjus*, keeping the heat high. It will bubble up and reduce quite quickly. Stir in the stock, then lower the heat and add the grapes, if using. Press a piece of baking paper over the meat and cover with a lid. Simmer for 20–25 minutes until tender.

Remove the rabbit to a warm dish. Increase the heat and boil the juices to reduce them by half. Taste for seasoning and add salt if necessary. Stir in the parsley, then return the rabbit to the pot and stir to coat well with sauce. Serve immediately.

Leftovers are great warmed through in any jellied juices and served with salad leaves and some sautéed potatoes or *pommes sarladaises* (see page 284).

Variations

This simple dish can be made with wild rabbit, but the meat will take longer to become tender. If using wild rabbit, it might be a good idea to add some diced pork fat or pork rind to make the dish more unctuous. It is just as delicious, too, when made with jointed chicken or veal. I have also tasted something similar featuring frogs' legs.

Entrecôte Steak in the Bordeaux Way

The steaks I bought in Le Bugue were enormous – easily three times the size of any porterhouse I have ever seen. One slice weighed 1 kg (2 lb)! They were from Limousin beef and, as explained on pages 231–2, these animals are much larger than those that provide the beef available to Australian butchers. To me, *entrecôte* had, up until that moment, always meant the upper cut of the porterhouse – that is, the sirloin. At home I had a discussion about it with butcher Vince Garreffa from Perth, who supplies me with special veal. He believes that a French butcher would have cut this prime section differently and it would have included some of what we know as the scotch fillet. He says that a good butcher will know what you mean if you request steaks cut from between the seventh and the thirteenth rib with the cap left on. I would be interested to hear what in fact happens if readers ask for this.

This luxury steak should be cooked over glowing coals, not flames, and is eaten rare, or medium–rare at a pinch. Depending on the design and depth of your barbecue or fireplace, the fire should be timed so that it has burned down to coals 15 minutes before dinner. A handful of dried vine prunings is traditionally thrown on the fire just before the meat. These burn very quickly and give a distinctive aroma and, after all, this is a steak as eaten by winemakers – fast, no fuss and with minimum garnish.

When buying marrow bones, don't let the butcher give you the end bits of the shin bone – it's impossible to extract the marrow.

Soak the marrow bones overnight in salted water. Remove the steak from the refrigerator several hours before you plan to eat. Rub it with the olive oil, grind over some black pepper and sprinkle with sea salt and set aside to rest, covered. Soak the shallot in the vinegar for 30 minutes.

While the fire is burning down, poach the marrow bones in simmering water for 8–10 minutes until the pinkish colour fades. Remove the pan from the heat and set aside. Put the meat on a grill no more than 6 cm/2½ in from the coals and grill for 5–7 minutes per side. Transfer to a hot dish and allow to relax for 5 minutes. Meanwhile, drain the marrow bones, grind over a little fresh pepper and add a sprinkle of sea salt. Put the meat on a chopping board, carve diagonally into thick slices and quickly transfer to a very hot serving plate. Strew generously with the shallot and garnish with the marrow bones.

Note

You may have to buy 3 pieces of porterhouse steak to approximate the weight given here. The thickness is more important than it being a single slab of meat.

Serves 3

6 × 2 cm/¾ in thick slices marrow bone
sea salt
1 × 1 kg/2 lb well-aged porterhouse steak, 3 cm/1 ¼ in thick (see Note)
2 teaspoons olive oil
freshly ground black pepper
3 tablespoons finely chopped shallots
2 tablespoons red-wine vinegar

Blood Sausage and Apple Parcels

BOUDIN NOIR ET POMMES FEUILLETÉES

Serves 8 as a first course

2 eating apples, peeled and
   quartered
1 tablespoon unsalted butter
500 g/1 lb puff pastry, rolled out to
   a thickness of 5 mm/¼ in
1 egg, lightly whisked
2 teaspoons mustard of your choice
2 blood sausages, each cut into
   4 pieces

The range of *charcuterie* in the markets seemed infinite. Blood sausages were popular in autumn, as were apples. In fact, the apple orchards intrigued us as we drove about. Often pruned as espaliers, both the trees and the ground were laden with golden and red fruit, leaving us to wonder why these windfalls seemed abandoned. The puff pastry I bought in the supermarket was made with butter and was of outstanding quality. I put all of these elements together and came up with this little treat to serve with a glass of wine as an appetiser.

Sauté the apple chunks on both sides in the butter for 4 minutes until coloured and just starting to soften. Remove and drain on kitchen paper until quite cold.

Cut the puff pastry sheet into eight 12 cm/5 in squares, then brush each square with egg, being careful not to let it drip down the edges. Divide the mustard between the squares. Put 1 chunk of sausage diagonally in the centre of each square, then rest 1 piece of apple next to the sausage. Bring 2 corners of the pastry up and squeeze together over the sausage. Brush the exposed pastry carefully with egg. Chill for 20 minutes. Preheat the oven to 220°C/425°F.

Bake the parcels for 15 minutes. Serve hot with a little mustard on the side, if desired. I chose one made with honey, but any mustard or fruit chutney would be a good accompaniment. You could even spoon it onto the sausage after it comes from the oven – the mustard will soften a bit and spread into the pastry.

Croustade of Peach

Serves 6–8

6 large ripe peaches (*or* 3 peaches
    and 3 nectarines or apricots)
3 tablespoons eau-de-vie de prune
    or peach liqueur
2 tablespoons almond oil *or*
    walnut oil
½ cup castor/superfine sugar
1 teaspoon cinnamon

Croustade pastry
250 g/9 oz plain/all-purpose flour
1 large egg, separated
pinch of salt
2 teaspoons olive oil
100 ml/3½ fl oz tepid water

Every food writer has a version of how to make the blow-away pastry essential for these typically south-western fruit tarts. They are easily recognisable in *pâtisseries* with their crumpled pastry petals, but not nearly so easy to construct at home. In France they are usually filled with apple or apple and prunes, but once back in my own kitchen I was inspired during the summer months and decided to make one with peaches.

I followed the quantities for the pastry given in one classic book but simply could not achieve the results promised. My first effort was a very sad affair, with pieces of dough all over the table and floor – the dog loved it, but I was disappointed. The author of the book suggested working and stretching the dough thinly over a printed bedsheet until you could see the pattern through the dough. Years ago an Austrian friend of my mother's told me that when making strudel dough you should be able to read a love letter through it. I mention this to emphasise how thin the stretched pastry should be in both cases.

The second attempt was more successful, but still a bit tough. And then I happened to eat at the restaurant of a friend in Sydney – Janni Kyritsis at MG Garage – and found that he had a *croustade* of mulberries on the menu. Janni and I have commented over the years that our menus often show similar interests, as if we communicate subliminally. I asked him about the pastry and he said his recipe came via an employee who had worked for Pierre Koffmann at La Tante Claire in London – and Koffmann is from Gascony in the south-west of France. So I tried his recipe, inevitably making a few personal adjustments. It worked well and although I did not have a love letter handy I could read the newspaper headlines through it!

I made my *croustade* hours before my guests arrived but found that if I put it in the plate-warming drawer of my oven it tasted just-baked on serving.

Peel the peaches and cut them into bite-sized pieces. (If using nectarines or apricots, do not peel, but do cut them into bite-sized pieces.) Put the fruit into a bowl with the *eau-de-vie* and almond or walnut oil and turn to mix well. Cover with plastic film and leave until needed.

To make the pastry, sift the flour and transfer it to the bowl of an electric mixer fitted with a dough hook. In 2 separate bowls, whisk the egg white with the salt until stiff, and slowly but steadily whisk the oil into the yolk as if making a mayonnaise. Fold the egg white into the egg yolk mixture, then gradually add the water and mix until smooth. With the motor running, slowly add the liquid mixture to the flour until all the flour is taken up. Increase the speed so that the dough is being well kneaded and allow to knead for a full 5 minutes or until the dough is smooth and shiny. Wrap the ball of dough in plastic film, put it in a bowl and leave for 4 hours in a warm, draught-free place.

To stretch the dough, remove your watch and any rings. You will not succeed with this if you have long fingernails, either! Cover a 2 m/6 ft square table or bench with a cloth and then with a clean bedsheet. Liberally smear the sheet with flour. Roll out the dough on the bedsheet with a thin rolling pin, using flour to prevent the pin sticking to the dough. It should roll easily to a thin sheet. Lift the sheet of pastry and allow it to rest over your loose fists and the backs of your hands, then start stretching it by constantly shifting the weight of the dough over your fists so that it doesn't drag unevenly to one side. The dough will stretch quite easily and will grow to about twice its original size in a few minutes. At this stage it will be too difficult to hold it up in the air, so settle it back on the floured bedsheet.

Still using your loosely clenched fists and the backs of your hands, slide your hands under the dough and, starting from the centre, work it thinner and thinner, moving around the dough as you go so that it stretches evenly. It is exciting to see it thin, just like strudel or filo pastry. Don't be afraid to really stretch it as the dough is pretty elastic. A few small holes won't matter. It took me 20 minutes to achieve a rather uneven square of about 1 m × 1 m (3 ft × 3 ft). At this stage, leave the pastry to dry for about 1 hour. The drying stage is important because if the pastry is wet it will be very tough. It should not, however, be so dry that it breaks (think of filo pastry).

Preheat the oven to 180°C/375°F. Drain the fruit and keep the juices nearby. Grease a 22 cm/8½ in round cake tin with a little extra oil (walnut, almond or olive). Mix the castor sugar and cinnamon. Trim any thick edges from the pastry. From the centre of the pastry square, cut a round large enough to fit the base and sides of the cake tin, of a diameter of about 32 cm/12½ in. Settle this into the tin. Cut another round alongside the first, this time of a diameter of 22 cm/8½ in, then cut 7 same-sized strips from the remaining pastry, working out from the edges of the cut rounds. These shapes will be narrow where they join the rounds and widen to the edge of the stretched pastry, like long triangles with the point missing.

Drape 1 long triangle across the base of the tin, the widest part in the tin, the narrow piece dangling. Sprinkle the pastry with some of the reserved juices from the fruit, then sprinkle with some of the cinnamon sugar. Lay a second strip of pastry across the base in the opposite direction from the first, so that its widest part is in the tin and the rest dangles over the edge. Sprinkle with juices and cinnamon sugar as before. Repeat once more. You now have a base of 4 layers of pastry.

Scatter half the fruit over the pastry. Cover with 2 more sections of pastry, cut, draped and crossed over in the same way as before. Sprinkle each layer with juices and cinnamon sugar as previously. Add the rest of the fruit. Cover with 2 more overlapping strips, sprinkling and scattering as before. Put the second pastry round on top and lift and settle all the overhanging pastry onto the top of this in loose, crumpled folds (some cooks are able to make the top look like a full-blown rose). Brush generously with the last of the juices and scatter with the last of the cinnamon sugar. Bake for 1 hour and serve warm.

OVERLEAF Another version of the local *croustade*, filled with apples and prunes. Here the pastrycook has compromised, using the *croustade* pastry just for the top section. When making my own version at home with juicy yellow peaches, I had great fun attempting the pastry. Months later, at the 2001 Melbourne Food and Wine Festival, I watched pastry queen Rose Levy Beranbaum demonstrate the very similar stretching of strudel dough, and felt that my technique had been pretty good.

Truffles

*P*robably nothing in the food world evokes more intrigue, controversy and mystery than the black truffle (*Tuber melanosporum*). Maybe part of my fascination with the Périgord, this region of deeply green oak forests, is the thought of what might lie beneath the surface. I am not alone in this fascination. Many French writers and poets have pronounced on the flavour and perfume of the potent fungus and once upon a time it was mandatory to include it in any dish belonging to *haute cuisine*. Things have changed, principally the availability of the truffle. Annual harvests had drastically diminished from 800–1000 tonnes at the beginning of the 20th century to 40 tonnes in the 1990s. At the time of writing, the best *T. melanosporum* was selling in France for approximately 3000 francs per kilogram. The Australian price was $A1800 per kilo, two and a half times the French price.

What has not changed is the mystery, the theories and the folklore, including a belief that 'the knowledge' rests with the old-timers. The story of the truffle, from its history in the time of ancient Greece up to the use of agricultural technology in the mid-1980s to try to unlock the secrets of successful cultivation, is told most clearly in *Le Grand Livre de la truffe*, a fascinating book written by Pierre-Jean and Jacques Pébeyre. The house of Pébeyre is synonymous with the finest luxury products of the south-west – truffles, *foie gras* and *confits* – and supplies many of the most prestigious restaurants in Europe with black truffles, delivered in baskets woven from chestnut leaves to allow a free flow of air.

In 1982 I had the privilege of spending an extraordinary week at the three-star Michelin-rated Restaurant Troisgros in Roanne, near Lyon, which was then presided over by the late Jean Troisgros and his brother Pierre. I watched as Jean Troisgros opened a parcel from Pébeyre and held my breath as a large basket of aromatic truffles was lifted from the packaging. Many of these would have gone to make the then-famous and supremely wonderful Restaurant Troisgros dish of a layered terrine of vegetables generously banded with thick slices of truffle.

The Pébeyres deliver some important facts in their book. In order to grow, a truffle needs a tree, suitable terrain and a precise climate. *T. melanosporum* and *T. brumale* are the only varieties allowed to be called *truffes de Périgord* and *melanosporum* is the superior variety. *T. aestivum* – the so-called 'summer truffle' – has no culinary interest for the Pébeyres, although to be controversial I would have to say that I had a salad of *écrevisses* in the summer of 1999 onto which freshly

OPPOSITE A morning's harvest from La Truffière de la Bergerie (see page 267) yielded several truffles. As can be seen in the photograph, a mature truffle can vary enormously in size from about that of a marble to that of a fist.

gathered *T. aestivum* was shaved at the last moment (as can be done with *T. magnatum*, the white truffle from Piedmont). The slices were curled and speckled and had an intriguing crunchy texture and a pleasant woodsy fragrance. I asked the waiter to bring me one so that I could see it whole and it proved to be brownish and quite small. He said that few people bother to gather them because they are not considered valuable. Tourists beware: I have often seen *T. aestivum* on sale in markets in the months when you could never expect to find a fresh *T. melanosporum*. Either leave them there or buy them for a modest price and expect a 'texture food' rather than any suggestion of truffle magnificence.

Truffles develop in symbiosis with the roots of a suitable tree: hazelnut, evergreen oak or regular oak. Mycelia (microscopic white filaments of vegetable origin) spread in the soil between the roots of the tree like a spider's web and contact between the mycelia and the roots (mycorrhization) causes the development of little bumps. Through these bumps passes the nourishment that permits the possible development of a truffle. The little bumps are *not* truffles in the making, but they are evidence that mycorrhization has taken place.

This natural process is imitated by the Union Régionale de Trufficulture d'Aquitaine (URTA) in Périgueux, a part of the Department of Agriculture. Truffle cultivation is big business and excites a great deal of interest in France and elsewhere. When I visited URTA in early December 1999, it was absolutely enthralling to hear about the efforts to cultivate *T. melanosporum* in France. Research has been going on for at least 20 years (some suggest even longer than this) and the scientist I spoke to, M. Patrick Regou, stated most excitedly that a great deal had been discovered in the last five years. Six months before my visit, the first truffles had been discovered on a *truffière* (a property dedicated to cultivating truffles) in Tasmania, seven years after the planting of hazelnut trees inoculated with mycelium spores. I had watched this project with great interest from its very beginning and was delighted that there was now physical evidence that the scheme was not a fantasy. It had not been easy to convince Tasmanian farmers to plant trees that *might* yield a valuable, if unheard-of, crop eight years hence.

Two years later I can report that a steady trickle of truffles (*T. melanosporum*) has been harvested in successive seasons in Tasmania, and that there are now six producing *truffières* in New Zealand. A friend and restaurateur in Christchurch, Lisa Scholz, holds an annual truffle dinner and last season purchased 1.2 kg from her supplier. In 2000, NZ truffles were fetching NZ$3000 per kg, and in 2001 it was closer to NZ$4000. Luxury food indeed, even though a kilo will go a long way.

At URTA Patrick stressed that truffles need light and warmth to develop and then need cold to mature. The soil should be chalky, with a high pH, and well drained. The season commences in late November and continues until the end of February. Truffles do not like to be disturbed, nor do they like insecticides. I was interested to hear that the soil influences the flavour of truffles and that, to an

OPPOSITE Truffles develop in symbiosis with the roots of hazelnut, evergreen oak or regular oak trees. At the truffle research laboratory in Périgueux we saw an infant hazelnut tree just days after its first inoculation with the spores of *Tuber melanosporum* (top right) and containers full of young oak and hazelnut seedlings.

expert, no two truffles smell the same. At local truffle markets you can choose your truffle according to your individual response to its perfume.

At the French research station, the practice is for 1.5 g (0.05 oz) of mycelium spores to be put onto the roots of tiny seedlings in the European spring (April). Before the seedlings are planted out two years later, the scientists examine microscopically a percentage of each batch to ascertain whether mycorrhization has occurred or not. The trees are sold to anyone interested for 60 francs (about A$17) per seedling. The research body has also undertaken to investigate trees that have been in the ground for four or five years to check whether mycorrhization is still actively present. This is obviously of great interest to farmers considering planting more trees on their land. It is understood that no more than 25 per cent of trees planted will yield truffles and that, according to URTA's fairly recently collected statistics, on average after 10 years of planting a *truffière* might yield 3–4 kg (6½–9 lb) of truffles per hectare. The maximum yield can be expected after 30 years (the anticipated productive life of an oak tree), at which time it will rapidly tail off unless new plantings have been carried out. As the Pébeyres state, we will never cultivate truffles as we cultivate mushrooms, but today we can plant truffle oaks with some hope of real benefit, thanks to new methods of cultivation and greater understanding of the terrain and conditions needed for success.

The explanation given in *Le Grand Livre de la truffe* for the disappearance of substantial truffle harvests is fascinating. As I had learned at URTA, an oak tree is productive for only 30 years and on average it takes 15 years for a tree to produce truffles. After widespread failings of the vines in south-west France in the 1870s, and the massive vine pullout due to a phylloxera epidemic, peasant farmers no longer cultivated their vineyards, nor did they prevent wild oaks from invading the vineyards. They turned instead to truffle gathering, on land that had been meticulously cultivated for generations. They planted many more oak trees on this land and 15 years later the result was an impressive harvest of truffles. This continued until the end of the First World War (in fact, the productive life of an oak tree), at which time the land was emptied of manpower and there were no new plantings of oaks and no cultivation of the land. And so, from the 1930s onwards, the truffle harvest began to decline.

The Pébeyres firmly believe that, contrary to some local beliefs, truffles flourish on land that has been well tended, not on land that has been left undisturbed. The first attempts to restart truffle farming relied on machines to clear and cultivate the land and these machines destroyed the delicate root structure, leading peasant farmers to deduce wrongly that truffles appeared more often if they did not cultivate the terrain. The Pébeyres believe it was the *type* of cultivation that was the problem. In any event, many farmers decided to concentrate on crops that offered more certain returns and in a shorter time. The few truffles that continued to be found were a bonus.

OPPOSITE When we were working on the last few shots for this book back at home, we needed a truffle. Simon Johnson's gourmet food store obliged with a tin of them, and even loaned me an extra tin to show the different sizes available. These were genuine 'first cooking' truffles (see page 272) and the larger can would retail for about A$275. At the right of the photograph is a truffle slicer – for fine slivers and slices the truffle is pressed down and across the blade.

Truffle Hunting

My first visit to a *truffière* was a bit of a farce. It was summer and therefore I knew that there was no likelihood of seeing a truffle, but I was nonetheless interested in looking at the trees. An Englishman called Harry met Julie and me in the bar of the only hotel in Vergt, a small town about 13 km (8 miles) south of Périgueux. Harry, who could well have been the model for one of Peter Mayle's characters, had retired and had lived in this part of France since 1987. He said he does nothing at all but 'live the life of a retired gentleman', but that he does take part in the social life of the town. One of the groups to which he belongs is the local truffle association, which holds regular meetings to discuss methods of cultivation. Harry said it is not unusual for about 30 people to attend a meeting, but more than triple this number turn up to the periodic social lunches held.

When there were overtures of interest in truffle growing from Australia, Harry implied that he had been the go-between in order to facilitate communication. He was vague about the connection. Someone called Didier seemed to be the one with the scientific knowledge, the spokesperson for the industry and the man who had come to Australia with a small team of 'experts' to talk with some Tasmanians at the beginning of their project in 1992. Didier was nowhere to be seen now, but we were to be shown his *truffière*.

Harry confirmed that everything to do with truffles, including their cultivation, is shrouded in secrecy, but claimed that there are a few farmers – Didier among them – who consistently find truffles among their inoculated trees. However, he also said that at least one of the farmers had planted trees in an area known to host truffles anyway. And, he said, there are many farmers who invested up to 10 years ago and are disgruntled because they have found nothing at all.

We drove down the D8 and turned onto the C201 (you are really deep in the rural heart of France when you are on a C road!) and then onto an unmarked track before bumping to a halt in front of a nondescript stone building. There were no fences, no gates and no signs and it would be difficult to find it again.

Truffles are dug only in the winter, when the ground temperature is no more than 8°C (46°F). Because of this, in high summer we expected to see nothing but trees and that is exactly what we saw. There were two plantations, one more advanced than the other. One was of hazelnut trees and the other a mix of hazelnut and oak. The *truffière* was lightly irrigated and under the 7-year-old trees we could see distinctive bare circles in the grass. These are known as *brulés* and are due to the fact that, as truffles grow, they compete with the weeds and grasses growing around the host tree. The truffles create a natural herbicide that kills off these weeds and grasses, resulting in the bare circle. Apparently some trees develop a well-marked *brulé* but still do not produce truffles in that season – 'or maybe never', we were told, with a Gallic shrug.

PREVIOUS PAGES The hunt commences at La Truffière de la Bergerie. As onlookers and novices, we were told to stay well clear of the *brulés* (bare circles) beneath the trees because the first truffles of the season mature high in the ground and an inadvertent footstep might crush one.

My second *truffière* visit, in the company of Maggie Beer, was the real McCoy. It was the first day of December 1999 and our guide was Roger Haigh, co-director of the École Hôtelière at Périgueux (see page 15). In a notebook entry I recorded that there was barely a tourist in sight and the weather was crisp with blue skies. The time of year not only meant that it was the moment for black truffles and *foie gras*, but that we were able to enjoy the lighting of Périgueux's Christmas decorations.

Convinced of my genuine interest regarding truffles, Roger opened many doors for me. We had a preliminary discussion over our first lunch, at which he told us that the local people rarely use truffles because they are considered far too expensive and, besides, the younger people in the community don't know how. This is a concern of the École Hôtelière, which wants to convince local chefs to include truffles in their dishes, but also to show them that it is not necessary to buy a kilo in order to do this.

The full story began to unfold the next morning, with a visit to the Truffière de la Bergerie, owned by Hugues Martin and his wife, near the village of Sainte-Foy-de-Longas. '*Nous allons au cavage* [we are going to hunt truffles],' said Roger. '*Caver*' was a verb I had never heard before. It literally means 'to excavate' or 'to undermine' and rhymes perfectly with *gavage*, which, of course, refers to the force-feeding of geese and ducks – a bit of trivia for the linguistically minded.

LEFT In early winter, the evergreen oaks at the *truffière* still kept some leaves.

The early-morning sun was low in the sky and blindingly white. A frost overnight had crisped the grass and left the hillsides looking ghostly. M. Martin commenced by saying that he believes he paid too much for his property four years earlier and that the harvest of truffles since then has not borne out the accounts of the vendor. But he also admitted that the entire business of truffle cultivation fascinates him and that he is totally hooked. He said that while a great deal is now known, there is still a lot that is not. The old-timers have secrets they will not reveal, despite the fact that many of them are well into their eighties and may not be around for many more years.

It was interesting to hear M. Martin tell his story and compare his account of growing truffles with the conversations I had had at the research station and with my reading of the Pébeyres' book. A cultivator must expect to wait 10 years before commercial quantities of truffles are found; M. Martin said 8–10 years for hazelnuts, 10–12 for evergreen oaks and 12–15 for traditional oaks, but sometimes a tree will do nothing for 20 years and then start to produce. He said that as the population has moved away from farming to the towns, and agricultural land has been taken over for intensive cultivation of strawberries and the felling of the oak forests has continued, the once-plentiful supply of truffles found in the wild has diminished dramatically.

'In my own village there were eighteen families 50 years ago,' he said. 'Today there are two. Once there were goats, cows, horses, lots of grass and plenty of activity. Wood was and still is the main heating fuel, so mature trees were felled and young ones grew with plenty of space around them. Truffles need light to develop. Many locals believe these changes have influenced the supply of truffles. I am constantly experimenting because no one method of cultivation seems to give better yields than another. Currently I tend to think that those trees that are not disturbed around the root area – to keep grasses down, for example – seem to bear better than those that have been tended more closely. But then . . .' He shrugged his shoulders and lit another Gitane.

An article in the *Sud Ouest* newspaper in late 1999 had more information on efforts to revive the ailing truffle industry. The journalist, Gilbert Garrouty, claimed that research into truffle cultivation has been continuing for 40 years. Like the Pébeyres, he underlined the connection between the considerable harvests of truffles at the end of the 19th century and the pullout of vines affected by phylloxera. Left fallow, that land had produced impressive quantities of truffles. Nowadays, however, without the development of the necessary technology for truffle cultivation, there is little doubt that the 'black diamond' will become just a memory. 'But', he hastened to add, 'we are a long way from producing truffles like potatoes' – *heureusement* (happily), I should think everyone would say. The truffle's rarity and hence its value are a great part of its charm. I was interested to read in this article that because the European autumn of 1999 had yielded an exceptional harvest of

OPPOSITE Scenes from La Truffière de la Bergerie: digging gently for fear of damaging the prize (top left); a stone shelter for ducks or geese (top right); the *brulés* clearly visible under the trees.

cèpes, it was likely to be a good year for truffles. (Autumn 2000 was a terrible year for *cèpes*, and I wondered if that meant perhaps it would be a poor year for truffles in the winter of 2000–01.)

There is an official truffle market and an unofficial one. Everyone admits quite cheerfully that it is impossible to ascertain the quantities of truffles – cultivated, wild and poached – that are sold on the black market. M. Martin said that he would guess that 80 per cent of all truffles harvested are sold in small quantities direct to a client rather than to large concerns. As far as the official market goes, more than 50 per cent of truffles that come to it are cultivated and somewhat less than 50 per cent are from the wild.

We proceeded with the hunt. The dog, Mickey, was very excited. M. Martin spoke to him gently and we were asked not to pat him – he needed to understand that he was now going to work. 'It is the first few hunts of the season, so he is not really serious yet,' said his master. Once in the *truffière*, Mickey seemed to understand his task and it was only a few minutes before he stopped and pointed with his front leg. A little gentle digging and there was the first truffle I had ever seen dug from the ground. The dog was rewarded (not with truffle, as he doesn't like them) and then we all crowded around for a good sniff. It was mossy and musky and damp-smelling and glorious, as large as a mandarin.

Poaching of truffles is extremely common and for a quick return poachers are prepared to dig up specimens that have not yet attained their full size and perfume. If they replant these immature truffles somewhere else in a satisfactory spot (on their own land, for instance), in 80 per cent of cases they will continue to ripen, thus giving an even better return for no outlay. It is not surprising that poaching is a big problem. The old-timers think M. Martin is completely crazy to show people around his farm and even more so to include on his stand at the local market, where he sells truffle products made on the farm, photos of his *truffière*, including shots of individual trees. He readily admitted to patrolling his land with a gun and said that every year from November onwards he never leaves the farm for a day. 'All of France is at table on Sundays at eight in the evening – prime time for poachers. I have caught them at it at this time. I fired my gun but unfortunately I missed them. They were scared off, however.'

Another interesting piece of information I learned is that there is a small insect (*Suillia gigantea* Meig.) that lays its eggs in a truffle and when the worms hatch they attract flies. These flies are a sure sign that there is a mature truffle underneath. Once dug up, it is soaked in salt water for 2 minutes to rid it of worms. Both Patrick Regou and M. Martin said that these wormy specimens were often those with the best flavour. Experts never look for smooth, round truffles.

Mickey found three more truffles and then we returned to the farmhouse to watch M. Martin brush them clean. He stores them in a screwtop jar in the refrigerator before sending them to a client. Should one ever be in a position to have

PIGS VS DOGS
Before dogs became the norm for hunting truffles, pigs were used. They are very efficient hunters because they love to eat truffles, but this is one of the major disadvantages of using them: the farmer has to distract the pig at the critical moment or he risks losing the truffle. The other disadvantage is the difficulty of transporting a fully grown pig to a truffière *if the* truffière *is some distance from the pig's stall. It was reported in the Australian press in December 2000 that one of the hopeful truffle farmers in Tasmania was experimenting with an electronic truffle finder called an 'E-nose', which he hoped would take the place of a pig or dog.*

OPPOSITE Truffle hunting: M. Martin and clever Mickey the dog (top) make a 'find' only a few minutes into the hunt – a very respectable *Tuber melanosporum* (bottom left), of which I was permitted a good sniff.

too many truffles (dream on!), freezing is the best way to preserve the perfume. Some cooks and chefs prefer to poach the truffles in goose or duck fat before freezing them (presumably, that perfumed fat would make delectable *pommes sarladaises* later on; see page 284). The traditionalists prefer to bury their truffles in clean duck or goose fat and store them in a very cool place or in a jar covered with the minimum amount of neutral-flavoured oil. Restaurateurs whom I know in France freeze their truffles in airtight containers.

Like many small producers, M. Martin sells a few conserves produced on the farm. He showed us his truffle juice, tinned truffles of genuine first pressing (see below), truffle oil and two other interesting products, which I bought: a small tin of cooked onions mixed with truffles and another of crushed hazelnuts mixed with truffles to form a paste. M. Martin recommended that this last product be added to the stuffing for a goose neck (not something you would do every day), or whisked into a warm vinaigrette as a sauce for vegetables or beans, or included in a stuffing or sauce for chicken, veal or pork.

Back home in Melbourne, on the last day of 1999 I hosted a dinner party for 10 special friends. The main course was a mushroom and hazelnut risotto (see page 286). I included dried *cèpes* and opened M. Martin's small tin just as the risotto was approaching a creamy perfection. The scent was marvellous and I stirred the whole lot in. We all agreed that the risotto was one of the most delicious dishes I had ever cooked. I wish I had bought dozens of the little tins.

Buying and Selling

A good-sized truffle will lose 15 to 20 per cent of its weight in the brushing and peeling process (peelings are canned separately and are excellent for sauces). It is then usually put into a can and sterilised. At this point it can be sold to restaurants or to those in the know, but it cannot have a label or net weight on the can as it will have lost up to a further 25 per cent of its weight during the sterilisation process. Such truffles are known as *première cuisson* (first cooking) and they are what you should look for if you are buying truffles in the south-west. In every small town in Périgord there is someone who cans truffles for local consumption. They will always be 'first cooking' and are rarely for sale, unless you visit a *truffière* and buy canned truffles prepared on the premises. For selling in boutiques, the cans are opened and the juice is extracted and canned and sold separately. The truffles are weighed and the cans are labelled, resealed and then re-sterilised: they will lose no more weight but a great deal of aroma.

The first truffle market of the 1999 season was at Excideuil the day after our outing to the *truffière* and Patrick Regou, the scientist we had met at URTA, was at

OPPOSITE At the truffle market at Excideuil, baskets of truffles were openly displayed for potential buyers – what a contrast to the fabled 'dark lane and bulging pocket' transactions of the black market. The truffles were quickly divided into *melanosporum* and *brumale* and then, within these two groups, into first and second quality. Prices varied accordingly.

a table officially verifying the truffles. Many of the producers (of both cultivated and wild truffles) from five *cantons* in the *département* have decided to work and sell cooperatively through this market, one motive being to try to minimise unscrupulous practices and make the whole procedure more transparent. Again, as soon as Patrick told me this, there were lots of shrugs. No-one truly expects that shady or black-market deals will stop.

Men with weathered faces and pulled-down caps approached with a bag or jar of truffles to sell and spilled them onto the table. Patrick quickly divided them into *melanosporum* or *brumale* (there were quite a lot of the latter), then took a tiny slice from each to determine, based on smell and colour, whether it was premium quality or second quality. Based on this, he put them into separate baskets. Sometimes the farmer had only two or three *melanosporum*, and maybe four or five *brumale*, to sell, but at the current prices (which were high because it was the very first market – apparently they would go higher as Christmas approached and then rise or fall depending on whether it turned into a good or bad season), even a few truffles yielded a good return, especially if they had just 'happened' on the person's land without the expense of cultivation.

After Patrick verified each truffle, one woman brushed it and another handed over the money and issued a certificate of authentication. Each specimen sold was identified by the name of the producer or gatherer, place, type and category. The previous season only 18 kg (40 lb) of truffles had been sold through the market as it was a terrible year, but it was expected that before the end of this season the market would sell up to 200 kg (440 lb).

I noticed one woman standing apart from the action, obviously not keen to have her jar of truffles officially investigated. I went over to speak to her and she introduced herself as Mme de Gaulle. She was happy to open her jar so that Roger and I could have a deep sniff and said she would sell them at the highest price offered. Mme de Gaulle was pleased to talk about the old days, when her grandfather used to bring a heaped basket of truffles to sell at the market, 'sometimes even a sack on his back', she assured us. She was also happy to tell us that she had collected her truffles from an abandoned vineyard on her property (which had been allowed by her lazy husband to fall into disrepair, she said, indicating a handsome elderly man with a luxuriant moustache), planted the year of her birth 73 years earlier.

OPPOSITE Truffle selection at the market is serious and the buyers sniff as well as look. Locals gathered to discuss the price – maybe they had a few truffles in their pockets – and the atmosphere in the buying shed was very particular, with heightened excitement but a lot of poker faces. Mme de Gaulle (top left) stood apart and would have none of the official prices. She wanted to sell all – for the best offer – or nothing.
OVERLEAF This farm building at La Truffière de la Bergerie was typical of the area. The attractive stone structures orgininally served as shelters for gooseherds and duckherds, as well as for the birds themselves. Most of them seem still to be in excellent repair, but nobody I spoke to could be specific about when they had been constructed. 'Certainly before my time' was the vague impression I received.

On Eating Truffles

A truffle is intensely perfumed, but the perfume escapes very quickly, which means that truffles should never be left in the open air. They smell and taste of decaying leaves, of damp forests, of mushrooms, of mystery, and are best with simple foods such as potatoes, eggs or fresh pasta. They are excellent with butter and cream, but reward restraint. Truffles add richness and a smell of ripeness to poultry and sauces and, it must be said, are almost impossible to describe.

Too many chefs feel that they must add ingredient after ingredient to justify the huge price they have to charge for a dish including truffles. In my experience, simple is best. One of the loveliest dishes I remember eating that featured truffles was a salad of curly endive and celeriac over which had been shaved thin slices of fresh truffle. The salad was dressed with modest quantities of full-flavoured walnut oil and wine vinegar, and was accompanied by a slice of grilled country bread. This dish was served to me in 1982 by Alain Dutournier when I spent an exciting day observing in his delightful restaurant Au Trou Gascon, in Paris's 12th arrondissement. This was before he opened his grand restaurant Le Carré des Feuillants in the Place Vendôme, but Au Trou Gascon is a place I still visit almost every time I am in Paris.

Strolling in the Palais-Royal in midsummer 1999 after an exquisite lunch at another great restaurant, Le Grand Véfour, I was thinking of one of my literary heroes, Colette. She spent her last years in an apartment in the Palais-Royal and the illustrious chef–proprietor of Le Grand Véfour at the time, Raymond Oliver, sent delicious little meals to her every day (including her last meal, on 3 August 1954 – a vegetable broth). Colette's love of food was well known and somewhat excessive. In earlier times she had had plenty to say about truffles:

> . . . you have purchased your truffle, now eat it on its own, all pungent and grainy, eat it like the vegetable it is, in generous helpings. Once it has been pared, it will not give you much trouble; its incomparable flavour disdains elaborations and combinations. Cover with a good white wine, very dry – keep your champagne for parties, truffles don't need it – salt lightly, pepper sparingly and cook in your black covered casserole. Keep at a constant boil for twenty-five minutes, adding to the swirling foamy liquid . . . twenty or so cubes of bacon, half-fat, half-lean, to enrich the sauce. No other spices! . . . Your truffles should be brought straight to the table in their liquor. Serve yourself without stinting; truffles stimulate the appetite and they aid the digestion . . .

Paysages et Portraits

OPPOSITE A luxurious apéritif – *foie gras* croutons topped with freshly shaved raw truffle and just a touch of sea salt, and a glass of sweet wine.

Colette's recipe is an extravagant method of cooking a whole truffle and is a dish I hope to eat one day. *Truffes sous la cendre* is another traditional delicacy where a large, peeled truffle, seasoned and sprinkled with Cognac or Armagnac (or *eau-de-vie*, according to La Mazille), is wrapped in a thin sheet of pork fat and then in baking paper (it could be aluminium foil today) and buried in the embers of a fire. La Mazille specifies 40 minutes for a truffle of 100–130 g (3½–4½ oz), which would be an enormous one – a smaller truffle would do me!

Had our December 1999 visit been a little later in the season, chef Pierre Corre at L'Auberge de la Truffe in the village of Sorges, where we lunched after our visit to the Excideuil market, would have made us *truffes sous la cendre*. Sorges is north of Périgueux on the N21, conveniently close to Excideuil, and has a small museum devoted to the truffle. L'Auberge de la Truffe is its best-known restaurant and has built its reputation on its use of truffles, canned out of season but fresh when available.

As it happened, Patrick Regou had sent ahead a gift for our lunch, which became an exquisite appetiser: freshly gathered truffle, finely shaved and served raw on thin slices of toast spread with a little *foie gras* and sprinkled with a grain or two of finest *fleur de sel* (sea salt), as shown in the photograph on page 279. This was a pure introduction to a Périgord truffle. Next came a golden *omelette baveuse*, bulging with truffles and buttery juices. There was very little conversation as we ate with reverence. We were later told by the chef that each of us had consumed four eggs and 12 g (½ oz) of truffle. (An *omelette baveuse* is a 'moist' or 'runny' omelette or, as more descriptively translated and immortalised in the Australian classic *Oh, for a French Wife!* by Ted Moloney, a 'slobbery' omelette.)

RIGHT The omelette cooked for Maggie, Roger and me at L'Auberge de la Truffe was stuffed with truffles and lavishly decorated with extra slices. As we cut it, juices speckled with small black chunks flowed out and the musky, earthy smell demanded our instant attention.

A DISH FOR A SPECIAL PARTY

I mentioned earlier (see page 67) that André Deroeux's parting gift to me was a large and aromatic 40 g (1⅓ oz) truffle canned in its own juices – I only hope it was not one that he and Henriette were saving for their Christmas treat. I used it to make a slow-roasted loin of pork (page 283) for our farewell-to-Lavalade party. The peelings gave intense flavour to the sauce and I was able to cut sufficient not-so-thin velvety slices so that everyone got one. The next day, when we were clearing out the refrigerator, I made a memorable potato salad combining the last of the truffle sauce from the pork with the last of the yellow waxy potatoes.

Not many people will have a truffle on hand, but this is a delicious roast even without one. As already mentioned, the season for truffles in Périgord is December and January. Some specialist food suppliers in Australia, such as Simon Johnson in Sydney and Melbourne, the Essential Ingredient in Sydney and the Vital Ingredient in Melbourne, import truffles at this time of the year and the pork is just as appetising eaten cold as it is hot, so why not contemplate buying one for a special Christmas dish?

As described in the 'Markets' chapter, the side of pork I saw at Le Bugue market was much larger than any I had seen in Australia. I asked Jonathan Gianfreda about this and he explained that the size difference was because pigs in France come from carcasses of 100–120 kg (220–265 lb) dressed weight, while the largest pigs in Australia dress out at 65–70 kg (140–155 lb). What should people do if they wanted to reproduce the dish I cooked in France, I wondered. Jonathan advised that the loin is cut a different way in France, with the shoulder division happening at a different point. It was all getting a bit too technical. He said to ask for a boneless rib-eye of pork but to request that your loin be cut from the shoulder end. In France, the shoulder end includes a portion that we would normally call 'neck of pork'; if you have an obliging butcher, and you give them plenty of notice, they may be prepared to cut the shoulder end of the loin to include some of the neck. Another of Jonathan's suggestions was to ask your local European butcher (if you have one) for 'l'échine de porc' or to tell them you want to make the dish known as l'enchaud de porc. Failing that, he suggested telling them you want to make Stephanie's 'slow-roasted loin of pork with truffle' recipe! I can't imagine that this last suggestion will get you very far, except perhaps at Jonathan's. He insists that he will send special cuts of meat to clients.

The recipe calls for a sheet of pork fat. The pork I purchased in France had been completely denuded of its layer of fat and because of the long, slow cooking, it needed protection to stop the outside surface becoming dry. A good butcher can provide a sheet of pork fat with plenty of notice. Jonathan made another suggestion: Vietnamese and Chinese butchers have plenty of pork fat because they shave the rind from the meat to use in other ways. An easier option, although not as strong, is caul fat.

Slow-roasted Loin of Pork with André's Truffle

L'ENCHAUD DE PORC TRUFFÉ

Trim the fennel bulbs. Finely chop the trimmings and reserve them for the stuffing. Cut the bulbs in half and set aside. To make the stuffing, heat the butter and olive oil in a heavy-based frying pan and add the onion, fennel trimmings and garlic. Cook gently for 15–20 minutes until very soft. Stir in the parsley and allow to cool.

Spread the pork fat or caul fat on your work surface and put the meat on top. Season the meat well with salt and pepper and cut a small channel in it for the stuffing. Peel the truffle (if using) as thinly as possible and reserve the peelings (and any juice from the can, if you are using a canned truffle) to add to the reduced stock later. Cut the truffle into thin slices and place along the channel you have made in the meat. Cover the truffle with the cooled stuffing – it doesn't matter if the stuffing oozes a bit over the rest of the meat.

Cut 6 lengths of kitchen string. Slip one underneath the centre of the sheet of pork fat and, bringing the fat up over the meat, tie it tightly. Tie the remaining string in the same fashion at 6 cm/2 in intervals along the meat. You will have a neat 'bolster'. Put the pork bones in a baking dish (one with a lid, if possible) and settle the meat on top. Arrange the fennel chunks around and put the dish in the refrigerator until you are ready to cook (it can be refrigerated for 2–3 hours in this state).

Preheat the oven to 200°C/400°F. Put the meat in the oven for 30 minutes to start the cooking, then pour over the wine. Cover the dish with a lid or aluminium foil and lower the heat to 180°C/375°F. Roast for 1 hour, basting every 30 minutes with the juices and adding at each basting 2 tablespoons of the reduced stock. Turn the meat and roast for another hour, basting and adding stock as before. You will have used about half the stock at this stage. Remove the lid or foil, settle the meat right-side up and test for tenderness – a skewer should slip through without resistance. Roast for an additional 30 minutes, then transfer the meat and fennel to a warm plate, cover loosely with aluminium foil and rest in a warm place.

To make the sauce, pour all the juices from the roasting tray into a glass jug and allow to settle. Spoon off the fat that rises and reserve for another use. Meanwhile, return the roasting tray to the top of the stove and deglaze the pan (still with the pork bones in it) with the remainder of the reduced stock, scraping hard to dislodge all the little stuck-on bits. Strain into a small saucepan and add the reserved truffle peelings and truffle juice, the reserved skimmed juices and any additional juices that have oozed from the resting meat. Boil hard for a few minutes to concentrate the sauce. To serve, carve the meat into thick slices.

Serves 8

8 small fennel bulbs, with tops
1 sheet of pork fat or caul fat, large
    enough to wrap around the meat
1 × 2 kg/4½ lb boned loin of pork
    (cut from the shoulder end of the
    loin), skinned
sea salt
freshly ground black pepper
1 fresh or canned truffle (optional)
several pork bones (ask your
    butcher)
1 cup dry white wine
2 cups reduced veal or chicken stock

Stuffing
2 tablespoons unsalted butter
1 tablespoon olive oil
1 large onion, finely chopped
2 tablespoons reserved chopped
    fennel trimmings
2 cloves garlic, finely chopped
3 tablespoons freshly chopped young
    parsley (preferably flat-leaf)

OPPOSITE This special roast was generously stuffed with truffle and tasted superb. Background details about the recipe are given on page 281.

Pommes sarladaises

POTATOES IN THE STYLE OF SARLAT

Serves 4

4 medium–large waxy potatoes
  (Desiree or Bintje are good)
4 tablespoons rendered duck fat
1 truffle (if you're lucky!), very finely
  sliced
sea salt
freshly ground black pepper
1 clove garlic, finely chopped
2 tablespoons freshly chopped young
  parsley (preferably flat-leaf)

No visitor to the south-west should leave without experiencing this wonderful potato dish. It traditionally accompanies *confit* and in the winter ought to include sliced truffle. In my experience it rarely does include truffle, but it is wonderful none-theless. I am guessing, but assume the dish's title reflects the importance to Sarlat of the commerce in everything to do with *confit* and truffles.

There are two basic ways to proceed: you can make everyday *pommes sar-ladaises* or a *galette* (cake) *de pommes sarladaises*. Both dishes start the same way and it is a good idea to have a go at both methods. The *galette* looks very fancy when served as a round of brown and crispy overlapping slices of potato, perfumed maybe with truffle. Both dishes have a final scattering of fresh garlic and parsley.

Peel the potatoes (do not wash them after peeling) and slice them thinly – I use a Japanese vegetable slicer for this. Pat the slices dry with a clean cloth. Melt half the duck fat and tip it into a large bowl. Add the potato and move the slices around with your hands so that they all become covered with a trace of fat.

Heat the rest of the duck fat in a 24 cm/9½ in heavy-based frying pan with a lid. Adjust the heat to medium and tip in the potato, spreading the slices around the pan with a flexible spatula. Add the sliced truffle. There will be plenty of layers of potato. Leave for a few minutes to allow the bottom slices to take on a bit of colour, then move these slices to allow others to take on some colour. Continue with this shifting and layering of coloured and not-yet-coloured slices for a few minutes, adding some salt and pepper as you go. At this point you need to decide whether you intend to make a *galette* or not.

For a *galette*, lightly press down on the slices to create an even thickness. Cover and reduce the heat to low. Leave undisturbed for 5 minutes. Lift the lid and slide the spatula under the bottom layer to allow some shifting of layers to occur. Press down again and replace the lid. Leave undisturbed for 10 minutes, then lift the lid again – the underside will be crispy and golden. Slip the spatula underneath to loosen the *galette* and invert it onto a plate. Slip it off the plate and back into the uncovered pan to crisp and brown the other side. After 5 minutes the *galette* will be compact and shining. Slide it onto a hot serving plate. Mix the garlic and parsley and scatter over the *galette*, then cut into wedges to serve.

To make everyday *pommes sarladaises*, continue lifting the slices so that you create a sort of 'hash brown' effect. Some slices will be crispy, others will be soft and tender. The garlic and parsley can be tossed in among the layers when you are just about ready to serve (if the garlic is added at the beginning, it will burn).

OPPOSITE A *galette sarladaise* such as this can be cut into strips for an absolutely marvellous addition to a green salad. Add a few fresh walnuts or a grilled *cabécou* for a sensational first course.

Millennium Mushroom and Hazelnut Risotto

Serves 12

140 g/5 oz hazelnuts
100 g/3½ oz dried cèpes (porcini)
500 ml/17½ fl oz boiling water
250 ml/9 fl oz dry vermouth
2.5 litres/4½ pints well-flavoured
  chicken stock
200 g/7 oz unsalted butter
2 onions, finely chopped
1 kg/2 lb arborio rice
8 flat black mushrooms, sliced
100 g/3½ oz tinned hazelnut and
  truffle paste *or* 1 truffle, finely
  sliced (optional)
6 tablespoons freshly chopped young
  parsley (preferably flat-leaf)
sea salt
freshly ground black pepper
150 g/5 oz freshly grated
  Parmigiano-Reggiano (optional)

Risotto in a book about south-western French cookery? This recipe is a complete interloper, but, as I have already mentioned, it was made and enjoyed on the evening of 31 December 1999 when I cooked a 'millennium supper' for 10 friends. The magic ingredient was the small tin of hazelnut and black truffle paste I had bought at La Truffière de la Bergerie in Sainte-Foy-de-Longas just a few weeks earlier (see page 272). There are many other ways this wonderful product could have been used, but it just happened to be with rice that night.

Spread the hazelnuts on a baking tray and roast at 180°C/375°F for about 10 minutes until the nuts are golden and smell toasty. Tip them into a clean tea towel and rub vigorously to remove the brown skins. Put the nuts and skins into a colander and shake, so that the skin fragments settle or sift out the bottom. Discard the skin fragments and roughly process the nuts in a food processor.

Rinse the dried mushrooms in cold water and then soak them in the boiling water for about 20 minutes. Heat the vermouth and stock together in a saucepan until hot. When the mushrooms have reconstituted, lift them from the soaking water and drain on kitchen paper. Discard any woody stalks, then chop roughly. Strain the soaking water thoroughly and add it to the hot stock.

Melt half the butter in a heavy-based pot and sauté the onion until it is soft and translucent. Add the reconstituted chopped mushrooms and cook for 1 minute longer. Stir in the rice so that it is evenly coated with butter. Add the sliced flat mushrooms and start adding the hot stock 1 cup at a time, stirring. Continue adding stock as the liquid is absorbed. There should always be a film of liquid over the surface of the rice. Taste the rice after 20 minutes; when it is ready, it should be creamy, with a slight resistance to the teeth.

Add the chopped hazelnuts (and any magic ingredient you may have secured, such as a tin of truffle and hazelnut paste or a fresh truffle). Stir in the parsley, salt and pepper to taste, the rest of the butter and the cheese, if using. Serve immediately.

Penne with Truffles

This is based on an idea given by Pierre-Jean and Jacques Pébeyre in *Le Grand Livre de la truffe* (see page 258).

Cook the pasta with the garlic cloves in plenty of lightly salted boiling water until tender (the French are not convinced about al dente pasta, so please yourself). Drain the pasta and set aside the garlic. Put the pasta in a heated bowl, cover and keep it warm.

Mash the reserved garlic to a paste. In a wide, deep pan that is large enough to hold all the pasta, heat the garlic paste briefly in the butter. When the mixture is aromatic but not at all coloured, stir in the cream and the truffle. Boil for 1–2 minutes until the cream starts to reduce. Return the cooked pasta to the pan and quickly stir to mix. Season with salt and pepper and pull the pan to the side of the stove. Add the Gruyère, cover and allow to infuse for a few minutes. Sprinkle with the chives and serve.

Serves 2–3

250 g/9 oz penne or macaroni or
   other tube pasta
1–2 cloves garlic, peeled
sea salt
25 g/1 oz unsalted butter
1 cup whipping cream *or* ½ cup
   cream and ½ cup milk
1 × 20 g/¾ oz truffle, finely sliced
freshly ground black pepper
40 g/1 ⅓ oz freshly grated Gruyère
1 tablespoon freshly chopped chives

Pot-roasted Guinea Fowl with Truffle and Figs

Serves 2 or 4

1 guinea fowl (approximately
    1.3 kg/3 lb)
2 tablespoons hachis (page 233)
1 truffle, sliced (optional)
2 tablespoons rendered duck fat
generous handful of thyme sprigs
2 bay leaves
2 tablespoons red-wine vinegar
Confit d'Oignons (page 327)
1½ cups veal stock or other
    well-flavoured stock
4 fresh cèpes or other wild
    mushrooms or flat cultivated
    mushrooms

Fig garnish
1 tablespoon unsalted butter
½ cup sweet white wine
½ cup water
8 small figs

This is a generous dish for 2 hungry people, or you can divide the legs into drumsticks and thigh and cut each breast portion in half, resulting in a dish for 4 people. Alternatively, serve only the breast fillet and save the legs and some of the figs to be eaten cold in a salad.

In *Le Grand Livre de la truffe* (see page 258) I read that you must *never* put truffles into the cavity of a bird, only ever under the skin. The authors say that truffle inside the cavity tastes like '*merde*' (excrement). I pass this on because no-one would ever want to waste a truffle!

Away from the south-west, you could substitute soft unsalted butter for the *hachis*. Mix the butter with some chopped garlic and parsley and introduce it under the skin exactly as described below.

Preheat the oven to 180°C/375°F. Remove the wishbone from the guinea fowl and loosen the skin over the breast by separating the skin from the breast meat with your fingers. Insert the *hachis* and spread it by pressing down on the skin with both hands. If using truffle slices, slip them on top of the *hachis* under the skin. Secure the legs of the bird with string.

Heat the duck fat in a cast-iron, ovenproof casserole with a lid. Once the fat is hot, drop in the thyme and bay leaves and then brown the guinea fowl well on both sides. Pour off the fat and discard. Still on a high heat, deglaze the pan with the vinegar, which will bubble up around the sides of the bird. Once the fumes have evaporated, add some Confit d'Oignons to the pan. Add one-third of the stock and allow to boil and reduce by half.

Meanwhile, cut off and discard the woody ends of the *cèpes*. Cut off and dice the stems and cut the tops into halves or quarters depending on their size. When the stock has reduced, add the *cèpe* stems and tops to the pan and pour in the remaining stock. Cover the casserole with a piece of baking paper and then the lid. Transfer to the oven and cook for 30 minutes. Meanwhile, make the fig garnish. Put the butter, wine, water and figs in a small saucepan and simmer for 15 minutes, then set aside until required.

Remove the guinea fowl from the oven and rest in its dish for 20 minutes before serving. To serve 2 people, detach the legs from the bird and reserve them for another occasion. Cut off the breast fillets and put 1 fillet in the centre of each diner's hot plate. Put some onion and *cèpe* mixture to one side of the meat and spoon over half the poached figs and half the juices. (Set aside the remaining figs to accompany the legs later.)

To serve 4 people, detach the legs and divide them into drumsticks and thighs. Cut off the breast fillets and cut them in half. Put 1 piece of breast fillet and 1 piece of leg meat on each plate. Divide the onion and *cèpe* mixture between the plates and spoon over the poached figs and juices.

Variations

During my summer visit I made a similar pot roast and sautéed a wedge of stuffed cabbage (see page 122) in some duck fat and served this 'bubble and squeak' alongside the guinea fowl instead of the figs. A *galette sarladaise* (see page 284) would be another fantastic accompaniment.

Foie Gras & Confit

I t would be difficult to decide which is the better-known gastronomic luxury of the south-west: the black truffle or *foie gras*. It is certainly easier to find the latter. '*Foie gras*' can be translated as 'fat liver' and that is exactly what it is: an enlarged liver from a duck (*canard*) or goose (*oie*) produced by force-feeding the bird large amounts of corn. Once it has been extracted, the *foie gras* can be eaten cooked – as a luxurious pâté – or it can be sliced and briefly sautéed for a rich and delicious hot entrée.

As *foie gras* is the exquisite by-product of a fattened duck or goose, there is an inseparable relationship between it and the equally important practice of preparing *confits* from the bird after it has given up its liver. The preparation of *foie gras* and *confit* has been a necessary part of the housewifery of this region for a very long time. In my conversations with Henriette Deroeux (see page 65), her memories were vivid of her mother making *confit* in the large copper pan that still hangs over the fireplace.

The cycle commences with the purchase of the young birds and ends at the regular *marchés au gras* held weekly throughout autumn and winter, where both the livers and the processed ducks or geese are displayed and sold. The vendors at these markets are deeply suspicious of factory production and insist that it is only here that you can buy 'real' *foie gras* and 'real' birds. Few tourists can credit their first sight of the bulging, curved, buttery-pink livers at the markets, displayed so that would-be buyers can visually assess their quality. At *le marché au gras* at Excideuil, which I visited in November 1999, whole plucked and singed birds, as well as parts of birds and whole livers, were arranged in neat rows on long tables – an extraordinary sight.

Once the *foie gras* is removed there is still the rest of the fattened bird to enjoy. South-western cooks show great imagination and culinary brilliance in the way they do this. Local restaurants offer *confit* of thigh, gizzard, *manchon* (the part where the wing joins the body) and neck; they offer grilled *magret* (the thick, meaty breast fillet); they make *rillettes* and *fritons* and *grillons* using the skin and the fragments of meat still attached to the carcass (often with pork as well as duck or goose); they sell separately the thin and delicate *aiguillettes* (underfillets); and they have various ingenious ways with the carcass itself. Parcels of wingtips, gizzards and neck are offered in the markets as the base for soups and ragoûts. The

OPPOSITE Decorative signs advertising local specialities are everywhere in the south-west. Some of them represent major national industrial concerns, but there are plenty of others, tucked away down small lanes and minor roads, that invite passers-by to call at individual farm shops.

carcasses themselves, with *aiguillettes* still attached, were a bargain at 10–12 francs (A$3–$3.50) each. And, of course, every morsel of fat is retrieved and melted. The crispy bits of skin are called *grattons* and the strained melted fat is used to cook potatoes as well as to make the various *confits*.

Foie Gras

The practice of deliberately force-feeding a mature duck or goose large quantities of corn so that its liver becomes enlarged is one that has caused many non-French people to express all sorts of horror and misgivings. It is considered part of the *patrimoine* (inheritance) of this part of France and the inhabitants shake their heads in disbelief at the suggestion that they are maltreating the birds. They insist that the birds are handled gently at all times and that if they are maltreated or sick they will not produce fattened livers. If the force-feeding, or *gavage*, is stopped for whatever reason, the livers quickly revert to their usual size.

It is said that the phenomenon of a fattened liver was discovered by examining migrating birds that gorged themselves before taking off on their long flights. In a 1998 issue of his newsletter *The Art of Eating*, American food writer Edward Behr stated that Egyptian reliefs dating from more than 2000 years BC show geese being hand-fed balls of grain and that the ancient Romans fattened their geese with dried figs. By the 16th century there was plenty of evidence in France, Italy, Germany and Bohemia that Jewish producers were selling *foie gras*, mainly to Christians for feast days. However, I am sure that quoting historic precedent will not change the minds of those who consider the practice barbaric.

Another interesting fact comes from an American book called *Foie Gras: A Passion*, by Michael Ginor. He explains that the lining of the oesophagus of a duck or goose is 'keratinised' – that is, composed of 'fibrous protein cells that resemble bristles or fingernails, allowing large pieces of food to pass safely. Because of this anatomical feature, the feeding tube creates no discomfort for the ducks [or geese]'. The book gives comprehensive information on every detail of *foie gras* production. It is particularly focused on the American experience and is essential reading for anyone interested in the practical aspects of the industry – an Australian duck farmer, perhaps?

The production of *foie gras* is still a common cottage industry in France and the majority of signs you see along the roads are for small farm operations. There are also, of course, larger, more industrial businesses and as the whole of Europe becomes more and more concerned with uniformity and standardised procedures, it is likely there will be fewer small-scale home operators. When I was there in October 2000 I was told that many farmers are deciding to raise, feed and kill their

OPPOSITE At the *marché au gras* at Excideuil, we saw fattened ducks with their livers partially displayed (top) and duck bits, including beautifully trimmed breast fillets and legs (bottom left). The market hall was sparklingly clean, but being early winter it was very cold and the products were presented on long trestle tables without any need for refrigeration. They would all have been sold by the end of the day anyway.

own birds but, because of the high cost of upgrading their simple machinery and workrooms, then to hand them over to the big firms for further processing. And some farmers prefer to buy birds that are a few weeks old, rather than just born, and then commence force-feeding.

During our autumn holiday Maggie and Colin Beer went to cast a professional eye over the procedure of raising, feeding and processing the birds. As niche marketers of high-quality gourmet products and specialist farmers of game birds, they had given more than a few moments to considering whether the production of *foie gras* could be of interest to them. Their conclusion was that it was not. Colin pointed to the labour-intensive nature of the feeding: for a flock of 150 geese, it took two people three hours, three times a day, to feed them and that was seven days a week. And it seemed critical to have close access to a processing plant, which, according to Colin, would be an expensive outlay, especially given the already stringent standards imposed on all farming of birds in Australia. The price charged for the resultant fattened livers would have to be very, very high.

It seems certain, however, that were the Beers or someone else to make the investment there would be plenty of customers. Again quoting Edward Behr in 1998, the two American companies that have gone into the business of producing high-quality duck *foie gras*, Sonoma Foie Gras and Hudson Valley Farms, were selling 2000 and 7500 *foies gras* per week respectively!

In the European winter of 1999, Roger Haigh of the École Hôtelière at Périgueux (see page 15) took me to meet M. Guy Meynard, who has a prize-winning goose farm at Sorges, to see for myself the process of raising and feeding the birds. The silver-grey geese moved around silently and were practically invisible in the morning fog. M. Meynard whistled to his dog, which bounded off to round up the flock and drive it closer to us. The dog turned and dashed and stopped, instantly responding to commands, in just the same way as an Australian working sheepdog. This farm processes 1400 geese per year and grows all the corn it needs to feed them. The Meynards also grow walnuts and the walnut trees provide shade for the geese in early summer.

M. Meynard stressed that the geese develop trust in the person who feeds them (the *gaveur*). The same trusted person must feed the birds three times a day for 21 days and must be calm and gentle so that the birds will remain calm. I saw no flapping of wings or squawking, attempts to evade M. Meynard's arm, widening of the eyes or any other overt signs of distress. I asked about *foie gras* in the United States and whether the birds there are fattened in the same way as they are in France. M. Meynard laughed and said with deep irony, 'The geese stuff themselves in the United States!' (In fact, the birds are stuffed in exactly the same way in the United States as in France, as explained in Ginor's book.)

The Meynards process their own birds to prepare many products, including goose fat; *rillettes*; *confits*; canned *cassoulets*; goose neck with a luxurious stuffing

OPPOSITE, TOP At the Meynard goose farm at Sorges, penned geese wait for feeding (left) and M. Meynard feeds softened corn to the birds.

OPPOSITE, BOTTOM Commerce in *foie gras* and related products is important to the region. Here, tastings are offered at a local market stall (left). As the stallholders are the actual producers, they are very happy to answer questions. The sign at right refers to 'Périgord in the olden days' and uses an image of a stone-roofed gooseherd's hut to reinforce the producer's claim to using artisanal methods.

of pork, *foie gras* and truffle; pâtés and, of course, *foie gras mi-cuit* and *en conserve* (see page 302). Another important resource is the birds' down and feathers, which are washed and dried and sold at a high price to fill quilts.

M. Meynard had assembled a selection of his products for us to try for a simple *casse-croûte* (snack). Even though it was only 10 o'clock in the morning, a bottle of Bergerac red was produced. It was a bit early for red wine for me, but I did enjoy the *rillettes* and terrine spread onto a slice cut from a giant country loaf, all set out on a simple table in front of a roaring log fire and accompanied by a few walnuts from the farm trees. The bread was cut by holding the loaf against the chest and drawing a sharp knife through the loaf towards the body. I saw this done a few times during my visits to the south-west and always found it alarming.

Wherever I went to meet and talk with specialist producers I encountered concerns about authenticity and quality assurance. There has been *foie gras* emanating from other places claiming to be '*foie gras de Périgord*' in the same way as there has been more extra-virgin olive oil sold as 'Tuscan extra-virgin olive oil' than is actually produced in Tuscany. In both cases the solution has been to institute a system of identification and labelling. For *foie gras*, there is now a logo that guarantees that the duck or goose was raised, *gavé* (force-fed), killed and cut up and processed in Périgord. *Foie gras* is also produced in other parts of France, where it carries its own appellation, but for a citizen of Périgord there is of course no question of where the best *foie gras* comes from.

Far more duck *foie gras* is produced than goose. Ducks are fattened for one week less than geese, and usually only twice a day, so both time and corn are saved, and geese are more temperamental, it is claimed. The majority of ducks that are fattened are *mulards*, or 'mules' as these sterile birds are referred to in English, a cross between a Barbary male and a female Pekin. Some farmers prefer Muscovy ducks. Although time and money are saved raising ducks rather than geese, the returns are less. An average duck liver weighs around 500 g (1 lb); in a goose it is much larger, up to 1.5 kg (3 lb).

OPPOSITE We enjoyed a *casse-croûte* with M. Meynard: *pâté de porc* (front) *rillettes* (in jar) and truffled *pâté de foie gras* (back) with toast grilled on the fire, accompanied by a glass of Bergerac red.
OVERLEAF The Meynards' geese looked stately and beautiful in the morning fog. They were herded by working dogs in the same manner as Australian sheepdogs round up sheep.

MI-CUIT AND EN CONSERVE

It is important to understand the difference between *foie gras* that is *mi-cuit* and that which is *en conserve*. Both are sold in tins and preserving jars, and *mi-cuit* is also obtainable in vacuum packs.

Mi-cuit (literally, 'half-cooked') is applied to two *foie gras* products, each of which is cooked to a different internal temperature. *Mi-cuit foie gras* cooked in a terrine in a water bath, or steamed in a vacuum bag, is taken to an internal temperature of 46–50°C (115–125°F) and then removed from the heat source. It is pale pink in colour and melting in texture and is generally agreed to have the best flavour. This is the most expensive type of *foie gras* and is the luxury product that a huge number of French insist on for their Christmas celebrations. *Foie gras* is prepared in this manner by the best restaurants, the best *charcuteries* and on the farm, and is always clearly described as '*mi-cuit*'. Such a terrine is best consumed within a week.

Mi-cuit foie gras intended for export (certainly to Australia) is required to be cooked to an internal temperature of 70°C (160°F) and held at that temperature for 92 minutes, or to an internal temperature of 80°C (175°F) and held for 16 minutes. AQIS, the Australian quarantine service, does not distinguish between *foie gras* presented in a can, jar or vacuum pack as long as these requirements have been guaranteed on the certificate of authorisation that precedes an import permit. Such a product has a comparatively short shelf-life of a maximum of 6 months, and must be stored under refrigeration. It tastes pretty good but does not have the finesse of the less-cooked product enjoyed in its home territory. This relatively long-cooked *mi-cuit foie gras* is also widely available in boutiques and markets in the southwest, sold in both preserving jars and cans.

En conserve means that the *foie gras* has been cooked to an internal temperature of 105°C (221°F) and completely sterilised. It is shelf-stable and can be stored anywhere for 1–2 years. It is beige in colour and has a denser, somewhat more granular texture and a much stronger flavour than *mi-cuit fote gras*. For my palate it is of little interest and I would not waste my money on it, but there are many French people who positively prefer it.

To clarify the distinctions, the most delicate *mi-cuit* product, cooked at the lowest temperature for the least time, has a very short shelf-life of about 1 week. That which is cooked longer at a higher temperature and then canned or put in preserving jars, but still labelled '*mi-cuit*', has a shelf-life of 6 months. The product that is cooked at an even higher temperature and then sterilised is shelf-stable for 1–2 years; it will not be labelled '*mi-cuit*' and the words '*en conserve*' may or may not be on the label.

BUYING FOIE GRAS

Anyone holidaying in Périgord or nearby will almost certainly buy a slice of *foie gras* terrine or a product in a jar or tin. Prices vary a great deal and for good reason.

FOIE GRAS CUIT AU TORCHON
Sometimes you see foie gras *advertised or described as* 'cuit au torchon', *which means* 'cooked in a cloth'. *This is a minor variation of the method of cooking* mi-cuit foie gras: *the cleaned lobes will have been wrapped in a cloth before being placed in the terrine, the idea being to absorb any fat that comes from the liver during the cooking.* Foie gras *cooked in this manner will probably be wiped clean once it is cold, replaced in the cleaned terrine and the gaps filled with a flavourful jelly, or it will be sliced and surrounded by aspic jelly. This is a luxurious way of serving* mi-cuit foie gras, *but the jelly or aspic also has a short shelf-life – about 1 week.*

In addition to the distinction between *mi-cuit* and *en conserve*, there are strict regulations controlling the content of tinned products and the prices reflect this. It pays to understand the differences and to read the label carefully.

Category 1 products must be 100 per cent *foie gras*.
1. *Foie gras d'oie entier* and *Foie gras de canard entier* are made from whole lobes of liver (this is the best Category 1 product).
2. *Foie gras d'oie* and *Foie gras de canard* are made from pieces of liver assembled together.
3. *Bloc de foie gras d'oie* and *Bloc de foie gras de canard* are made from *foie gras* reconstituted by machine (minced or puréed and pressed together).

Category 2 products must contain a minimum of 75 per cent *foie gras*.
Parfait de foie d'oie and *Parfait de foie de canard* are made from processed *foie gras*. They may have up to 25 per cent added chicken liver or *foie gras* fat and may be a blend of duck and goose.

Category 3 products must contain a minimum of 50 per cent *foie gras*.
1. *Pâté de foie d'oie* and *Pâté de foie de canard* are made from *bloc de foie gras* surrounded by minced forcemeat, and can be a blend of goose and duck.
2. *Galantine de foie d'oie* and *Galantine de foie de canard* are made from *foie gras* mixed with forcemeat, 35 per cent of which must be visible pieces of liver. These products can be a blend of goose and duck
3. *Purée* or *Mousse de foie d'oie* and *Purée* or *Mousse de foie de canard* are made from *foie gras* and forcemeat mixed or assembled to produce a purée or mousse.

Category 4 products must contain a minimum of 20 per cent *foie gras*.
All products described as '*au foie d'oie*' or '*au foie de canard*' are in this category. They are made from *foie gras* (the percentage must be stated) mixed with forcemeat.

This information relates to Decision no. 83 approved on 9 July 1987 by the French ministers of State, the Economy, Finance and Privatisation, and Agriculture. I am reliably informed that Decision no. 83 is unchanged to date.

For the visitor it is interesting to try both goose and duck *foie gras*. Each has its own character – goose *foie gras* is paler, silkier and has a more refined flavour; duck *foie gras* is more rustic, definitely 'ducky' and has more of a golden hue. (The colour is also influenced by the feed. Yellow corn is grown in Périgord, but elsewhere in the south-west the corn is white and that *foie gras* therefore has a lighter colour.) I think both are delectable and would claim that a slice of a well-made *mi-cuit foie gras* terrine and a slightly chilled glass of Monbazillac are perhaps the best beginning to a meal I can think of. Certainly as I sit here writing this sentence

I can feel the texture of the *foie gras* slipping and melting on my tongue, taste the incomparable flavour and remember the glorious golden wine. It was only a few weeks ago and already I am missing it!

It has become very popular in French restaurants to offer a quickly sautéed slice of *foie gras* – or escalope, a thick slice cut slightly on the bias from a chilled, raw *foie gras* – often paired or deglazed with something acidic to counteract its undeniable richness. Apples or grapes are popular choices, as are *verjus*, port or a late-picked wine. It takes experience to cook such a dish well: if the pan is too hot the liver will melt, leaving a sea of fat and a small lump of hard liver. I have included a recipe for *foie gras* sautéed with *verjus*, apple and grapes (see page 317) for those who want to have a go when in France.

La Mazille writes of sautéing an escalope of *foie gras*, implying that this dish was a local speciality and a good way of using livers unsuited for terrines. She recommends a quick sauté in a pan brushed with duck or goose fat and then serving the escalope with a green salad, perhaps with sliced hard-boiled eggs, or else with a truffled sauce. I was interested to read her comments as it confirmed that escalope of *foie gras* was not an invention of *nouvelle cuisine* in the 1970s as might have been thought, given the proliferation of sautéed *foie gras* on menus in France at that time.

Some combinations I have seen on menus in the south-west and, more often, in English-language cookery books seem to me to be bizarre and pointless. When you are presenting such a stand-out ingredient, why complicate and confuse it with too many other strong flavours? Black truffles are permitted and mushrooms and maybe caramelised onion, or a compote of apple or quince. A customer at Richmond Hill Cafe & Larder told me of a soup he had eaten in Paris that was a thin cream of lentils, puréed and strained so that it was as smooth as cream and a beautiful taupe colour, garnished with an escalope of sautéed *foie gras*. I thought that sounded ambrosial.

I would choose as my favourite combination soft salad leaves or wilted spinach leaves dressed with sharp sherry vinegar and a dash of walnut oil, topped with one modest slice of *foie gras* that has been slightly caramelised on the edges and maybe a few crisply sautéed slices of *cèpe* as well. This style of dish cannot be achieved with cooked *foie gras*, whether *mi-cuit* or *en conserve*. It works only with a fresh liver.

OPPOSITE Examples of the local produce widely available in the south-west are *bloc de foie gras*, *confit* of duck and goose, *foie gras en conserve* and duck *rillettes*. Even when the labels are professionally printed, some producers opt for the handwritten look because there is definite market advantage in seeming to be 'artisanal'. Similarly, preserving jars with rubber seals (such as those at top right) have the connotation of being 'made on the farm' – and many of them are indeed farm-made.

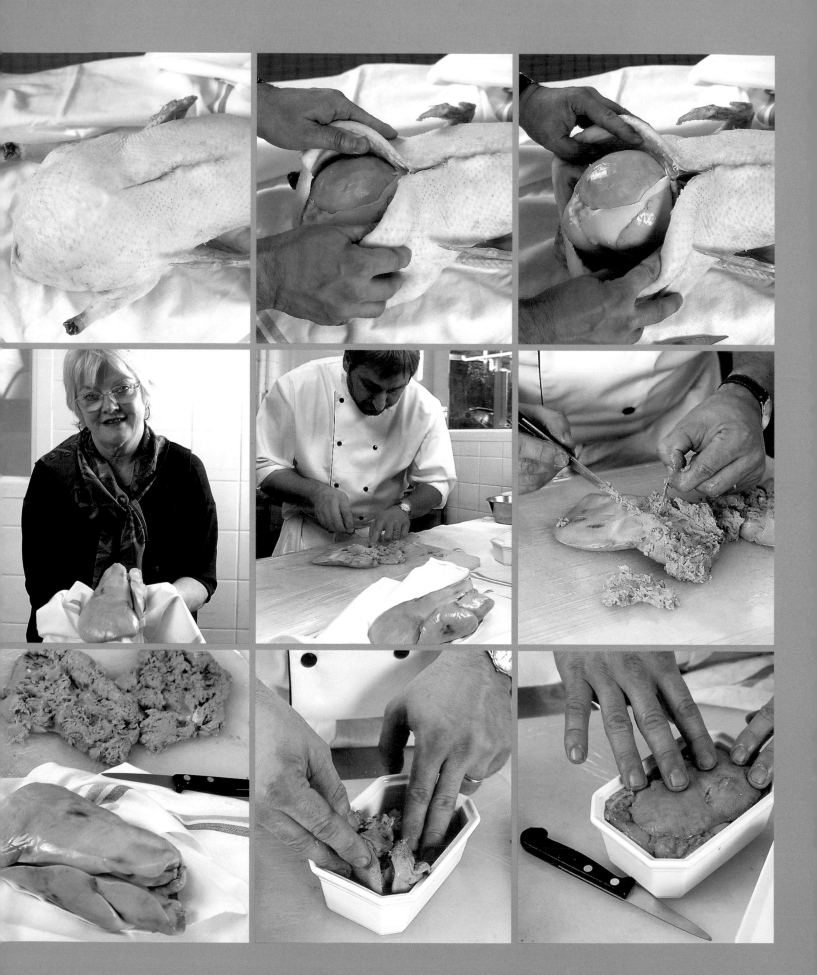

Terrine de foie gras

At the École Hôtelière in Périgueux during my winter 1999 visit, chef Claude Dussaigne gave me a demonstration of how to make a terrine of *foie gras mi-cuit* – the most sensual food I know. He started with a whole fattened duck weighing around 6 kg (13 lb) and slowly opened it to reveal the pale pink liver. This was carefully lifted out and the guts were removed. The gizzard and heart were put to one side for use in another dish, the legs were used later in a demonstration of how to prepare *confit*, and the monster breast fillets (*magrets*) were saved for an explanation of the best way to cook them.

Claude said that for a terrine it is best if the liver is removed from the bird quickly after its death while it and the bird are still warm. (For an escalope of *foie gras* this is less important, as the liver must be chilled before it can be sliced.) This is, of course, a counsel of perfection as most people buy their *foie gras* at a market or from a retailer and have no access to a liver that is warm!

The chef carefully examined the liver in order to remove all the tiny veins that run through the two lobes. This was good to watch as the exposed surface of the lobes looked a complete mess after he had probed and scraped and lifted out the tiny fragments. Had I done this at home, I would have been certain that I had ruined a very expensive product. The liver was seasoned to a precise ratio that was given per 1 kg (2 lb 3 oz) of liver:

Salt: 18 g (³⁄₅ oz) per kg
Freshly ground white pepper: 5–7 g (¹⁄₅–¹⁄₄ oz) per kg
Sugar: 15–20 g (¹⁄₂–³⁄₄ oz) per kg
Freshly grated nutmeg: 5–7 g (¹⁄₅–¹⁄₄ oz) per kg

Some cooks add a little alcohol, such as Armagnac, with the seasoning, but chef Claude feels this is unnecessary, saying that a well-made *terrine de foie gras mi-cuit* is so sublime that the flavour of Armagnac can be intrusive.

After seasoning, one lobe was pressed, smooth-side down, into a porcelain terrine and then covered with the other lobe, smooth-side up, which was pressed in firmly with the fingertips. The lid was put on and the terrine was cooked in a water bath in a convection oven set at 150°C (300°F) until the centre of the terrine registered 46°C (115°F) when tested with a probe. Then a light weight of exactly the dimensions of the terrine was substituted for the lid and the dish was set aside to cool. I wondered if the staff or students of the college would later get to taste this delicacy.

OPPOSITE Watching chef Claude Dussaigne making a terrine of *foie gras mi-cuit* was a very special experience. He commenced by removing the large, fattened liver carefully from the duck, then extracted all the nerve tissue and threads of blood vessels from each lobe. He pressed the seasoned lobes into a porcelain terrine, which was then cooked in a water bath until the internal temperature reached 46°C (115°F).

Confit

Before the days of refrigeration, households needed to stock up on food for the long winter and *confit* was the answer. This method of preserving meats has become synonymous with the cooking of the south-west. '*Confire*' means 'to conserve or preserve', and the products of this conservation are known as '*confits*'. The meat is slipped into warm fat and brought slowly to near-simmering point (90°C/195°F), cooked very gently until tender and then allowed to cool, still in the fat. The finished product should never be dry or splintery; it should be soft and melting and should not taste greasy.

There is little evidence that *confit*'s popularity has declined in these days of freezers and refrigeration. When in France a good local poultry stall, such as at the Sarlat market, is the best way of seeing how resourceful the *confit* method is. The breast is sold either as a *confit* or as a thick steak for grilling (*magret*), or cured and smoked to be thinly sliced. The thigh, considered the choicest portion, is sold as a *confit*, as are the wing, the gizzards, the heart and the neck, which has usually been stuffed with a pork sausage mixture. You can buy the carcass and the fat and the skin as well.

I do not think it is properly understood that *confit* improves with keeping. You *can* salt, cook and eat the product quickly, but it will not have mellowed as it ought. Paula Wolfert wrote in *The Cooking of South-West France*, 'People . . . can taste their *confit* within a week or so, or for that matter as soon as it finishes cooking, but what they are eating won't really be *confit* any more than freshly drained curds are ripe cheese.' Providing the fat and the storage pot are scrupulously clean, *confit* will keep for several months in the refrigerator.

Australian cooks do not usually plan to keep *confits* for months and months, as French cooks do. In addition, Australians would almost certainly store them under refrigeration rather than in a cellar or similar, which means that we do not need to use quite as much salt as is sometimes recommended in recipes. And often we resort to pork fat because our ducks and geese do not have the plentiful layer of thick, firm, yellow fat found in French birds.

Having seen the size of the usual thigh from a fattened duck in France, weighing a minimum of 400 g (14 oz), I wonder why we bother to make *confits* from Australian ducks. It takes great skill to create something soft and succulent when the duck legs are as lean as ours are (average size 200 g/7 oz). I am not saying you shouldn't do it, but be aware that the cooking must be extra gentle, with the fat never at more than a murmur, and that the result will never achieve the succulence of the French product.

The technique of cooking meat products in fat to preserve them is not restricted to ducks and geese. You occasionally encounter *confit* of rabbits or game

---

COOKING WITH FAT

In The Cooking of South-West France *Paula Wolfert devotes several pages to discussing all aspects of cooking with fats. They make for fascinating reading. She states that the temperature at which fat is used affects both its digestibility and whether it can be removed after it has given its flavour to a dish. For example, by cooking a dish very gently you allow the flavours to mingle but the fat will not emulsify with the juices, so the fat can readily be lifted off at the end of the cooking process. Paula also makes the point that rendered poultry fat contains 9 per cent cholesterol compared with butter's 22 per cent, and that you need less poultry fat for the same cooking process than butter, thus further reducing your intake of saturated fat. I urge interested cooks to read her full account.*

birds. Rabbit *rillettes* (see page 321) is a classic *confit* dish where rabbit and pork are well seasoned, gently cooked in pork fat and rabbit fat, then shredded and potted with the fat. And I remember a supper cooked for me some years ago by Damien Pignolet where we feasted on *confit* of quail with a purée of sorrel.

Confit is also widely made with pork. The annual killing of the pig was a major event in the year and every morsel would be used. Some parts were salted and slowly cooked and put down in glazed earthenware crocks to last through the winter. Preserved pork rind is used over and over again in south-western cookery and every butcher in the region today has a roll of it for sale. Customers can indicate how many centimetres they want in the same manner as Australians might show their butcher at home how much sausage they want cut. Strips of this product find their way into all manner of braises. In Australia it is a good idea to order a large sheet of rind from the butcher – it is easier for a butcher to supply it this way than to provide little pieces without notice. Trim away any fat attached, cut the rind into strips and freeze both the fat and the rind in clearly marked parcels, or prepare it according to the recipe on page 314.

Still on pork, in the markets you can buy a roughly chopped product called *fritons*, resembling coarse *rillettes*, which is made from the muzzle, ears and cheeks of the pig. *Fritons* can also be made from the scraps of duck or goose that fall off the larger pieces and are left behind in the preserving pan once the large pieces are removed. They are always fairly loose and crumbly, and whether of pork or poultry are good sautéed and added to a dish or soup of lentils or dried beans.

Grillons, chunks of pork cooked in pork fat, are another speciality of Périgord. The relationship between *grillons* and *fritons* is not clear. *Les grillons périgourdins*, according to La Mazille, are the delicious little morsels that break off and sink to the bottom of the pot after cooking lots of *confit*, either duck, goose or pork. This is exactly how she describes *fritons*, too, so I am taking it that the two terms are synonymous. Where *confit* is being prepared in large quantities, there will be a great deal of this savoury debris and it makes good sense to pot it for sale. The bits are retrieved from the cooking vessel, chilled and then chopped quite coarsely and seasoned with pepper, *quatre-épices*, and a little finely chopped garlic. This mixture is returned to the stove together with a glass of water and cooked gently for 1 hour, stirring often as it has a tendency to stick. It is then potted and covered with a layer of melted fat. It can be used as a rustic spread, just like *rillettes*, or chopped and added to stuffings or refried with other ingredients and added to a fricassée.

La Mazille is very enthusiastic about *les grillons périgourdins* and I found it helpful to read her discussion on the relationship between *grillons* and *rillettes*. She says that *grillons* were either chopped finely or made with coarsely minced meat, while *rillettes* were always made with pieces of pork that were cooked and then shredded. (In the Loire you can also buy the pieces of cooked meat before shredding, when they are known as *rillons*.)

In these days of creative culinary terminology, menus list non-meat *confits* of onions, tomatoes, beetroot, and so on. In every case the term implies long, slow cooking. It may or may not imply that the finished product can be stored for a long time. I have included a recipe for a *confit* of onions as an example (see page 327).

MAKING CONFITS

I have described at some length the process of making *confits* in *Stephanie's Feasts and Stories*. Having now carefully read the writings of La Mazille on every aspect of preparing *confits*, it seems a good idea to give a brief description of the process here, adding any of La Mazille's hints or observations that are helpful to my basic recipe. As it is easier for Australian cooks to have access to ducks than geese, I shall restrict my remarks to ducks.

Essentially, the process begins by portioning a whole bird into quarters (unless you are reserving the breast fillet for grilling). Separate each leg and wing bone with a portion of the breast meat attached, then season the quarters with thyme, a bay leaf, a mixture of spices and coarse salt – 50 g (1¾ oz) per kg is a good rule of thumb. Leave the pieces overnight or for up to 24 hours and then brush or rinse away the salt and seasonings.

Slip the pieces into warmed, rendered poultry fat and cook gently at barely simmering point for at least 2 hours until the flesh is very tender and no more juices escape from the meat. La Mazille believes that, as ducks have less fat than geese, it will always be necessary to augment the duck fat with pork fat. Certainly this is the case in Australia.

Allow to cool a little, then put some of the strained fat into a scrupulously clean glazed pot or a wide-necked glass jar, followed by the cooked *confit*, then cover with more fat and store until required. The *confit* can be stored for at least a month in the refrigerator. In country France, pots like this would be expected to keep for a year.

La Mazille says that the final sealing should be done with fat that has been heated separately (after the pieces of *confit* have been put in the pot). Allow this fat to come to boiling point and boil just until a scum containing all the impurities forms on the top. Pull the pan from the heat at this point, allow it to stop bubbling and then carefully skim the scum, leaving perfectly clear fat. Cool it a little and then cover the *confit* with this fat to a depth of 3 cm (1 in). Once it has set, cover the pot with clean paper and put the lid on.

When you want to use some of the *confit*, warm the fat sufficiently to dislodge the required number of pieces. To do this, the traditional earthenware *confit* pot would have been warmed over the fire until the edges of the fat started to melt, at which point it would have been a simple matter to lift out the required number of pieces without damaging the rest. Modern cooks, if they have used an enamelled cast-iron or fireproof pot as a storage vessel, can put it over a low flame for a few

OPPOSITE Making *confit*: a duck is opened out (top left), showing the generous fat deposits over the thighs, and then portioned (top right) into breast fillets (*magrets*), wing sections and legs (*cuisses*). The pieces are salted and seasoned (bottom left) and left overnight before being put in a pan with the skin from the back, the internal fat and all the trimmings, and slowly rendered for the precious duck fat.

minutes to achieve the same result. However, if you have stored your *confit* in a plastic container you will have no alternative but to gouge out the pieces required and accept that it is likely the remaining ones will be torn.

Scrape the excess fat from the dislodged pieces and heat the fat in a heavy-based pan. It should be hot but never smoking – poultry fat that is smoking is spoiled and cannot be used. Add the meat to the pan skin-side down and cook gently, turning once, until the skin is thoroughly crisped and the meat is warmed right through. The meat should not be prodded or poked during cooking. You must still go through this process even if the *confit* is to be served cold – in a salad, for example. The skin *must* be crisp. Serve the hot, crisped *confit* with an accompaniment of your choice: a green salad, some potatoes separately sautéed, maybe with mushrooms as well (see the recipes for potatoes with dried or fresh *cèpes* on pages 171 and 173, and *pommes sarladaises* on page 284), or with cabbage previously blanched, drained and tossed in a little poultry fat with garlic and parsley.

If a *confit* is to be an ingredient in a stuffing or added to a *cassoulet*, the skin will usually be removed first. I cannot imagine any housewife in the south-west throwing the skin away, however. She would crisp it and toss it through a salad or maybe a dish of potatoes or green beans.

In France the neck skin, gizzard and heart are treated the same way as the rest of the duck or goose but are stored (and sold) separately. They are collectively called *les abattis* and take only about 30–45 minutes to cook. A gizzard salad has become one of the most popular starters in small restaurants, while the neck is frequently stuffed with seasoned pork and cooked as a separate speciality. To serve, the neck is crisped and heated through in the same manner as other *confits* and cut into thick slices.

As part of the initial preparation of a duck or goose, all excess skin from the back and any loose fat from inside are rendered to provide the fat for the preserving process. At the completion of the rendering the pieces of skin will have become golden and crispy and these special treats often find their way into salads. Again, they are available in markets, where they are packaged in cellophane bags and sold as *grattons de canard* or *d'oie*. Away from the south-west, you can buy imported rendered goose or duck fat in cans from specialist food stores.

Australian and English cooks will probably also buy their *confit* from a specialist food store. It should be sold with a layer of fat attached to it. At the Richmond Hill Cafe & Larder I have a vacuum-pack machine that provides an ideal way of storing *confit*. We slip a pair of duck legs and some of the flavourful fat into a vacuum bag and seal it. The bag contains enough fat for the reheating and to sauté a few potatoes or cabbage leaves.

OPPOSITE This pot of duck-and-pork *rillettes* was made using the rabbit rillettes recipe on page 321. *Rillettes* are easy to make and soften quickly to room temperature and spreadable consistency, which makes them an ideal filling for a split baguette. You won't need any butter, though! The little pot and knife in the picture were bought long ago at a French market stall.

Preserved Pork Rind

Makes 4–5 rolls

1 sheet pork rind (approximately
    1.5 kg/3 lb 4 oz)
salt
1 kg/2 lb pork flare fat, trimmed of
    any membrane
reserved trimmed fat from pork rind
1 cup water

Throughout these pages I have often mentioned *confit* of pork rind. This is a fantastic resource and so easy that it is worth making a reasonable quantity. I have given quantities sufficient for 4–5 long rolls, but if you prefer them shorter, cut the strips of pork rind in half crosswise to make 8–10 short rolls.

Any other part of a pig can be salted and cooked in fat in the same manner as pork rind, although it is not common to have the prime pieces of meat prepared using this method. But ears, muzzle and belly do find their way into the *confit* pot. And I thought it might also be helpful to give a few hints on rendering fat.

Pork flare fat, also known as 'flair fat' and '*la panne*', is the softish fat surrounding the kidneys. It is used for making superior sausages and melts readily.

Trim all fat from the sheet of pork rind and set the fat aside. Weigh the trimmed sheet and then measure out 22 g/¾ oz salt for every 500 g/1 lb 2 oz pork rind. Cut the rind lengthwise into strips about 8–10 cm/3½–4 in wide. Put the strips on a tray and sprinkle with salt. Leave for at least 12 hours.

Cut the pieces of pork flare fat into small squares and put them in a heavy-based pot with the reserved fat trimmings from the sheet of pork rind. Add the water to prevent the fat sticking. Put over moderate heat and from time to time press down on the squares of fat with the back of a ladle or similar to encourage the fat to render. The rendering process is complete when the pieces of pork fat have become a dark gold in colour and have just begun to give off a faint smoke. Strain the fat through a coarse-meshed sieve set over a heavy-based saucepan that will be large enough to hold all the pork-rind rolls in 1 layer.

Brush the salt from the strips of pork rind and roll up each strip tightly, as you would roll up a carpet, and tie firmly with string in the centre of each roll. Slip the rolls into the hot, rendered pork fat and cook steadily for about 3 hours until quite tender. Remove the string and transfer the rolls to a clean, sterilised container. Pour over a little strained fat. To make sure the rolls do not float to the surface, allow the fat to set before adding more. Refrigerate.

Once they have been cooked and chilled, you can freeze the rolls, individually bagged with some of the fat and clearly labelled. Use them within 6 months.

Les Grillons de ménage

HOME-STYLE POTTED PORK

This recipe is based on a description given by La Mazille. She makes the point that the average housewife would not have access to the resource of a huge pot in which to find plenty of savoury bits – she must start from scratch. She does, and makes *les grillons de ménage*.

Mix the pork with the salt and leave it for several hours. Put the meat and salt in a heavy-based pot with the water and bouquet garni and cook over a gentle heat, stirring often, for 1 hour. Add the garlic, shallot, pepper and *quatre-épices*, stir well and taste for salt. Cook for another 1½ hours, stirring from time to time. Cool a little, then strain. Press the solids into small pots and allow to cool. When cold, cover and seal with some of the strained fat. Spread on hot toast and enjoy as a snack with cornichons or a pre-dinner drink, or serve in the pot as part of a selection of cold dishes for lunch. I like to combine *grillons* with spiced cherries or prune-plums.

Makes approximately 3 cups

2 kg/4½ lb lean pork (I would
    suggest a mixture of belly and
    shoulder), coarsely minced
60 g/2 oz coarse salt
1 cup water
1 good-sized bouquet garni (bay
    leaf, several parsley stalks, large
    sprig of thyme)
2 cloves garlic, finely chopped
3 shallots, finely chopped
pinch of freshly ground black pepper
pinch of quatre-épices

LEFT Colourful, practical earthenware pots are inexpensive and available in many shapes – we bought several at the market. They are not at all traditional to the south-west and are more typical of the south of France, while similar pottery is also seen everywhere in southern Spain. Unfortunately they do not travel well, as I found out to my cost – it is best to buy, use and appreciate them in situ.

Escalopes of Foie Gras with Verjus, Apples and Grapes

This dish was made by chef Claude Dussaigne (see page 307) at the École Hôtelière in Périgueux. *Foie gras* cooked in this manner is quite extraordinary – the outside is crusty and caramelised but when it is cut, the centre seems to be liquid. 'Moving molecules' is how a colleague of mine once described it.

Escalopes of *foie gras* combine well with the natural sugars and acidity in fruit. Apples and grapes are used here, but sautéed quince or pears make good accompaniments, too. The pan can be deglazed with sherry vinegar or an aged red-wine vinegar if *verjus* is not available.

Blanch the grapes in boiling water for 1 minute and set aside. Heat the duck fat in a non-stick frying pan. Add the apple and sauté until golden on both sides, turning once. Transfer the apple to a warm plate and keep warm. Wipe out the pan and reheat it. Add the escalopes of *foie gras* and turn after 30 seconds. The turned side should look a little caramelised. Quickly return the apple to the pan, then add the grapes and the *verjus*. Remove the *foie gras* to a heated serving plate and arrange the apple slices next to the *foie gras*. Allow the *verjus* to reduce almost completely, then add the stock and reduce until syrupy. Taste for seasoning. Spoon the grapes and sauce over and around the *foie gras* and apple and serve immediately. Chef Dussaigne added a final flourish of diced tomato and mixed sliced vegetables, but I don't think this is necessary.

Serves 2

1 handful peeled grapes
1 tablespoon rendered duck fat
1 Granny Smith apple, peeled and
　cut into thinnish slices
4 thick slices from a very cold raw
　foie gras, refrigerated until needed
3 tablespoons verjus
100 ml/3½ fl oz duck stock
freshly ground black pepper
sea salt

OPPOSITE To make this dish, escalopes (slices) are cut from a raw *foie gras* and quickly coloured in a hot pan (top). Grapes and apples contribute sweetness and acidity to balance the richness, and the pan is deglazed with *verjus*.

Salad of Haricots Verts and Foie Gras from Le Centenaire

Serves 4

1 large carrot, peeled
400 g/14 oz green beans of the
   smallest and best quality possible
   (preferably home-grown)
sea salt
freshly ground black pepper
2 slices mi-cuit foie gras
freshly chopped chives
sprigs of chervil
sprigs of dill

Dressing
1 teaspoon Szechuan pepper,
   coarsely crushed
3 tablespoons hazelnut oil
1 tablespoon balsamic vinegar
1 teaspoon Dijon-style mustard
sea salt

This lovely dish was one I ate at Le Centenaire restaurant at Les Eyzies during the summer trip. When chef Roland Mazère shared his recipe with me, he did not give specific quantities. I imagine that in his restaurant the dressing would be made in a fairly generous quantity sufficient for the day's needs, but here I have suggested quantities for a salad for 4 people. Chef Roland suggested an alternative dressing using truffle purée and truffle juice. If you find yourself with either of these ingredients, feel free to substitute or add.

At Le Centenaire the curls of *foie gras* would have been taken from a chilled terrine. It was a very generous portion. In Australia I would buy 2 slices of *mi-cuit foie gras*, which is obtainable in this quantity in vacuum-packed form, and divide them between the 4 salads.

To make the dressing, mix all ingredients except the sea salt. Taste for salt.

Using a potato peeler, cut the carrot lengthwise to make long, thin slices. Top and tail the green beans and, unless they are very slender, slit lengthwise. Bring 2 generous pots of lightly salted water to a boil. Drop the carrot slices into 1 pot and cook for 2 minutes only. Drain quickly, then immediately season with salt and pepper and moisten with some of the dressing. Drop the beans into the second pot and cook rapidly, uncovered, until they are barely tender. Drain quickly and immediately season with salt, pepper and some of the dressing.

Arrange a pile of dressed beans on each plate. Divide the *foie gras* between the plates, settling it on top of the beans, and sprinkle with a grain or two of sea salt. Drape the carrot slices over and drizzle with a little more dressing. Garnish with chives, chervil and dill and serve.

Rabbit Rillettes

Long ago, in the mid-1960s, I lived for a year in the Loire town of Tours, famous for its pork *rillettes* and for a rabbit-and-pork version named for the nearby town of Le Mans. *Rillettes du Mans* became a great favourite of mine. In the town *charcuteries* it was piled into attractive taupe stoneware bowls. Frequently I bought a small quantity to spread on a baguette and take for an afternoon by the river. When I opened my first restaurant in Melbourne in 1976 I made and served *rillettes*. They were greeted with enthusiasm and I found it embarrassing that my customers believed I had made a culinary breakthrough and invented a wonderful new dish. In vain I protested that this simple product was a classic. I still love *rillettes* and make them often. Restaurant trends being the way they are, the dish is now rarely offered, but it should not be too long before it is considered revolutionary again. In the south-west I was pleased to find that rabbit *rillettes* and pure pork *rillettes* were just as ubiquitous as they had been in the Loire Valley.

If you have a whole rabbit, joint it into pieces. Cut the belly pork into strips about 2 cm/1 in wide. Liberally season the rabbit and the belly pork with salt and pepper. Bury the garlic, bay leaf and thyme in the meat. Leave for 6 hours or overnight.

Preheat the oven to 150°C/300°F. Transfer the meat and seasonings to a heavy-based, ovenproof container with a tight-fitting lid. Add the pork fat and water and stir to mix. Put into the oven and cook for 2½ hours or until both the rabbit and the pork are quite tender. Lift the contents of the dish into a strainer set over a bowl and leave to cool for a few minutes. Discard the garlic, bay leaf and thyme. Strain the liquid fat and juices into a glass jug and allow the fat to rise.

Separate the rabbit meat from the bones and discard the bones. Shred the rabbit and pork meat with 2 forks and transfer to a scrupulously clean and dry container. Spoon over the risen fat, leaving the juices behind. At this stage the mixture should be quite moist but not sloppy. Mix well with the forks and taste for seasoning (*rillettes* need to be well seasoned). Press down to expel any air. There should be a layer of fat that rises above the level of the pressed-down meat shreds. Chill until completely set and eat within 1 week. Serve cold with toasted country bread, preferably sourdough, and small, crunchy cornichons.

Longer keeping

The *rillettes* will keep for longer than a week if the pot is thoroughly sealed with an extra layer of completely clarified fat, as described on page 311. Using this method, the *rillettes* can be stored for at least 1 month. However, once the fat layer has been broached, the contents should be consumed within 1 week.

Makes plenty for a first course for 6 people

1 kg/2 lb rabbit (weighed on the bone)
500 g/1 lb skinned, boned belly pork (not too lean)
sea salt
freshly ground black pepper
2 cloves garlic, peeled and lightly crushed
1 bay leaf
large sprig of thyme
100 g/3½ oz minced pork back fat
2 tablespoons water

OPPOSITE A few olives, some sharp and crunchy radishes, *saucisson sec*, pickled cherries and cornichons are excellent accompaniments for rich, savoury *rillettes*.

Zuzu's Confit and Cèpe Tarte Tatin

Makes 4

unsalted butter
1 sheet puff pastry, approximately
    24 cm/9½ in square
1 egg, lightly beaten

Filling
1 confit duck leg *or* 100 g/3½ oz
    other cooked poultry
250 g/9 oz cèpes *or* assorted
    mushrooms
2 teaspoons olive oil
2 shallots, finely chopped
2 tablespoons crème fraîche
freshly ground black pepper
1 tablespoon freshly chopped young
    parsley (preferably flat-leaf)

I met Zuzu Fel at the home of Jean and Lorraine Lagarde near Montauban (see page 145). She is an enthusiastic home cook, who told me proudly about being a finalist in the nationwide Sofitel–*Le Figaro Magazine* cooking competition in 1998 and its winner in 1999. Her winning dish was a leg of lamb cooked with a series of garnishes, of which this *cèpe tarte Tatin* was one. She cooked a large tart for dinner that evening, which was enthusiastically received. It was also very rich. I prefer to make it in a smaller size and serve it as a substantial first course.

If you are using frozen wild mushrooms, blanch them in boiling water for 2 minutes and drain them well before you chop them. Frozen puff pastry is fine to use, but read the packet carefully and try to buy one made with butter. The filling is good to use as an alternative stuffing in the recipe for stuffed mushrooms (see page 177). The tart is nearly as good made with chicken and cultivated mushrooms as it is made with *confit* duck and *cèpes*.

Preheat the oven to 220°C/425°F. Generously butter 4 × 12 cm/5 in fluted tart tins, preferably non-stick (do not use loose-bottomed moulds). Cut 4 circles of puff pastry the same size as the largest diameter of the moulds – most non-stick fluted tart tins have sloping sides and you need to cut the pastry to fit the diameter of the top, not the base. Put the pastry circles in the refrigerator while you prepare the filling.

To make the filling, remove the skin from the duck leg (reserve the skin for another use) and cut the meat from the bone. Chop the meat finely and set aside. Cut off and chop the stalks from the *cèpes* and cut the caps into 5 mm/¼ in slices. Heat the oil in a frying pan and sauté the caps for 1 minute. Drain on kitchen paper. In the same pan, sauté the chopped stalks and the shallot for 2 minutes. Add the crème fraîche and stir for about 2 minutes until it has bubbled and reduced. Stir in the chopped duck meat. Season with pepper and add the parsley.

Distribute the sautéed mushroom slices among the 4 moulds. Remember that this is the layer that will be visible when the tart is turned upside down, so arrange them with care. Cover with the filling. Remove the rounds of puff pastry from the refrigerator and settle them on the top of the filling, easing them inside the rim of each mould to create an edge. Brush the pastry with the egg, trying not to let it run down inside the tin (this may make it hard to remove the tarts from the moulds). Bake for 15 minutes, then flip the tarts out onto individual plates and serve.

If you like, spread the reserved duck skin on baking paper and bake in a hot oven (200°C/400°F) for about 5–8 minutes until crisp. Allow to cool, then chop or crumble and scatter over a salad to serve alongside the tarts.

Confit d'oignons au vin de Pécharmant

CONFIT OF ONIONS IN PÉCHARMANT WINE

Being slowly cooked, these onions are often referred to as a *confit d'oignons*. They make an excellent side dish for a simply roasted leg of lamb, can be used as a topping for a steak, and add a bit of magic to any stuffing or to a potato and mushroom dish – and that's just a few ideas.

The wine of Pécharmant (see page 369) is rich and full bodied. If you are a long way from the south-west, use your favourite full-bodied wine instead.

The onions I used at Lavalade were not much bigger than marbles. If you can't find small onions, use large ones halved and cut across into thinnish slices.

Heat the duck fat over moderate heat in a stainless steel or enamelled heavy-based pan with a lid. Add the onions and turn to coat with fat, then stir in the herbs and wine. The onions will be piled high at this stage. Cover and adjust the heat to low. If the wine starts to boil over, set the lid ajar. Cook very gently for about 1 hour, stirring frequently, until the onions become soft and shiny and the flavour has mellowed. After an hour the onions will have shrunk in size and the wine will have become a syrupy glaze.

Confit d'oignons will keep for weeks in a covered container in the refrigerator. To reheat, sauté gently in a tiny bit of fat or olive oil, or put in the oven at 160°C/320°F, covered. Alternatively, add some to pan juices to give a further dimension to a sauce for veal, beef or poultry.

Makes approximately 1 cup

1 tablespoon rendered duck fat
  or olive oil
20 whole small onions, peeled *or*
  4 large onions, peeled and sliced
few sprigs of thyme
1 bay leaf
250 ml/9 fl oz vin de Pécharmant
  or other full-bodied red wine

PAGES 324–5 *Confit d'oignons* can be made just as successfully with shallots or even garlic, or a combination of the two. These bundles of shallots displayed at Sarlat market were called 'chicken-thigh shallots', a charming and apt description. The shallots and the violet garlic are of the *département* of Lot-et-Garonne – all produce in Europe is now legally required to show where it comes from.
OPPOSITE Here the little onions have started to shrink, but they will reduce and soften a lot more and the *confit* will eventually look more 'jammy'.

Eating Out

*N*o traveller need ever go hungry in France. Apart from the culinary delights on offer in markets and food stores and the infinite number of perfect picnic spots, restaurants are everywhere – not just in the obvious places, but up country lanes, on the top of mountains, in hotels, in deserted medieval villages and on farms. What follows is an abbreviated account of a few of the eating experiences I enjoyed in the south-west during the visits described in this book, chosen to show the different styles that exist.

For a Francophile, there is something marvellous about the formality with which any meal is offered, no matter how humble the surroundings. The table will be set just so, even though the 'cloth' might be a piece of paper torn to accommodate the central pole of the sun umbrella, and the cutlery might be the cheapest aluminium variety. For example, at one humble *auberge*, Chez Crouzil, visited in summer at Masclat, we started with an apéritif, the local peach wine – herby and definitely peachy, somewhere between a sweet vermouth and a late-picked wine – and our simple menu for 90F (A$25) offered soup, pâté, gizzard and walnut salad, a choice of meat, cheese and dessert. The salad was enormous and would certainly have been enough for a substantial lunch. The lamb was flavoursome and modest in quantity and the Bleu d'Auvergne cheese was delicious, as was the bottle of 1994 Franck & Jacques rosé (Rigal, Vin de Pays du Lot), which cost around A$10.

Price should not be the only deciding factor when you are choosing a place to eat: good experiences are possible at all price points. As always, doing a little prior research will pay big dividends. Almost every French restaurant, whether large or small, simple or fancy, will have a fixed-price menu (*menu fixe*) or a range of such menus, which offer excellent value and are a good way of sampling the chef's style and specialities. They are often the preferred choice of French travellers, who know that the day's menu will be well balanced, with seasonal ingredients, and promptly served.

We questioned French acquaintances regarding *prix nets* (net prices), a phrase that appears on almost every restaurant bill – these days it is rare to see the more helpful *service compris* (service charge included). They told us that all restaurants include in their prices a 15 per cent service charge, so technically you are not obliged to add more. In practice, French customers 'round up', so if the bill is 265F they might leave 280F, but probably not 300F.

OPPOSITE Our favourite place to eat was Le Pont de l'Ouysse, a hôtel-restaurant rightly described as 'a little corner of paradise'. One of the specialities was this mighty veal shank, which weighed 1.5 kg (3 lb 4 oz) and fed four people. The recipe is on pages 356–7.

At the time of writing, Europe is readying itself for the introduction of new currency. The old currencies will no longer operate after 28 February 2002 in the 11 member states of the European Union (France, Belgium, Germany, Spain, Ireland, Italy, Luxembourg, the Netherlands, Austria, Portugal and Finland) and in Greece. They will all be using the euro after that time.

Fermes Auberges

Once upon a time the best eating experiences in rural France were said to be had at truck drivers' stops, known as *les routiers*, along the major roads. The reality nowadays is that few of these are memorable, although they do offer substantial meals for comparatively little cost. Lately I have read that the *ferme auberge* (farm inn) is where to go for authentic French country cooking. Here you will find simple and attractive accommodation on the farm, locally produced dishes of tradition and local wines. Apart from the lovely food, it is a most delightful way of meeting country people and putting real faces and stories to the memories of flavours and landscape.

However, it is of the utmost importance that you recognise the genuine article. The real *ferme auberge* will be a member of the network Bienvenue à la Ferme and can be identified by a sign that is half red and half green, with a yellow stylised daisy or marguerite. The proprietors of these admirable establishments are required to guarantee that 80 per cent of the ingredients used to prepare the meals are grown or raised on the farm itself. Other places might call themselves *fermes auberges*, but these pretenders or imposters do not have to comply with the standards set by the parent organisation. They might have a menu offering several courses (frequently far too many) and a reasonable inclusive price, but customers may well find that they are served with flavourless soup, ordinary pâté, sloppy salads and main dishes that never seem to vary.

Careful cooking will always be elusive and the best you can do is have a personal recommendation from someone whose tastebuds you respect. This is not easy to obtain when touring, so it is best to take a chance and approach every meal with goodwill and a spirit of optimism.

LA FERME AUBERGE FORT DE LA RHONIE

During my travels in 1999 and 2000 it was always a particular pleasure to be offered something I had not tasted or heard about before. I know I ought not to rail against the sameness of the menus in the *auberges* and restaurants of the south-west – after all, isn't this what I am lauding when I talk about regional food and culinary tradition? – but I know that ordinary local families do not eat *foie gras* and *confit* several times a week, as tourists can easily find themselves doing. You need to put

OPPOSITE In the kitchen at the Coustaty *ferme auberge* (see page 335), Madame was preparing melon jam to serve at breakfast time. Any melon can be used in this way and it is a common method of using excess fruit. Some jam recipes specify underripe melons, but the ones being used here were large and looked completely ripe.

a bit of effort into finding alternatives or risk returning home with feathers and quacking!

One *ferme auberge* where I had an outstanding meal during my visit in late 1999 was La Ferme Auberge Fort de la Rhonie, which is in the village of Meyrals near Saint-Cyprien, and is run by four generations of the Coustaty family. Geese were strolling and grazing in the early winter sunshine. On inspecting the factory kitchen, it was obvious that the processing of the entire bird was a central activity and an important source of revenue for the Coustatys. Here the family prepares *foie gras*, pâtés and *confits*, including an unusual *confit* of *cèpes* preserved in goose fat, and a goose breast stuffed with *foie gras* to be thinly sliced. M. and Mme Coustaty also sell the feathers and down of their geese, which go to make soft, warm bed-covers. In addition, they sell walnuts in the shell and walnut kernels, make jam from their own fruit (peach, melon, quince and fig), press walnut oil, make walnut wine, sell fresh goose cuts, make and bake their own bread in a wood-fired oven and give cooking classes, not to mention running the residential side of the business and cooking three meals a day for the family and guests. No wonder there are four generations still actively involved!

Lunch started with a terrine of *foie gras*, which was brought to the table and left there. I had to control my greed but allowed myself to be persuaded to have a second slice. We were then privileged to eat one of the great Périgourdin dishes, *la poule avec sa mique* (see page 350). It belongs to that tradition of country cooking where one pot holds everything and each ingredient adds complexity and subtlety to the whole. The golden, clear broth was served first. The grandfather unselfconsciously poured a little of his red wine into his broth and drank it out of the plate. This is a custom known as *faire chabrol*, in which the acidity of the wine is supposed to overcome any greasy residue in the mouth. It is especially appro-priate if the soup is a fatty one, such as the many cabbage and pork soups of the region. The usual soup plates are shallow and rounded rather than having a flat edge, making them easier to sup from, especially if you have a substantial mous-tache, as many Frenchmen do.

After our broth we went to the kitchen to see the *mique*, a football-sized dumpling that bobbed in the pot alongside two big hens and plenty of vegetables. La Mazille says that it was customary for the man of the house to cut the *mique* at the table, which is how it was done on this occasion. (She also says that the definition of a henpecked husband is one whose wife cuts the *mique*.) With this dish was served a lovely local Bergerac wine, a 1995 Domaine de Golse (Jean-Marie Bertrand, Port Sainte Foy). After copious helpings of chicken, vegetables, *mique* and all the accompaniments (cornichons, mustard and coarse grey salt), I felt a bit like one of the farm's geese as I waddled back to the car.

OPPOSITE As good as it gets: homemade *terrine de foie gras* and hot toast, as eaten at the Coustatys' farm. Madame told me that the youngest member of the family, Vivien, who was about 8 years old, loves *foie gras* and it is his preferred after-school snack.

Hôtel-restaurants

Our lunch on one summer's day epitomised another of France's greatest assets, the hôtel-restaurant. With just a bit of research you can find a charming small establishment almost anywhere, where you will be greeted with a smile and served pleasant-to-exceptional food at a prettily set table under trees or umbrellas, all for a modest price. Driving into such a place and hearing the clinking of glasses and glimpsing aproned waiters moving briskly among the well-filled tables is enough to set my gastric juices flowing!

My notebooks from the 1970s record a meal at a hôtel-restaurant in the Bergerac area, where my husband and I chose from the day's menu. I had superb country ham with cornichons, then vineyard snails, followed by a thin and very rare steak and then crêpes sandwiched with crushed walnuts. Maurice had a duck-liver parfait, followed by a freshly caught trout, then a local dish of tripe bundles with pork stuffing, which had been simmered in a light stock, and to finish, a classic caramel custard. How did we eat all this, I now wonder?

LE PONT DE L'OUYSSE

The best dining experiences of the summer and autumn holidays (other than home cooking) were at Le Pont de l'Ouysse, a hôtel-restaurant deep in the countryside at Lacave, not too far from Rocamadour in the Lot (you will need your yellow Michelin map for this one). We went four times in all to a place that is a perfect example of what I hinted at in the first paragraphs of this chapter. Without prior knowledge I doubt anyone would stumble upon it, but as the extremely charming wine waiter told us on our first visit, we had unexpectedly arrived at '*un petit coin du Paradis*'. The restaurant is reached via one of the spectacular D roads that follows the valley of a river, in this case the Ouysse, with awesome and magnificent cliffs topped by limestone plateaux (*les causses*) rising on both sides of the valley. This landscape is completely different to the gentle character of the hills and valleys and plains of the *département* of the Dordogne. 'A little corner of paradise' seemed an apt description.

On our first visit, in summer, the tables were set under giant *tilleul* and *marronnier* trees. The tablecloths were palest green – the colour the French refer to as *eau-de-Nil*, supposedly the colour of the Nile – and old-gold pleated fabric (very Issey Miyake, Julie thought) and there was a pleasant murmuring and clinking of glasses from guests already lunching. In front of the tables was a narrow garden bed full of cabbages, lettuce, silver beet, cherry tomatoes and herbs. The flower beds are planted further away at the foot of the old stone bridge, now crumbling, that once crossed the Ouysse, and there is a more extensive kitchen garden alongside the river so that the chef is able to offer just-picked produce in his dishes.

OPPOSITE A view on the way to the Pont de l'Ouysse hôtel-restaurant. The wild landscape, rushing river and isolation were somehow living evidence that a romantic dream of rural France can still come true now and then.

Daniel Chambon and his wife, Marinette, have been in charge here since 1977. Mme Chambon's family has owned the property since 1886. She told me that the bridge over the river was built in 1900 when the property was a farm, and the family had decided to open a restaurant to feed the bridge workers. The bridge was destroyed in a major flood in 1966 and was later rebuilt 300 metres (330 yards) downstream.

Both of Daniel and Marinette's sons are chefs and they will become the fifth generation of the same family to run the place when their father has had enough. Le Pont de l'Ouysse has no doubt become more elegant and its cuisine perhaps more refined over the years, but I sensed that the welcome has always been warm and that there has always been a genuine desire to use the best products available in the region. We noted that the menu thanked several key suppliers, including '*Hemmy, qui élève amoureusement nos poulettes*' ('Hemmy, who raises our chickens with love') and '*les petits ramasseurs qui nous apportent quotidiennement les meilleurs champignons*' ('the small gatherers who bring us the best mushrooms every day'). The dishes offered covered a wide range of the products a visitor would hope to experience.

Four variously priced menus were available as well as a small à la carte menu. I had a stunning beef dish: fillet roasted (not grilled) alongside a *crépinette* of delicious oxtail meat, the dish scattered with tender and mild cooked shallots, bone marrow and parsley, and on the side a tiny and perfect potato gratin. Our angelic wine waiter suggested a red from Cahors, a 1995 Clos de Triguedina, which proved to be a chewy wine, dark in colour, fruity and quite tannic. It was perfect with the light-bodied but winey sauce accompanying my beef and the gutsy oxtail flavour. We both chose Roquefort as our cheese from the trolley, watching with interest as *fromage blanc* was served at the next table with two small bowls, one of finely chopped shallots, the other of *fines herbes*, and a pepper grinder – the only time we saw pepper or salt at the table here.

Dessert decisions then had to be made and we wondered whether we could manage one more mouthful. Fortunately, we pressed on. Julie had a trembling slice of rose-pink berry jelly in which were embedded wild strawberries and garden strawberries, accompanied by an ice-cream made from Monbazillac. For me, dessert was raspberries on a *sablé* biscuit with a miraculous, silky-textured sorbet that was described as '*caillé de vache*'. (On reflection some hours later I decided that this must mean 'junket'.) And just as we were gasping, we were each served a thimble-ful of a baked Calvados custard. Our very reasonable bill was 320F ($A90) each, plus drinks.

We drove home silently, digesting all this food both physically and mentally. I reflected on the pleasure of seeing the French experience at its best: nothing hurried but nothing lagging, smiles all round, proper concern for how the dish was received, but no obsequiousness. Our sommelière had been exceptional, moving swiftly and gracefully among the 60 or so guests without any sign of pressure or

OPPOSITE Le Pont de l'Ouysse is part of the Châteaux et Hôtels de France group. It has one Michelin star and would be a perfect place to stay for travellers wishing to visit Rocamadour on one day and maybe the marvellous Romanesque abbey of Sainte-Marie at Souillac the next. The restaurant's kitchen garden is next to the river (bottom left). In fine weather, the preferred place to eat is outside on the terrace (bottom right). **OVERLEAF** The hôtel-restaurant is built right alongside the River Ouysse, and you can see the remains of the bridge that was destroyed in a flood in 1966.

anxiety and smiling warmly, and her recommendations had been outstanding. We ate too much, of course, but how else do food writers do research? It was a most delightful experience – so much so that we cancelled a reservation we had made elsewhere for Bastille night and resolved to return there. The sky was light until 10 o'clock at night and it was a joy to drive through the valley again with the afternoon sun lighting the cliffs; later, over dinner, the light turned pink and tinted the clouds – so very beautiful. Wild ducks from the river came to pay a visit and walked unconcerned on the driveway in front of the restaurant. 'They even lay their eggs in the garden,' said the waiter.

We had half-expected the restaurant to be decorated and the mood one of fête. Not so. There were no flags or special dishes and no special menu. Bastille Day seemed remarkably low key. Earlier in the day we had seen a few flags over the doors of a few public buildings, and there was to be a *bal* in our local square later that night (which we would have a look at on our way home), but otherwise nothing at all.

The sommelière suggested another local wine this evening: a 1997 Moulin des Dames Bergerac Sec. It was big and round, deep gold in colour and perfect with our selection for dinner. We had decided to choose à la carte and to start with shellfish, followed by poached, then roasted, *poulette de la ferme demi-deuil* ('farm chicken in half-mourning'), a classic dish where a fine chicken is stuffed with black truffles. The chicken was certainly in heavy mourning, not half-mourning, with many black bands. Truffle slices were stuffed beneath the skin of the drumstick, thigh and breast and, just for good measure, appeared on top of the dish as well. There was a small quantity of stuffing, made with the blond liver of the bird, a few spoonfuls of poaching juices simmered with a touch of cream, and a tumble of tiny orange *girolle* mushrooms. I bent my head to inhale the aroma and it almost made my head swim – I had never before experienced a positive *cloud* of truffle scent. Amazing! It was months after the last black truffles would have been harvested, but this dish proved that it is indeed possible to successfully freeze truffles.

My dessert was marvellous. I ordered the *fine tarte aux pommes* (thin apple tart), a classic in many French restaurants. This one was exceptional. The puff pastry was incredibly thin and baked really hard so that it had the crunch of a biscuit and the colour was dark tan. The apples were intensely flavoured and the pastry shattered as I cut it. On top was a small portion of cinnamon ice-cream, a slick of caramel was evident on the plate, and there was a scattering of toasted almonds. The recipe is on page 360.

On our last summer's day in the country, with the packing almost complete, Julie and I looked at each other and said, 'We could go for a quick lunch . . .' This time we chose the 160F (A$45) menu. It was as satisfying as the other experiences and, by happy chance, the thin apple tart was the dessert of the day. We enjoyed another local wine, a 1997 Château Puy-Servain (Marjolaine, Montravel) that was a

blend of sauvignon, muscadelle and sémillon. Julie had a terrine of duck livers (not *foie gras*) interleaved with thin slices of fig and then pressed; I had a fillet of river trout with crispy skin and a wafer-thin slice of bacon lard, also very crispy. We both then had a poached veal shank, sliced from the bone, with a lovely fresh veal *jus* and served with long spirals of macaroni – a most successful dish (see pages 356–7).

And then came the autumn visit. I wanted to return to Le Pont de l'Ouysse for Sunday lunch and had no difficulty persuading the others to join me. Julie and I had been so enthusiastic about our summer experiences that anticipation was high. The autumnal weather meant that we ate indoors, not underneath the linden trees as we had done in the summer. But we did linger outside and lean on the stone wall and listen to the sound of rushing water, and walk down the steep steps to inspect the restaurant's kitchen garden alongside the river. There must be other restaurants that are as beautifully situated, but I don't know where they are.

Autumn menu selections included a frothy chestnut soup sprinkled with powdered wild mushrooms, *foie gras* in various forms, hare, *écrevisses*, quinces, venison, the famous lamb of Quercy, partridge, pigeon, chicken and goose. Decisions were as difficult as they had been in summer! Again I ordered the massive veal shank, this time served with fresh young vegetables, to be shared with Simon and Julie. Maggie raved about her warm custard of hare and duck liver, followed by a whole veal kidney roasted in its own fat and a poached fig with almond-milk ice-cream.

As we had travelled from Lavalade in the Dordogne to Le Pont de l'Ouysse in the Lot, we felt we should change our wine experiences also. The white wine was Domaine Cauhape 1999, a Jurançon Sec that the wine waiter (alas, not our sommelière from summer) told us was made with large grapes of the manseng variety. The red was marvellous: Prince Probus, a 1993 Vin de Cahors from Château de Triguedina that was 100 per cent malbec. It was a big, powerful wine with a mushroomy, mossy nose. Later I did some research and discovered that manseng comes as both gros manseng and petit manseng and is a Basque variety. It gives the tangy, rich character to the wines of Jurançon, which are well known in the region of the French Pyrénées and in nearby Gascony.

So that was it. Four marvellous experiences of wine and food, true to the best French tradition but with a light hand and entirely contemporary in feeling. Perfect service, enchanting atmosphere, charming hosts.

OPPOSITE I chose the poached veal shank at Le Pont de l'Ouysse on two separate occasions. The first time it was served with long, tubular pieces of pasta that had been tossed in the well-reduced cooking liquid; the second time, with shaped vegetables, as shown here, and carved into thick slices, showing its exceptional texture and the slightly sticky juices.

Restaurants

LA RAPIÈRE

A few days into our summer holiday Julie and I made our first visit to the market in Sarlat. After three hours inhaling the scents and staring at pieces of duck and goose in various shapes and sizes, we were ravenous. The terrace of La Rapière looked inviting and in we went. It was pretty predictable that we would order the set menu because it started with *foie gras*, was followed by *confit* and finished with a walnut cake.

The price was quite reasonable and I should have known better – the *foie gras* was canned and mediocre. However, the *confit* was the genuine article, with meltingly soft (but very salty) flesh and crisp skin. It came with a mound of glistening and savoury *pommes sarladaises*, soft with crispy bits. The walnut cake was pleasant, served with crème anglaise and chocolate sauce. We loved our meal, but were enormously thirsty for the rest of the day. Later we both confessed to not wanting to eat again for hours. My advice is not to eat *confit* for lunch unless you are able to follow it with an hour's walk.

LE PRÉSIDIAL

In summer the long evenings were languorous and seductive. Julie and I wanted to linger under swinging lanterns suspended from trees, watch the French at table and, of course, taste wonderful things. We first noticed the green lawns and shaded terrace of Le Présidial restaurant as we strolled through Sarlat on market day. Situated in a restored grand building dating from the 17th century, it had only recently become a restaurant.

At dinner, we ordered a *vin de pêche* as an apéritif. Its colour was yellow-gold rather than the bronze of others we had sipped, but it was just as refreshing. I had superb goose *foie gras* that was of the palest pink and silky in texture (and, here, luxuriously priced). Julie ordered a sautéed escalope of *foie gras de canard* with *verjus* and received a huge portion – dangerously large, we agreed. During my *stage* (training course) in the kitchens of Restaurant Troisgros at Roanne (see page 258) in the heyday of *nouvelle cuisine*, a dish of quickly sautéed escalope of *foie gras* was the height of culinary fashion, but the carefully measured portion served at Troisgros was about one-third of what Julie received that night.

L'AUBERGE DU SOMBRAL

Another happy summer experience was lunch at the Auberge du Sombral in Saint-Cirq Lapopie. Once again we were attracted by tables set outside, this time under a tiny terrace shaded by vines and edged by window boxes filled with scarlet geraniums. We each ordered the *salade paysanne*, which proved to be a

OPPOSITE La Rapière restaurant in Sarlat is a popular choice on market day. Many local specialities are featured on its menu and the service is swift and friendly.

generous plateful of soft, tender salad leaves dressed with thin, moist slices of *jambon de Bayonne*, tomatoes, freshly crumbled Roquefort and a few walnuts – so good, so beautifully seasoned. It was served with a basket of fantastic chewy bread.

LE CENTENAIRE

This restaurant is near Lavalade in Les Eyzies de Tayac, a town that is world-famous as the centre of prehistory in Europe, and has two Michelin stars. We had an introduction to the restaurant's English sommelier, Tim Harrison, and were able to tap into his extensive knowledge of local wines. He did better than advise us: he purchased on our behalf a wide selection so that we came away from our holiday a great deal better informed regarding the local wine styles than would otherwise have been the case.

We also had a memorable dinner at the restaurant. The menu was bursting with local flavour and references: wild duck, *foie gras*, suckling pig, rabbit, goose steak, partridge, *écrevisses*, chestnuts, apples and walnuts. We were all silent for a long time as we tried to choose from the wonderful dishes. Tim suggested that, as we had been drinking Pécharmant and Bergerac wines almost exclusively up to that evening, we move a little further afield. Our apéritif was a glass of Montravel 1997, a lively 50/50 sémillon/sauvignon blanc that had been specially blended for chef Mazère. The next wine was a surprising white grenache from the Roussillon, followed by a Côtes du Roussillon Rouge 1998 (Domaine Gardies, La Forre) made from mourvèdre grapes, and then a cabernet/syrah blend, 1995 Domaine de la Grange des Pères (Vin de Pays de l'Hérault). Colin detected a Hunter Valley echo in this one, but not everyone around the table concurred. It was interesting to note the different style and lighter weight of this wine compared with well-known Australian cabernet/shiraz blends.

Unable to resist *foie gras* (and anyway, the holiday was drawing to a close and opportunities would soon disappear!), I started dinner with a salad of tiny green beans topped with curls of duck *foie gras* (see page 318), and continued with a rabbit main course that was very special (pages 182–3). It combined a trimmed rack with its minuscule bones Frenched and trimmed, the loin and the foreleg and the kidney, a little custard made with rabbit *jus*, and *cèpes* – a successful blend of delicate and robust flavours.

CHÂTEAU DE MONBAZILLAC

For anyone interested in wine, particularly the glorious golden wines of Monbazillac, a visit to the 16th-century Château de Monbazillac is a must. It has come unscathed through centuries of turbulent history and is today listed as a Monument Historique. You can visit the original kitchens to see the vast fireplace, the bread oven, stone sink and collection of old kitchen utensils. And you can also have a fine lunch. The restaurant has been converted from a 12th-century wine store and has a magnificent view over the vineyards.

The day we visited in autumn we were treated to a tasting of some of the finest wines, with, of course, *foie gras*. The wine is variously described as having *une robe de Louis d'or* ('a cloak of gold') and *le nez de Cyrano*, referring to the impressive nose of both the wine and one of Bergerac's heroes. The goose liver was accompanied by a well-reduced purée of apple with a hint of cinnamon. Roasted pigeon came next, then a portion of Bleu des Causses cheese from the Lot and, finally, strawberries. Every course was matched with a different vintage of Monbazillac. We drank Château Monbazillac 1994 Domaine de Pecoula, Monbazillac 1996, and a 1995 Grande Maison Cuvée du Château Monbazillac. I was unconvinced by the pigeon with the sweet wine, but otherwise thought the food and wine partnered very well.

LE BISTRO D'EN FACE

On the last night of the autumn house party, having scraped the cupboard bare, we dined at Le Bistro d'en Face in Trémolat, opposite its well-known parent establishment, Le Vieux Logis. There was a tinge of sadness to the evening, with all of us knowing that this particular adventure had run its course. I ordered the country terrine and was taken back nearly 40 years to one of my very important seminal eating experiences in France. The entire terrine was brought to the table with a knife stuck in it and left there, just as used to happen in my student days when I lived in Tours in the Loire Valley and worked as an *assistante de langue* at the local École Normale des Filles. I can remember how amazed I was all those years ago – and how delighted. Not only could I be as hearty or delicate as I wished, but there was added pleasure in admiring the shiny brown crust of the terrine and appreciating the texture as I cut into it, and noticing the patina on the simple brown pot. No doubt in 2000 the effect had been carefully calculated, but it is such a winning way of offering a dish. Rarely would a French person do more than cut a modest slice, and nor did I on this occasion.

La Poule avec sa mique

HEN WITH ITS SAVOURY DUMPLING

This dish is central to an appreciation of the cookery of Périgord and its neigh-bouring region, Quercy. A selection of meats, or one alone, is simmered in broth with plenty of vegetables, and a large dumpling (*la mique*) is added to the pot about an hour before all is ready. The local custom was – and still is at La Ferme Auberge Fort de la Rhonie (see page 335) – to drink some of the broth first, either with a slice of the dumpling or with *pain de campagne*, then to serve the meat, vegetables and dumpling, all moistened with more broth. The dish was traditionally eaten with mustard, cornichons and coarse grey salt, and any leftover *mique* was fried the next day and eaten as a bread. Leftover meats were served cold, again with cornichons, coarse salt and mustard and a variety of cold sauces.

Because the dish is so important, there are variations throughout Périgord and Quercy. Sometimes the meat preferred is a large piece of salt pork, sometimes it is a large hen, sometimes a shin of veal. The vegetables will be those grown on the farm. Many years ago I tasted a scaled-down version of this classic at Le Centenaire restaurant at Les Eyzies. Chef Roland Mazère had devised a dish in which the meat was a cabbage-wrapped *crépinette* of oxtail with a rich sauce, the vegetables were all neatly trimmed and each dumpling had been individually shaped and poached. I thought it was a most successful way of encouraging sophis-ticated travellers to try an important but very rustic dish that they would almost certainly never taste otherwise.

As for *la mique*, there are many versions. Recipes might include yeast or baking powder, or neither. The recipe given to me at the Coustaty farm included pork fat and day-old bread but no raising agent. Leftover bread is always a valuable resource, so it is not surprising that it appears as an ingredient in some dumplings. *La mique* can also be made with fine cornmeal, but more often contains wheat flour, or half cornmeal and half wheat flour. The recipe I give on the following pages is for a dumpling with yeast added.

La mique relies heavily on a savoury broth to make it interesting. I like the suggestion in Anne Penton's lovely book, *Customs and Cookery in the Périgord and Quercy*, of adding a bit of something to the basic dough. Penton mentions *rillettes*, which would be delicious, as would be, I think, some *grillons* (see page 315), crumbled *confit* or minced bacon. On one occasion when I made the dish back in my own kitchen, I stepped right outside the traditions of the south-west and suc-cessfully added freshly grated horseradish to the dumpling dough. Penton also gives an alternative name for the dumpling in Quercy: *la farcidure*, which hints at this idea of adding something (*farce* is the French word for 'stuffing').

OPPOSITE I was privileged to taste this local speciality at La Ferme Auberge Fort de la Rhonie – a poached hen in broth with a savoury dumpling and assorted vegetables, seen here still in the cooking pot. The green vegetable in the centre is silver beet (Swiss chard), or *blettes* as it is called in France.

The chicken for my version is boned, for which I give the instructions opposite – it sounds much more complicated than it is. Ask your butcher to bone the bird if you really feel you cannot do it. You can leave the chicken unboned and simply stuff the cavity, but if you do this it will take 1 hour longer to cook because of the bones – see the notes at the end of the recipe on page 354. Whether you or the butcher does the boning, or even if you leave the chicken unboned, you will still need a 50 cm (20 in) square piece of doubled muslin, poultry pins and some string.

Parts of the dish can be prepared the day before you plan to serve it: you can make the stuffing, bone the chicken and make the broth in advance.

RIGHT Each diner is served a portion of *la mique* and it is traditionally cut by the man of the household. It is intended to be very substantial, like the dumplings in other similar dishes. I imagine that in days gone by there would have been less chicken served than there is today.

THE RECIPE

To make the stuffing, soak the bread in the milk until all the liquid has been absorbed. Transfer to a food processor with all the remaining stuffing ingredients except the salt and pepper. Process until well mixed, then taste for seasoning – it may not need salt (especially if you have used pork sausage mince rather than plain minced pork). Refrigerate until needed.

To bone the chicken, put it breast-side down on your workbench and, using a sharp knife, slit the skin from the neck cavity to the tailbone. Working with the knife always pointed towards the bone, separate the flesh from the carcass, freeing the thigh ball joint and the wing ball joint and pulling out the wishbone. When you have freed all the flesh on one side of the bird and have exposed half the breast-bone, do the same on the other side. Release the flesh by cutting carefully down the breastbone. Lift out the carcass. Carefully remove the thigh bones by working the knife around and down the bone, pulling the flesh and skin down as you work to expose the next bit of bone. You should now have an opened-out chicken with the wing bones and drumsticks the only remaining bones.

Chop the carcass into 4–6 pieces and put into a stockpot with the thigh bones, pork rind, whole carrots, leeks, celery sticks, bouquet garni, chicken stock and water. Bring slowly to a boil, then skim the surface. Adjust the heat to a simmer and cook for 3 hours. Strain the broth, discarding the solids, and set aside until needed.

On the day you plan to serve the dish, start making *la mique* 4 hours before dinner. Remove the skin from the *confit*, then roughly chop the *confit*. If you like, crisp the skin in a moderate oven (180°C/375°F) to add to the dough later. Mix the salt and yeast into the flour and transfer to an electric mixer with a dough hook. In a bowl, lightly mix the eggs, butter and water. With the motor running, add the egg mixture and the *confit* (and the crisped skin, if desired) and mix until the dough becomes a smooth ball. Transfer to a lightly floured basin and sprinkle with a little extra flour. Cover and leave in a warm place for 3 hours or until *la mique* has doubled in size.

Meanwhile, spread a 50 cm/20 in square doubled sheet of muslin on your workbench. Put the boned chicken on top, skin-side down and opened out. Season the flesh with salt and pepper. Form the stuffing into a rough sausage shape, then pinch some off and fill each drumstick cavity. Put the rest of the stuffing down the centre of the chicken and pin the bird securely with poultry pins, paying special attention to the cavity and neck openings. Bring up the muslin to form a firm, compact bolster shape and tie, not too tightly, with string. Refrigerate until needed.

One and a half hours before dinner, bring the reserved broth to a simmer. Taste and adjust the seasoning and slip in the muslin-wrapped chicken, *la mique* and the turnips, carrot chunks, onions, celeriac, potatoes and silver beet. Cover the pot and simmer very gently for 1 hour. Do not lift the lid.

Serves 8–10

1 × 2 kg/4$\frac{1}{2}$ lb roasting chicken
1 × 100 g/3$\frac{1}{2}$ oz piece pork rind, fresh or preserved *or* 1 split pig's trotter/foot
2 whole carrots
2 leeks
2 sticks celery
1 bouquet garni (thyme, bay leaf, parsley stalks)
2 litres/3$\frac{1}{2}$ pints chicken stock
2 litres/3$\frac{1}{2}$ pints cold water
sea salt
freshly ground black pepper
16 small turnips, peeled
16 carrot chunks, peeled
16 small onions, peeled
8 celeriac chunks, peeled
8 waxy potatoes
10 sticks silver beet/Swiss chard

Stuffing

100 g/3$\frac{1}{2}$ oz day-old bread, cubed
$\frac{1}{3}$ cup milk
50 g/1$\frac{3}{4}$ oz ham, diced
200 g/7 oz minced pork or pork sausage mince
$\frac{1}{2}$ onion, finely chopped
2 cloves garlic, chopped
1 egg
1 tablespoon brandy
2 tablespoons freshly chopped young parsley (preferably flat-leaf)
1 teaspoon freshly chopped tarragon
sea salt
freshly ground black pepper

La mique

60 g/2 oz duck confit or rillettes or finely chopped bacon
$\frac{1}{2}$ teaspoon salt
1 teaspoon instant dry yeast
250 g/9 oz plain/all-purpose flour or 125 g/4$\frac{1}{2}$ oz fine cornmeal and 125 g/4$\frac{1}{2}$ oz plain/all-purpose flour
2 eggs
50 g/1$\frac{3}{4}$ oz butter, melted and cooled
3 tablespoons warm water

To serve, have ready a hot serving dish and, for each guest, a wide soup plate. Retrieve the chicken bundle and put it on the serving dish. Unwrap it and remove the pins. Lift out the cooked vegetables with a slotted spoon and transfer to the serving dish. Cut *la mique* into fat slices and put 1 slice in each soup plate. Ladle over a little of the broth. Slice the chicken and serve each guest an equal amount of meat and stuffing. Offer a jug of the poaching juices for additional moistening.

Using a whole chicken

If you are using a whole chicken, stuff the cavity with the stuffing, but not too tightly as it will swell. Pin the opening and wrap the chicken in muslin and tie as instructed above. Bring the broth to a simmer 2 hours before dinner. Taste and adjust the seasoning, then slip in the muslin-wrapped chicken and simmer very gently for 1 hour. Add the vegetables and *la mique*, then cover the pot and cook for a further hour. Do not lift the lid.

Smaller dumplings

It is not traditional, but if you like you can break up the risen ball of *mique* dough and form individual balls somewhat smaller in size than a tennis ball. Allow them 15 minutes to recover after reshaping and then add them to the broth and cover and simmer as above, although they will be ready in 20 minutes rather than 1 hour. If you don't feel like making *la mique* – although I would encourage you to give it a go – serve the dish by adding a slice of really good country-style bread to each bowl instead.

Leftovers

We had quite a bit of chicken left over when I cooked this dish at Lavalade and it was delicious served cold with *aillade toulousaine* (see page 205) and thick slices of *la mique* fried in a little oil. In fact, I could say that this 're-fried' *mique* was more enjoyable to my palate than when it was served with the hot dish. You could also serve any leftover chicken with a vinaigrette made from diced ripe tomatoes, small capers and plenty of fresh herbs mixed with olive oil and a good red-wine vinegar.

OPPOSITE This was my first helping of *la poule avec sa mique*. The golden hue of the hen's skin indicates that it was fed on maize. The dish was so mouth-wateringly good that I went back for more!

Milk-fed Veal Shank Poached in a Clear Stock

JARRET DE VEAU

Serves 4

1 veal shank on the bone weighing
at least 1.5 kg/3 lb 4 oz *or*
4 × 500 g/1 lb 2 oz veal shanks
6 black peppercorns
1 clove
sea salt
500 ml/17½ fl oz well-flavoured
veal stock

Mirepoix
1 leek, quartered
2 tablespoons unsalted butter
1 medium carrot, diced
1 large onion, diced
1 sprig of thyme
1 bay leaf
100 ml/3½ fl oz white wine

Vegetable garnish
2 tablespoons unsalted butter
8 small young carrots, peeled
8 small young turnips, peeled
8 small new potatoes, peeled
500 ml/17½ fl oz well-flavoured
veal stock
8 chunks young zucchini

This is one of the superb dishes we enjoyed at Le Pont de l'Ouysse restaurant. I have included the recipe here as given to me by chef Daniel Chambon, intended for a shank weighing at least 1 kg (2 lb) on the bone, but I have also included times and quantities for smaller shanks. As discussed earlier (see page 281), the animals bred for the table in France tend to dress out much larger than ours. There is one notable exception: White Rocks veal bred in Western Australia and marketed by Perth butcher Vince Garreffa. A shank from one of Vince's animals would weigh in the order of 2 kg (4½ lb) and would serve 6 people – think of a piece of meat roughly the size of a leg of lamb. It is far more usual, however, to be sold veal shanks that weigh around 500 g (1 lb 2 oz); one of these is a generous but not over-whelming portion for 1 person.

Most of the dish can be prepared at least 30 minutes–1 hour before dinner: you can make it up to the point where you have taken the meat out of the oven bag and reduced the cooking juices. You will then have just 15 minutes' finishing to do.

The very low oven temperature (70°C/160°F) given in the first line of the method is as recommended by chef Chambon. My home oven does not register below 90°C (200°F), but when I cooked 4 smaller shanks at this higher temperature they were perfect after 4½ hours.

Preheat the oven to 70°C/160°F. To make the *mirepoix*, wash the leek well and slice finely. Heat the butter in a heavy-based frying pan and add the leek, carrot, onion, thyme and bay leaf. Sauté until the vegetables have softened, then pour on the wine and stir to deglaze the pan.

Put the veal and the moist *mirepoix* in a large oven bag. Add the pepper-corns, the clove and a little salt, then pour in the veal stock and seal the bag carefully. (If you are using 4 smaller shanks, divide the meat, *mirepoix*, seasonings and stock between 2 oven bags.) Put the bag (or bags) in a cast-iron casserole with a tight-fitting lid and fill the casserole with boiling water. Put on the lid, transfer to the oven and leave undisturbed for 5–6 hours. It is relatively easy to inspect the meat through the oven bag and to prod it with your finger and assess if it needs any more cooking. Do not open the oven bag as it is easy to lose the juices and very difficult to retie.

Carefully remove the bag from the oven and settle it in a wide bowl. Snip open the bag and lift the shanks into an ovenproof pan or gratin dish. Tip the liquid through a strainer into a saucepan and reduce it over high heat by two-thirds until quite syrupy. Reserve until needed.

When you are ready to finish the dish, preheat the oven to 225°C/425°F. To make the vegetable garnish, heat the butter in a wide pan in which the vegetables will fit neatly. When the butter has just started to foam, add the carrots, turnips and potatoes and turn in the hot butter to colour for a few minutes. Pour in enough of the stock to barely cover the vegetables and cook for 10 minutes. Add the zucchini and cook for another 5 minutes. Watch the pan to ensure that the cooking is gentle and that the reducing stock is in no danger of evaporating.

Brush the veal with the reserved reduced cooking juices and put it in the oven for 15 minutes or so until the skin takes on a good caramel colour. Remove from the oven and, if you are using a single large shank, slice the meat lengthwise from the bone. Serve with the vegetable garnish and a good quantity of the reduced juices.

Variations

The vegetables used in the garnish can be varied according to what you have available or what is in season. If you wish, omit the potatoes from the garnish and serve the dish with macaroni or other pasta (see the recipe below), as it was served to me on the first occasion I ate it.

When I tested this dish at home I steamed the garnish – using carrots, zucchini and small turnips – and cooked a good handful of peas in boiling water as well. I used pappardelle pasta, which cooked as the shanks glazed in the oven, and then tossed the vegetables and the peas with the pasta and the rest of the veal juices.

Macaroni in Veal Juice

This delicious pasta accompanied the veal shank I had for lunch at Le Pont de l'Ouysse. Note that the French are not at all convinced by 'al dente' pasta and prefer their pasta (*les pâtes*) well cooked.

Peel and core the tomatoes, leaving them whole. Cook them with the pasta in plenty of lightly salted boiling water. When the pasta is nearly cooked, pull the pan to the side of the stove and let the pasta swell and finish cooking. Lift out the tomatoes with a slotted spoon and press them through a strainer set over a bowl. Drain the pasta thoroughly and return to the rinsed-out pan, then add the tomato purée and just enough veal stock to moisten the pasta thoroughly. It should be a bit sloppy. Return to the heat and bring to simmering point, shaking the pan to prevent sticking. Grind over some pepper, scatter with parsley and serve at once.

Serves 4

3 ripe tomatoes
300 g/10½ oz macaroni *or* other
   long tube pasta
salt
1 cup well-reduced veal stock
freshly ground black pepper
freshly chopped young parsley
   (preferably flat-leaf)

Pumpkin Cake with Caramel Orange Slices

I first tasted this lovely dessert at the Auberge du Sombral in the village of Saint-Cirq Lapopie. The chef, M. Gilles Hardeveld, very kindly gave me the recipe. He served it with a generous heap of candied orange zest, but I like to serve it with slices of navel orange steeped in a caramel and orange juice syrup.

To make the caramel orange slices, put the sugar and water into a small saucepan and stir over medium heat until the sugar has dissolved. Increase the heat and boil steadily until the mixture turns a rich caramel colour. Carefully pour most of the caramel into a cake tin 22 cm/8½ in round × 4 cm/1½ in deep and tilt to coat the sides as much as possible, then set the tin aside until needed. Even more carefully, add the orange juice to the saucepan (it will bubble and spit) and return it to a low heat to dissolve the rest of the caramel. Stir until smooth. Put the orange slices in a shallow dish and pour over the caramel orange syrup. Put in the refrigerator to macerate until you are ready to serve the cake.

Steam the pumpkin until just tender and drain in a colander for 10 minutes. Meanwhile, preheat the oven to 150°C/300°F. Melt the butter in a wide frying pan, then add the pumpkin and turn to absorb the butter and to evaporate any remaining liquid. Do not let the butter burn. Remove the pan from the heat and allow to cool for 5 minutes. Purée the pumpkin in a food processor. Using an electric mixer, beat the castor sugar, whole egg and egg yolks together until thick and pale, then add the lemon zest and flour. Add the pumpkin and beat to combine well. Pour the batter into the caramel-lined cake tin and cook for 45 minutes. Remove from the oven and allow to cool completely (even overnight) before unmoulding. Serve with the chilled caramel oranges.

Serves 8

1.5 kg/3 lb 4 oz pumpkin, peeled, seeded and thinly sliced to yield 1.2 kg/2½ lb
50 g/1¾ oz unsalted butter
150 g/5 oz castor/superfine sugar
1 large egg
3 large egg yolks
grated zest/rind of 1 large lemon
75 g/2½ oz plain/all-purpose flour

Caramel orange slices
½ cup white/granulated sugar
3 tablespoons water
juice of 2 oranges (preferably navels)
4 oranges (preferably navels), peeled and sliced thickly

Thin Apple and Cinnamon Tart

FINE TARTE AUX POMMES

Serves 1

½ teaspoon cinnamon
1 teaspoon castor/superfine sugar
1½ eating apples, peeled and cored
1 × 15 cm/6 in very thin round of
   puff pastry
20 g/¾ oz unsalted butter, softened
icing/confectioner's sugar (optional)
toasted flaked almonds (optional)

I ate this tart on three separate occasions at Le Pont de l'Ouysse, served with cinnamon ice-cream. It can be assembled in advance, part-baked and frozen, and is a spectacular but very simple dessert, ready in minutes. I have not given a recipe for puff pastry here as it is easy enough to find one, but I suspect many people will prefer to buy it. You should be able to find puff pastry made with 100 per cent butter in your supermarket deep-freeze, the sheets pre-rolled ready for cutting and shaping.

Put a baking tray/sheet in the oven and preheat the oven to 220°C/425°F. Mix the cinnamon and sugar together. Halve the whole apple and cut the 3 apple halves into very fine slices. Arrange the slices, overlapping, around the edge of the pastry round. Dot with the butter and sprinkle generously with the cinnamon–sugar mixture. Put the dressed tart directly onto the hot baking tray and bake for 15 minutes. Sprinkle with icing sugar and flaked almonds, if desired, and serve with a scoop of cinnamon (or vanilla) ice-cream (see page 363).

Making in advance
If you are intending to freeze the tart for another day, remove it from the oven after 10 minutes and lightly press down on the apple slices with a flexible spatula to flatten them. Cool completely, then wrap the tart in plastic film and transfer to the freezer. When you wish to serve it, sprinkle with a little more cinnamon mixed with castor sugar and bake for a further 5 minutes at 220°C/425°F. The pastry should be very thin and quite crisp and the apples may have just started to catch on the edges.

PÊCHE JAU

36,00 f LE PLAT

ET 8,90 f LE Kg

LO GARONNE   CAT

Cinnamon Ice-cream

Bring the milk and cream to simmering point in a heavy-based saucepan. Beat the egg yolks, sugar and cinnamon until thick, then whisk in the scalded milk and cream. Return to the rinsed-out pan and cook over a moderate heat, stirring constantly with a wooden spoon, until the mixture thickens and coats the back of a spoon. Strain into a bowl and allow to cool. Churn in an ice-cream machine according to the manufacturer's instructions.

Serves 6–8

250 ml/9 fl oz milk
250 ml/9 fl oz whipping cream
5 egg yolks
115 g/4 oz castor/superfine sugar
½ teaspoon cinnamon

Vin de pêche

PEACH WINE

This delightful apéritif quickly became a favourite of mine. It varied considerably from establishment to establishment, not only in flavour but also in colour. Having looked up a book of traditional recipes, I suspect that the colour variation depends on the wine used. My most recent homemade batch is a deep pink–gold, rather syrupy and very powerful. I enjoy it best of all in a tall glass with lots of ice.

I have translated this recipe from an old French food magazine, which said that the peach leaves should be picked towards the end of the season when they are starting to become a little yellow. I would add that they should be from a tree that has not been sprayed recently.

Mix all the ingredients in a glass or stainless steel container and leave in a cool place, covered, for 8 days. Strain through a fine strainer into a scrupulously clean bottle, cover or cork and leave for at least 1 week before serving. Serve chilled. The peach wine will keep for up to 2 years.

Makes 750 ml/26 fl oz

100 late-season peach leaves
1 bottle (750 ml/26 fl oz) rosé wine
1 wine glass (125 ml/4½ fl oz) eau-de-vie or vodka
300 g/10½ oz castor/superfine sugar

OPPOSITE Just looking at this photograph brings back the scent of the summer markets. Both white and yellow peaches and nectarines were available, almost all of them sold absolutely ripe. However, it is the leaves from the peach tree, not the fruit, that are used to make *vin de pêche*.

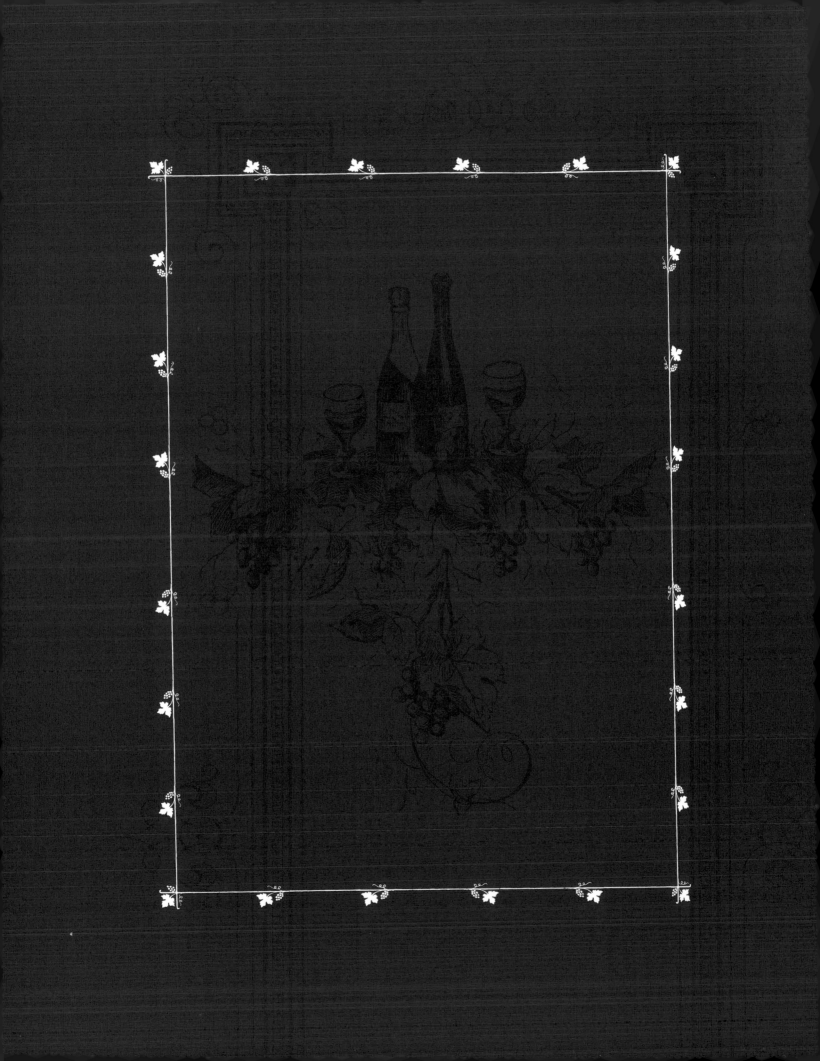

Drinking

One of the joys of travelling in rural France is seeking out the small local bars. Even the tiniest village will have a bar, and even the smallest bar will have at least one table set outside. Watching the world go by is a very popular activity. Inside, the locals lean on the counter and enjoy a chat as much as a drink. It seems to me that there is perhaps less drinking done in the bars these days and more watching of the inevitable small television, which is always switched on. The younger men are frequently to be seen playing table soccer or – as it is colloquially known in French – 'babyfoot', a game that involves much shunting of levers and pushing of handles and which I have always found to be incomprehensible.

Years ago there was a sign in French train carriages advising the population not to drink more than 1 litre (1¾ pints) of wine per person per day. The situation has definitely changed and today there would not be a need for such advice. It is quite common in bars nowadays to see people drinking flavoured non-alcoholic syrups with soda – brilliant green for peppermint, crimson for blackcurrant, and so on – or enjoying a coffee. Every bar these days has its coffee machine, although even the most committed Francophile would have to admit that the French haven't quite the facility with espressos that the Italians have.

French people have long enjoyed an apéritif in the late afternoon or before a meal and, although there are favourites that cross regional boundaries – such as the popular drinks flavoured with aniseed that originated in the south of France, the three leading brands being Pernod, Ricard and Pastis – the preferred tipple is often influenced by local produce. In the south-west, for example, you are regularly offered the lightly fortified *vin de pêche* (see page 363), or classics such as Kir (white wine with a dash of *cassis*) or Kir Royale (Champagne and *cassis*).

In autumn our group took to dropping into the bar at Sainte Alvère, about half a kilometre's stroll from our house at Lavalade, to be restored at the end of a day's walking or cooking. The locals largely ignored us, although we did think that they were a bit intrigued by our loud laughter. The French philosophy is to live and let live, so they looked us over and we smiled back in a friendly way, but it has to be said that there was no fraternisation. Julie developed a special liking for Suze, one of a group of liqueurs flavoured with mountain herbs such as gentian. It is deep gold in colour, syrupy with medium bitterness and, as with the aniseed-based drinks, served as a long drink with ice and/or water.

OPPOSITE Suze is one of the family of herby, syrupy drinks usually served over plenty of ice. It was first made commercially in 1889, with the brand being acquired by the giant Pernod Ricard company in 1965. Suze is packaged in an elegantly distinctive bottle.

Digestifs are taken after a meal and are supposed to aid the digestion. Here, local preferences definitely prevail. For example, you would not order a Cognac in the south-west. Instead, you would choose from an extensive range of Armagnacs, which the bar's proprietor would be pleased to describe, or you might choose a fruit-based *eau-de-vie*, especially La Vieille Prune (see page 151) or a liqueur made from walnuts (page 196).

It has always been customary for country people in France to drink local wine with their meals. They believe that wine is superior to water as it is nourishment in liquid form, containing all the goodness of the grape. The red wines of the south-west go particularly well with those meat and poultry dishes that are often rich with goose or duck fat and include the earthy flavours of cabbage, dried beans, garlic and onions.

I enjoy the experience of drinking local wines when I travel, and my experiences in the Dordogne, Lot and Lot-et-Garonne have confirmed that local wines are perfect partners for local food. They are eminently drinkable, cover many styles and are reasonably priced. The reds tend to be big, with strong tannins, the whites fruity and aromatic. The rosés are crisp, fresh and not too sweet, and the sweet wines are a glorious and perfect accompaniment to *foie gras*, blue cheese, fruit tarts or fresh berries. Local wine merchants offer free tastings, including their own bulk wines, which they will happily sell to you by the litre. Take an empty plastic water bottle along and they will fill it using something resembling an early petrol bowser. On the autumn holiday we enjoyed a rosé Colin found at the local butcher's shop for the princely sum of 14F (A$4) a litre.

Hopefully many of you will find your way to the south-west for a memorable holiday. However, once you arrive, staring at the wines in the local supermarket or wine shop on your first day can be very confusing and almost overwhelming. As with many other areas of France, local labels are not much help in understanding the wine. They rarely detail the grape varieties and are even less likely to give the percentage of one grape used to make the wine, and rarely does a back label exist to give any additional information. On an Australian label it is usual to read that, for example, 'this wine is made with 60% cabernet sauvignon, 20% merlot and 20% shiraz'. Although in France percentages are sometimes laid down by the AOC, the mix is not stated on the label. It seems to be assumed that local people will know.

The following notes on the wines we obtained and enjoyed are therefore provided to help visitors to the south-west to find good wines to drink. Back home in Australia my advice would be to take pleasure in the challenge of seeking out wines that will complement the savoury, hearty food of the region. As a starting point, you could try wines made from the same grape varieties as those listed here. However, wine and food matching is not an exact science, and ultimately the aim is to enjoy both the food and the wine. It is up to you!

Appellations of the Region

The wines of the south-west are considered as falling into two groups: the huge and prestigious Bordeaux region and the Haut-Pays. Haut-Pays wines include Cahors, Bergerac, Pécharmant, Monbazillac, Saussignac and others. These wines are little known outside of France – in fact, I do not know of any Australian wine merchant that imports the wines of the Haut-Pays. Maybe I can change their minds!

In the face of so many winemakers and such limited information on bottle labels, a useful guide is the AOC (Appellation d'Origine Contrôlée), which designates the specific area where the grapes are grown. The AOC also specifies the grape varieties to be used in blending the wine, although there is variation allowed in the percentage of each variety used (and, as already mentioned, this information does not appear on the bottle).

BERGERAC

This is the largest appellation in the region. The white wines (Bergerac Sec) are a blend of sémillon, sauvignon blanc and muscadelle, while the grape varieties used for the red wines (Bergerac Rouge) are cabernet sauvignon, cabernet franc, merlot and malbec. The reds range from high-tannin big wines with predominant cabernet elements to softer, more appealing blends with 90 per cent or even 100 per cent merlot. In general, the premium Bergerac reds contain 70–90 per cent merlot, but this varies from year to year depending on the quality of each grape variety at vintage.

Bergerac Rosé, a blend of the same varieties as Bergerac reds, is refreshing and not sweet – excellent for lunch. The one we liked best was Château Calabre (the second label of Château Puy-Servain; see page 373). It was 12 per cent alcohol by volume and was made from 30 per cent merlot, 60 per cent cabernet sauvignon and 10 per cent cabernet franc.

CÔTES DE BERGERAC

These wines are made from the best vines in the Bergerac AOC and are generally more full-bodied and longer lasting. The grape varieties are the same as for the standard Bergerac wines.

PÉCHARMANT

This is a small AOC, north-east of Bergerac, which produces elegant silky reds with soft tannins and cherry and berry flavours. The grape varieties blended are cabernet sauvignon, cabernet franc and merlot. They age well for up to 10 years.

OVERLEAF Sunshine reflected in some of the region's glorious sweet wines – moments before they were carefully stored in our cellar at Lavalade.

MONTRAVEL

The Montravel AOC produces only white wines. They are made from sémillon, sauvignon blanc and muscadelle, and are often more fruity and floral than the Bergerac Sec whites, with more sauvignon blanc than sémillon. Haut-Montravel is a delicious dessert wine made from 100 per cent sémillon.

MONBAZILLAC

This is the home of the signature sweet wine of the region, made from botrytis-affected sémillon grapes. The wine can vary from pale, young, lighter styles to more complex, deep amber stickies.

SAUSSIGNAC

Saussignac is a small AOC that produces outstanding sweet dessert whites.

Winery Visits

Don't miss a visit to Château de Monbazillac, not just to taste the exquisite sweet wines but to admire the view over the vineyards and beyond. The mists, fog and mild temperatures we experienced in autumn are ideal conditions for *Botrytis cinerea*, the magic ingredient that withers sauvignon, sémillon and muscadelle grapes to intense sweetness.

Apart from Château de Monbazillac, we visited two wineries in the Bergerac region. They were chosen by our guide for the day, Tim Harrison, sommelier at Le Centenaire restaurant (see page 348), as establishments that make excellent wine and are each owned by a passionate individual who was delighted to expound on his winemaking theories and practices before offering us a tasting.

CHÂTEAU PUY-SERVAIN

At this winery at Fougueyrolles, 24 km (15 miles) west of Bergerac, Daniel Hecquet explained that the name of his vineyard means 'at the top of a windy slope' and that the wind and fog give something special to the grapes. We looked over the vineyard and he pointed out small patches of chalky soil within one field, which he said would affect just that patch of vines. We could see that they were changing colour faster than the rest. His point was that a winemaker must always study the soil and read the messages in the vines.

At Puy-Servain the bunches are hand-selected and all grapes are sorted by hand to remove the stems before being crushed. We tasted the 1999 wines: Château Puy-Servain Marjolaine, Daniel's premium white; Puy-Servain Terrement red; and Puy-Servain Terrement cuvée Vieilles Vignes, at which Daniel rolled his eyes and

THE HAUT-PAYS WINE INDUSTRY
In considering the wines of the Haut-Pays it is helpful to note that in 1999 the region included 12 separate AOCs and that more than 12 000 hectares (29 600 acres) were under vines, of which 52 per cent were for red-wine grapes and 48 per cent were for white wines. There were more than 1240 growers, who between them produced 680 000 hectolitres (18 million US gallons).

OPPOSITE Some of our favourite wines from the region, including Bergerac and Pécharmant, which are both appellations of the area. Neither is as well known as the world-famous wines of close neighbour Bordeaux.

OPPOSITE Sampling the region's wines and apéritifs was one of the most enjoyable parts of the autumn house party. Colin Beer (top right) was interested in the comparisons between these wines and those of his home in the Barossa Valley. The local bar at Sainte Alvère (top left and bottom right) was a convivial place to which we often retired for an apéritif or two.

breathed to no-one in particular that it was '*superbe*'. The Vieilles Vignes consisted of 60 per cent merlot, 20 per cent cabernet franc and 20 per cent cabernet sauvignon and had an aroma of chocolate and coffee. During our two weeks at Lavalade we enjoyed the 1998 versions of these same wines, and Julie and I enjoyed the 1997 vintage of the Marjolaine during our summer holiday.

CHÂTEAU TOUR DES GENDRES

At Château Tour des Gendres at Ribagnac, about 10 km (6 miles) south of Bergerac, winemaker Luc de Conti explained his harvesting methods. For his premium wines he has 10 people 'negative picking' before the mechanical harvesters move into the vineyard. In other words, any suspect grapes or bunches are removed before the actual harvest. The grapes are then hand-sorted once again to remove all traces of stem or stalk before being crushed. Such care had Colin the Barossa vigneron shaking his head in wonderment.

Luc emphasised his belief that the winemaker must taste the grapes before deciding to pick, and not rely on chemical analyses of sugar content. He was adamant that the grapes could have achieved 13° Baumé (23° Brix) – a relatively high sugar level – but still be immature and not yet ready to pick.

More than half of Luc's vineyard is cultivated organically. He sprays what he called *tisanes* (a word usually meaning 'herbal infusions' or 'herbal teas') on the leaves to discourage insects, but admitted that French vignerons are on their guard against the beginnings of a terrible infection imported from the USA, Pierce's disease, named after the plant pathologist who unsuccessfully attempted to control it. Originally thought to be a virus, it has now been identified as the bacteria *Xylella fastidiosa* and is dreaded by vignerons for the devastation it causes. After hearing this, we all resolved to dip our shoes in bleach before returning to Australian soil.

We tasted the premium white, Moulin des Dames, the 1999 being a blend of muscadelle, sémillon and sauvignon blanc. Once again Julie and I felt at an advantage as we had already had recommended to us and very much enjoyed the 1997 Moulin des Dames Bergerac Sec during our summer stay. The premium red, the 1999 Gloire de Mon Père, was a big wine blended from 60 per cent cabernet, 30 per cent merlot and 20 per cent malbec. There were huge tannins in this wine, which I found a bit unapproachable.

A surprise was my first tasting of grape juice that had been in the barrel for just a few days. The malbec juice smelled of intense blackcurrants and tasted wonderful, almost creamy, and of blackcurrants rather than grapes, while the muscadelle juice had an equally lovely but more grapey flavour. The hit of sugar was necessary, as by then we were all starving and needed to leave for Lavalade, where Maggie was cooking guinea fowl for dinner.

Wines Tasted at Lavalade

For these tasting notes, Duffy Clemens was appointed scribe. It was a thankless task, as he found it quite difficult to extract sensible comments from the lively and unruly group around the table. What with eels in water jugs, loud music ranging from opera to Miles Davis to the Ink Spots, much laughter and even a scream or two, he regularly had to call for order. The following notes represent the best that could be extracted at the time. After all, as someone said to someone else, 'At the end of the day, it's only wine.' And we loved it! What follows is a list of the wines we drank, with 'family favourites' marked with an asterisk.

VINS ROUGES

L'Adagio des Eyssards (Bergerac), 1998 *

Château de la Colline, Carminé (Bergerac), 1998 (merlot) *

Château de la Jaubertie, Réserve Mirabelle (Bergerac), 1998 *

Château Puy-Servain Terrement (Bergerac), 1998

Château Puy-Servain Terrement, Vieilles Vignes (Bergerac), 1998 *

Château Tour des Gendres, La Gloire de Mon Père (Côtes de Bergerac), 1998

Clos des Verdots, Grand Vin Les Verdots (Côtes de Bergerac), 1998 (selon David Fourtout) *

Domaine de l'Ancienne Cure, L'extase (Bergerac), 1998 *

Domaine des Costes (Pécharmant), 1998 *

Domaine de Puy de Grave (Pécharmant), 1997

Famille de Conti, Moulin des Dames (Bergerac), 1998

K de Krevel, Vieilles Vignes (Côtes de Bergerac), 1997

Relais de Kreussignac (Vin de Pays de Dordogne), 1998

VINS BLANCS

Château de la Colline, Calista (Bergerac), 1997 (winemaker Charles Martin, sémillon) *

Château Puy-Servain Terrement (Montravel), 1999

Château Puy-Servain Terrement, cuvée Marjolaine (Montravel), 1998 *

Château Richard, cuvée spéciale (Bergerac), 1999 (winemaker Richard Doughty, organically farmed vines)

Château Tour des Gendres, cuvée des Conti (Bergerac), 1999

Clos des Verdots, Grand Vin Les Verdots (Bergerac), 1999 (selon David Fourtout) *

Domaine de l'Ancienne Cure (Bergerac), 1999

Domaine de l'Ancienne Cure, cuvée Abbaye (Bergerac), 1999

Famille de Conti, Moulin des Dames (Bergerac), 1999 *

K de Krevel (Montravel), 1998

ROSÉS

Château Calabre (Bergerac), 1999

Clos des Verdots (Bergerac), 1999

SWEET WINES

Château Puy-Servain Terrement (Haut-Montravel), 1998 *

Château Richard, Coup de Coeur (Saussignac), 1995, 1996, 1997 *

Clos des Verdots, Moelleux (Côtes de Bergerac), 1997 (selon David Fourtout) *

Domaine de l'Ancienne Cure, cuvée Abbaye (Monbazillac), 1997 *

Tirecul La Gravière (Monbazillac), 1998 *

LEFT Our last meal at Lavalade was a pot-luck affair intended to clear out the refrigerator. I especially remember the salad of truffled potatoes that was made using the last of the sauce from the pork (see page 283). Judging by all those pink cheeks we obviously proposed several toasts – the last one to the next adventure! Anna is at the front, kicking up her heels, then Colin to her left, then me. On the other side of the table is our wine scribe, Duffy, then Angie and last, but not least, Maggie.

Memorable Dinners and Their Wines

THE FIRST NIGHT

Grand Vin Les Verdots, Bergerac Sec, 1999
Five stars. Asparagus and pineapple on the nose. Complex and long on the palate. 'The biggest white since I arrived in Europe.' (Simon)

Château Tour des Gendres, La Gloire de Mon Père (Côtes de Bergerac), 1998
Blackcurrant and berry nose. Big tannin, front-palate loaded, tight and closed. Needs more time in the bottle. Good with goat's cheese.

Domaine de l'Ancienne Cure, cuvée Abbaye (Monbazillac), 1997
Delicious. Brilliant match with Roquefort.

THE EEL NIGHT

Famille de Conti, Moulin des Dames (Bergerac), 1999
Excellent white. Full-bodied. Great balance of sauvignon blanc and sémillon.

Domaine de Puy de Grave (Pécharmant), 1997
Soft tannins, refined with berry and cherry.

Château Richard, Coup de Coeur (Saussignac), 1995
Slightly spritzy. Possible secondary fermentation. The 1996 and 1997 showed no fizz. All were luscious.

THE BIG NIGHT

Château Puy-Servain Terrement (Montravel), 1999
Matched Maggie's artichokes (see page 243) perfectly.

Domaine des Costes (Pécharmant), 1998
Perfect with the truffled pork (page 283).

K de Krevel, Vieilles Vignes (Côtes de Bergerac), 1997
Balanced tannins and fruit. A very good Bergerac Rouge.

Château Richard, Coup de Coeur (Saussignac), 1996
Rich, light amber colour. Superb with the prune tart (page 159).

Glossary

aiguillette Long, thin slice, usually from the breast of poultry; also refers to the thin, delicate underfillet of a duck or goose.

aligot Dish of puréed potato and *la tomme fraîche de Cantal*, a soft, unfermented young cheese found in country markets in its native Auvergne and throughout Quercy.

AOC Appellation d'Origine Contrôlée; guarantees that a food or wine has been produced in the region claimed and that its production has followed established methods. For wine, AOC also establishes the grape varieties or percentage of a particular variety permitted for the appellation.

Armagnac Robust brandy from the Haut-Armagnac and Bas-Armagnac, distilled at a lower strength than Cognac. This method allows more flavour elements to remain in the wine. After distillation it is stored in black oak, which adds deep colour and powerful flavours.

auberge Simple country inn, usually offering rooms and meals. In recent years, some *auberges* have become quite grand.

baguette The universal French breadstick; long and thin with a crisp crust.

bastide Fortified town founded in the Middle Ages.

beurre manié Literally, 'worked butter'; simple thickening for sauces made by working two-thirds flour into one-third soft butter and whisking this mixture into simmering sauce until the desired consistency is reached. Ideal when you want a thicker sauce but do not want further reduction of flavours.

boudin noir Blood sausage; the French equivalent of the English black pudding. Usually made from pig's blood, cream, onion, pork fat and seasonings. The whole sausage or slices of it are fried or grilled (broiled) before eating.

boules Leisurely game played with heavy metal balls in practically every shady square in France, mostly by men; similar to but more formal than *pétanque*.

bouquet garni Classic flavouring for braises, stews and stocks, usually made up of a bay leaf, a good sprig of thyme and some parsley stalks, either tied together or put into a small muslin bag so that it can be retrieved from the pot after cooking. Sometimes extra flavourings are suggested, such as orange peel or celery.

brocante Second-hand market that can include valuable pieces as well as flea-market trash and treasure; also the second-hand goods themselves.

brou de noix South-western name for one of the various liqueurs and digestifs (q.v.) made from different parts of the walnut tree (nuts, husks, leaves).

Cabécou de Rocamadour Flat disc of goat's cheese produced in the south-west; considered so important gastronomically that it has AOC status (q.v.).

canard The French word for 'duck'.

canelé Little fluted cake found all over the south-west; notoriously difficult to make but should be glossy, dark and crunchy on the outside and smooth and almost custard-like inside. Always powerfully flavoured with rum or, in some cases, *eau-de-vie* (q.v.). Sometimes spelled *cannelé*.

cassoulet Probably the best-known bean stew hailing from the south-west of France; more prevalent in the southern towns of Toulouse, Carcassonne and Castelnaudary. The combination of ingredients varies widely, but a *cassoulet* will always include dried white (haricot) beans and feature a crust on the top. Other ingredients might be fresh pork, sausages, *confit* (q.v.) duck or goose, onions and carrots.

cèpes Prized wild mushrooms (*Boletus edulis*), also known in Italian as *porcini*.

chanterelle *see* girolle

charcuterie Collective name for all manner of pork products (sausages, *rillettes*, pâtés, and so on) and by extension also the name for the establishments that sell these products.

châtaignier Wild chestnut tree (*Castanea sativa*) that produces two or three nuts (*châtaignes*) to a shell.

citron pressé Freshly squeezed lemon juice served with powdered sugar, iced water and a long spoon for stirring; typically French and very refreshing in summer.

clafoutis Baked batter pudding that includes fruit such as cherries or plums.

compote Fancy name for 'stewed fruit' (although the fruit is often poached), where effort is made to ensure that the fruit keeps its shape. The syrup can be flavoured in many ways.

confire/confit Method of preserving meats that has become synonymous with the cooking of the south-west, in which the meat is slipped into warm fat and brought slowly to near-simmering point, cooked very gently until tender and then allowed to cool, still in the fat. *Confire* means to 'conserve' or 'preserve' and the products of this conservation are known as *confits*.

cornichon Small cucumber (*Cucumis sativus*), picked when not fully developed and then pickled and preserved in vinegar; traditional accompaniment to pâtés and *rillettes* (q.v.).

couenne *see* pork rind

crème de noix Another of the popular walnut liqueurs of the south-west. *See also* brou de noix.

crépinette Small, shaped meat patty, often of seasoned pork, encased in a veil of caul fat (*crépine*) ready for grilling (broiling) or frying.

croustade Frilly fruit tart easily recognisable in *pâtisseries* (q.v.) by its crumpled pastry petals; usually filled with apple or apple and prunes. Also known as *tourtière* or *pastis*.

daubière Heavy, lidded cast-iron or earthenware casserole traditionally used for cooking a *daube*, or rich stew.

digestif Alcoholic drink taken after a meal to aid the digestion; can be a fortified wine (e.g. port), spirit (brandy), or herb or fruit liqueur. In the south west, a digestif is often an *eau-de-vie* (q.v.) at 42 per cent alcohol-by-volume, or one of the many walnut liqueurs.

eau-de-vie Literally, 'water of life'; potent liqueur distilled from fruit or berries, normally sold in the south-west at 42 per cent proof. Also used in cooking; professional cooks' suppliers sell an *eau-de-vie* that is 50 per cent proof and intended solely for culinary purposes.

eau-de-vie de prune *Eau-de-vie* (q.v.) of plum.

eau-de-vie de pruneau *Eau-de-vie* (q.v.) of prune.

eau-de-vie de vieille prune Aged plum liqueur.

écrevisse Freshwater crayfish (*Astacus astacus*) similar to the yabby in Australia and crawfish in America; has a finer flavour than rock lobster.

élevage The breeding of animals, especially ducks and geese.

entrecôte Literally, 'between the ribs'. In Australia, the upper cut of the porterhouse, i.e. the sirloin; in France, includes some of what we know as the scotch fillet.

escalope de foie gras Thick slice cut slightly on the bias from a chilled, raw *foie gras* (q.v.).

fait When applied to cheese, means it is fully developed; if the cheese is one with a runny centre, it will be very fragile at this stage.

ferme auberge Farm inn offering simple accommodation, locally produced traditional dishes and local wines.

fines herbes Mixture of freshly gathered, finely chopped herbs. The traditional combination is parsley, chives and tarragon; sometimes chervil is included instead of chives.

fleur de sel The very finest sea salt; actually the 'crust' that forms on evaporated sea salt, which is raked off the salt pans separately. Thought to have the best flavour of any salt.

foie gras Literally, 'fat liver'; enlarged liver from a duck or goose, produced by force-feeding the bird large amounts of corn. Once extracted, the *foie gras* can be eaten cooked – as a luxurious pâté – or it can be sliced and briefly sautéed for a rich hot entrée.

frais When applied to cheese, means very fresh, soft and without noticeable rind.

fraises des bois Wild strawberries (*Fragaria vesca*); nowadays a cultivated variety. Smaller than standard strawberries, highly perfumed and very sweet.

fricassée Has a specific meaning in south-western cookery: fried bits and pieces served with soup, made by extracting some of the vegetables from the soup pot (or using fresh vegetables and bacon), draining and frying them in a little duck or goose fat and putting them back in the pot.

fromage blanc Fresh, soft, unsalted curd cheese. Sometimes contains seasonings such as herbs or pepper but is often eaten with fruit and sugar as a dessert.

fromage fermier de chèvre Farmhouse goat's cheese; falls outside the area of appellation and can therefore not be

called Cabécou de Rocamadour (q.v.), although it may be very similar in appearance and taste.

fromage frais Simple curd cheese with salt added, which draws out some of the moisture.

fromagerie The actual place – workshop or factory – where cheese is made; also refers to a specialist cheese shop.

gabarres Flat-bottomed river-cruise vessels once used as cargo punts.

gavage Force-feeding of ducks and geese.

girolle Small, bright yellow upturned mushroom (*Cantharellus cibarius*), formerly wild but now cultivated; also known as a *chanterelle*.

gratin Dish that has been sprinkled with breadcrumbs and/or cheese, dotted with butter and browned in the oven or under a griller (broiler) until the crust is golden. Can be made of almost anything, from potatoes or pumpkin to raspberries. A dish prepared in this manner is called *au gratin* or *gratiné(e)*.

hachis Minced pork fat mixed with chopped parsley and garlic, used to enrich soup or a casserole; from the verb *hacher*, meaning to 'chop' or 'mince'.

haricots verts Green beans (*Phaseolus vulgaris*), also known as French or string beans; best eaten when young and tender.

haute cuisine Fine style of cookery, presentation and service to be found in 'starred' restaurants. Quite different from home cookery (*cuisine bourgeoise*).

Laguiole Elegant, sharp folding knife with the motif of a fly, made in the town of Laguiole.

lait cru Unpasteurised milk.

lauzes Cut limestone slabs traditionally used for roofing in the south-west.

magret de canard Breast fillet taken from a fattened duck; weighs on average 400–500 g (14–18 oz). Always cooked rare or medium–rare and served thinly sliced.

manchon Meaty part of the wing that joins the breast of a duck or goose.

marché au gras Literally, 'fat market'. Held weekly throughout autumn and winter; both the livers and the processed ducks or geese are displayed and sold.

marché des producteurs de pays Farmers' market, where the produce sold has been exclusively grown by the stall-holders.

marronnier Grafted chestnut tree that has one large nut (*marron*) in the shell; considered superior to a *châtaignier* (q.v.).

menu fixe Fixed-price menu.

mi-cuit Literally, 'half-cooked'. *Mi-cuit foie gras* is cooked in a terrine in a water bath, or steamed in a vacuum bag, taken to an internal temperature of 46–50°C (115–125°F). It is pale pink in colour, melting in texture and generally agreed to have the best flavour of all *foie gras* (q.v.). When applied to prunes, *mi-cuit* means 'semi-processed'.

mi-frais When applied to cheese, means the centre is just starting to become creamy.

mique *see* pot-au-feu

mirepoix Common culinary term for diced vegetables (carrot, onion, celery and possibly turnip) that are fried at the beginning of a cooking process, such as when preparing a braise, and used as a seasoning or as a bed for meat or fish.

morille Pointy spring mushroom (*Morchella esculenta*) with a distinctive honeycomb structure; known in English as a morel.

moules de bouchot Tiny and very sweet mussels; cultivated on ropes and usually sand-free.

mousserons Small, pointy-capped mushrooms (*Marasmius oreades*) that appear in a circle on lawns after spring rain; also known as fairy-ring mushrooms.

nouvelle cuisine Mid-1970s change of direction in French restaurant cooking; identified and named by food writers Henri Gault and Christian Millau. Of major importance worldwide, it started the popularity of shorter cooking times, unthickened sauces, composed salads and many other techniques. Chefs Paul Bocuse, Alain Chapel, Jean and Pierre Troisgros and Michel Guérard were the pioneers.

oie The French word for 'goose'.

orange Mushroom (*Amanita caesarea*) with a bright orange rounded cap and bright yellow gills; also known as Caesar's mushroom.

pain de campagne Massive crusty loaf usually weighing 2 kg (4½ lb), also known as a *tourte*. Essential for making bread-based soups and in many south-western homes still served at every meal, often soaked or dunked either into a soup or a braise.

pain au levain Sourdough bread, raised using a natural starter rather than commercial yeast.

panne Softish fat surrounding a pig's kidneys, also known as pork flare fat or flair fat; melts readily and is used for making superior sausages.

pastis *see* croustade; also a very popular aniseed apéritif enjoyed widely in France, but typically coming from the south.

pâte brisée French version of the British shortcrust pastry.

pâtisserie Collective name for baked sweet and savoury items; also the name for the establishments that sell these products, including cakes and biscuits (cookies) and, sometimes, bread.

pigeonnier Dovecote; square or round tower either attached at the first floor of a farmhouse or built to one side originally to house pigeons bred for the table.

pork fat Usually refers to the hard, white fat attached to the skin (rind) of the pig, also known as back fat or fatback. Also comes from other parts of the animal and often has quite specific names, for example, 'flare fat'. Useful for wrapping game birds or small, lean joints of meat and ideal for lining a terrine. In some dishes it is used with the rind still attached, to add a gelatinous quality. French *charcuteries* (q.v.) and butchers in the south-west often sell back fat carefully pared from the skin in a smooth sheet and rolled up like a scroll. When a customer wants some, it is unrolled and cut to the length requested. In the recipes in this book you will also see references to 'rendered pork fat' – this refers to fat that has been gently rendered for use as a frying medium, also known as lard. *See also* panne; pork rind.

pork rind The skin of the pig; known as *couenne* in French. French *charcuteries* (q.v.) and butchers in the south-west sell it both fresh and preserved (*confit*; q.v.), carefully separated from the fat in a smooth sheet and rolled up like a scroll. Pork rind, either fresh or preserved, adds richness and a gelatinous quality to broths, stews and bean dishes. In days gone by the housewives of the south-west would have chosen to preserve their pork rind so as to always have

some available to add extra flavour to simple dishes. *See also* pork fat.

pot-au-feu Classic dish of simmered meats, poultry and vegetables, traditionally served as two courses: first the broth, then the meat and vegetables. The south-western version often has a dumpling (*mique*) included.

potage A more delicate soup than *soupe* (q.v.), but thicker than a consommé.

poule Hen or boiling fowl; often a bird no longer useful for laying.

prix net Net price.

prune The French word for 'plum'.

prunes d'Ente Plums from the Ente plum tree (*Prunus domestica*).

pruneau The French word for 'prune'.

pruneaux d'Agen Processed prunes named after the port town of Agen; *see also* mi-cuit.

quatre-épices Literally, 'four spices'; a frequently specified seasoning in French recipes. The combination of finely ground spices varies, but it usually includes black pepper, cloves and nutmeg and, sometimes, ginger.

ragoût Very loose term meaning 'stew' or 'mixture'.

rémoulade Mayonnaise sauce incorporating mustard and anchovies; popular with shredded celeriac, among other things.

rillettes Classic *confit* (q.v.) dish in which rabbit and pork (or just pork) are well seasoned, gently cooked in pork fat, then shredded and potted with the fat; usually served as an appetiser spread on toast or bread.

roux Thickening for sauces, made of butter and flour cooked together. Liquid is gradually added to the roux, then the sauce is slowly brought to a boil and simmered until ready. A 'blond' roux is unbrowned and used in white sauces.

sablé Means 'sandy'; refers to buttery biscuits (cookies), or pastry with such a texture. *Sablé* biscuits are often flavoured with lemon zest.

salade Collective French noun for salad leaves of whatever variety.

salade composée Literally, 'composed salad'; does not refer to a mix of salad leaves, but rather to various ingredients included in the salad.

saucisson sec Coarse-textured, salted and air-dried salami-style sausage, usually made of pork and eaten cold.

soupe A soup that is often eaten as the main meal; traditionally the poultry, game or meat that gave the soup its character was eaten as a separate course after the liquid. *See also* potage.

tarte Tatin Famous upside-down apple tart that was invented by Mme Tatin, one of two sisters who ran a hotel in Normandy in the early 1900s.

tilleul Lime-linden tree; the fruit is not eaten but the flowers can be dried and used to make a soothing infusion or *tisane*.

tourin Local onion soup served in many small restaurants. Unlike the better-known version of onion soup, it contains no cheese; stirred-in egg whites separate into fine shreds, giving the impression of cheese.

tourte *see* pain de campagne

tourtière Fruit tart with crumpled pastry 'petals'; *see* croustade. Also a shallow tart tin or flan tin.

tremper la soupe Soak, dunk or dip bread into soup.

truffière Property dedicated to cultivating truffles.

tuile Literally, 'tile'; thin biscuit (cookie) often served with ice-cream. Its curved shape resembles that of a traditional French roofing tile.

velouté Literally, 'velvety'; term used to describe a sauce or soup usually made from chicken stock and a roux (q.v.).

verjus Fermented juice of unripe grapes, widely used in medieval times in cooking and as a condiment; now experiencing a bit of a revival. May be used in mustard.

A South-West Pantry

This list of Australian, New Zealand and British suppliers might prove useful when you are shopping for certain ingredients and utensils needed to cook the dishes in this book. For a basic 'south-west pantry', make sure you have dried haricot beans, brown lentils (preferably du Puy), chestnuts, dried *cèpes (porcini)*, prunes, goat's cheese, sourdough bread, garlic-flavoured boiling sausage, bacon (smoked or unsmoked), ham (raw and air-dried), *rillettes*, preserved pork rind, rendered duck fat, rendered pork fat, garlic, *quatre-épices*, verjuice and walnut oil. Then, if your budget runs to it, you could add Armagnac, *eau-de-vie de prune* (or *eau-de-vie* of another fruit), *foie gras mi-cuit*, Roquefort (if available) and truffles (*Tuber melanosporum*). Wines to buy include crisp dry whites, full-bodied reds with plenty of tannin, and luscious dessert wines. As far as cooking equipment goes, earthenware dishes are the most important utensils to have in your cupboard. Alternatively, buy enamelled cast-iron pots – they are much more expensive but will last for a lifetime of cooking.

AUSTRALIA-WIDE

Barossa Farm Produce
11 Yalumba Terrace, Angaston 5353
Tel: (08) 8564 2050
Barossa Chooks and other high-quality poultry.

Cheznutz
Mountain View Chestnuts
5780, Myrtleford 3737
Tel: (03) 5756 2788
Web site: www.cheznutz.com.au
Fresh and peeled chestnuts.

Eels Australis
RSD 95, Montana Road, Deloraine 7304
Tel: (03) 6362 2539
Live eels.

Galloway Yabbies
Main Road, Inman Valley 5211
Tel: 0428 364 919
Live yabbies.

Maggie Beer Products
Tel: (08) 8562 4477
Web site: www.maggiebeer.com.au
Verjuice.

Mondo Di Carne (Vince Garreffa)
824 Beaufort Street, Inglewood 6052
Tel: (08) 9371 6350
Web site: www.mondo.net.au
High-quality meat, tripe, trotters, farmed rabbit.

Mulataga Aquaculture
Tel: (08) 9479 5288
Web site: www.mulataga.com
Live yabbies.

Périgord Truffles Tasmania
'Rockdale', Tasman Road, Grove 7109
Tel: (03) 6261 2213
Web site: www.perigord.com.au
Limited supply of truffles in season.

Simon Johnson Purveyor of Quality Foods
Tel: 1800 655 522
Web site: www.simonjohnson.com.au
Goose fat, truffles, dried cèpes (porcini), walnut oil, confit, eau-de-vie, verjuice.

MELBOURNE

Canals Seafoods
703 Nicholson Street, Carlton North 3054
Tel: (03) 9380 4537
Live eels, live yabbies.

Casa Iberica
25 Johnston Street, Fitzroy 3065
Tel: (03) 9417 7106
Raw ham.

The Essential Ingredient
Prahran Market
South Yarra 3141
Tel: (03) 9827 9047
Web site: www.theessentialingredient.com.au
Goose fat, truffles, dried cèpes (porcini), foie gras, walnut oil, confit, eau-de-vie, verjuice, specialist cooking equipment.

John Cester Poultry & Game
Shop 506, Prahran Market
South Yarra 3141
Tel: (03) 9827 6111
Duck fat, high-quality poultry.

Jonathan's of Collingwood
122 Smith Street, Collingwood 3066
Tel: (03) 9419 4339
High-quality meat, tripe, trotters, farmed rabbit, raw ham.

Mediterranean Wholesalers
482 Sydney Road, Brunswick 3056
Tel: (03) 9380 4777
Earthenware pots and dishes at very moderate prices. Outside Melbourne, similar vessels can be found wherever there are Italian or Spanish foodstores.

Prahran Market
177 Commercial Road, South Yarra 3141
Tel: (03) 8290 5822
Web site: www.prahranmarket.com.au
Walnuts and chestnuts in season, farmed rabbit, live eels, live yabbies, raw ham, high-quality poultry.

Queen Victoria Market
Elizabeth Street, Melbourne 3000
Tel: (03) 9320 5822
Web site: www.qvm.com.au
Walnuts and chestnuts in season, farmed rabbit, live eels, live yabbies, raw ham, high-quality poultry.

Richmond Hill Cafe & Larder
48–50 Bridge Road, Richmond 3121
Tel: (03) 9421 2808
Web site: www.rhcl.com.au
Confit, cheeses (Cantal, Bleu des Causses, chèvre etc.), peeled chestnuts, verjuice.

Scullerymade
1400 High Street, Malvern 3144
Tel: (03) 9509 4003
Specialist cooking equipment, e.g. canelé moulds, muslin.

Vietnamese butchers
Victoria Street, Richmond 3121
Pork bits, skin, fat, tripe etc.

QUEENSLAND

Black Pearl Epicure
36 Baxter Street, Fortitude Valley 4006
Tel: (07) 3257 2144
Web site: www.blackpearl.com.au
Goose fat, duck fat (locally produced), truffles, dried cèpes, foie gras, walnut oil, confit, cheeses, chestnuts (peeled), verjuice, live yabbies, farmed rabbit, high-quality poultry.

Palatable Partners
Tel: (07) 3899 5266
Web site: www.palatablepartners.com.au
Cheeses, walnut oil, high-quality meat products.

SOUTH AUSTRALIA

Adelaide Central Market
52 Gouger Street, Adelaide 5000
Tel: (08) 8203 7494
Web site: www.adelaidecitycouncil.com
   /CentralMarket/
*Walnuts and chestnuts (unpeeled) in
season, dried cèpes, high-quality meat,
tripe, trotters, raw ham, cheeses.*

Bottega Rotolo
7 Osmond Terrace, Norwood 5067
Tel: (08) 8362 0455
Web site: www.bottegarotolo.com.au
*Goose fat, truffles, dried cèpes, foie gras,
walnut oil, cheeses.*

Organic Market & Cafe
5 Druids Avenue, Stirling 5152
Tel: (08) 8339 4835
*Walnuts (imported and local) and
chestnuts (biodynamic) in season.*

Pallas Meat Store
Heading Avenue, Campbelltown 5074
Tel: (08) 8337 3308
Raw ham.

SYDNEY

AC Butchery
174 Marion Street, Leichhardt 2040
Tel: (02) 9569 8687
High-quality meat, tripe, trotters.

Accoutrement
611 Military Road, Mosman 2088
Tel: (02) 9969 1031
Web site: www.accoutrement.com.au
*Goose fat, dried cèpes, walnut oil,
verjuice, specialist cooking equipment.*

Chefs' Warehouse
111–115 Albion Street, Surry Hills 2010
Tel: (02) 9211 4555
*Goose fat, eau-de-vie, specialist cooking
equipment.*

David Jones Foodhall
Ground floor, 65–77 Market Street
Sydney 2000
Tel: (02) 9266 5544
*Dried cèpes, foie gras, walnut oil, cheeses,
high-quality meat and poultry, verjuice.*

The Essential Ingredient
6 Australia Street, Camperdown 2050
Tel: (02) 9550 5477
Web site: www.theessentialingredient.com.au
*Goose fat, duck fat, truffles, dried cèpes,
foie gras (preserved), walnut oil, confit
duck and goose, cheeses.*

Farmers Market
(Wednesdays and Saturdays)
Entertainment Quarter, Moore Park 2021
Tel: (02) 9383 4163
High-quality poultry.

The Nut Shop
25 The Strand Arcade, Sydney 2000
Tel: (02) 9231 3038
Web site: www.nutshop.com.au
Walnuts.

Penny's Quality Butchers
880 Military Road, Mosman 2088
Tel: (02) 9969 3372
18 Bungan Street, Mona Vale 2103
Tel: (02) 9004 1100
*High-quality meat and poultry, farmed
rabbit, tripe, trotters.*

Sydney Fish Market
Bank Street (cnr Pyrmont Bridge Road)
Pyrmont 2009
Tel: (02) 9660 1611
Web site: www.sydneyfishmarket.com.au
Live eels, live yabbies.

Wright's The Butchers
1111 Botany Road, Mascot 2020
Tel: (02) 9313 5228
High-quality meat, tripe, trotters.

TASMANIA

Bayside Meats
628 Sandy Bay Road, Sandy Bay 7005
Tel: (03) 6225 1482
*High-quality meat and poultry, tripe,
trotters.*

Chung Gon Greengrocers
66 Brisbane Street, Launceston 7250
Tel: (03) 6331 4166
Chestnuts in season.

W. Chung Sing & Co.
28 Warwick Street, Hobart 7000
Tel: (03) 6234 5033
Web site: www.chung.com.au
Walnuts and chestnuts in season.

Habitat of Hobart
70 Liverpool Street, Hobart 7000
Tel: (03) 6231 0555
Web site: www.yourhabitat.com.au
Specialist cooking equipment.

Salamanca Fruit Market
50 Salamanca Place, Hobart 7000
Chestnuts in season.

Wursthaus Kitchen
1 Montpelier Retreat, Hobart 7000
Tel: (03) 6224 0644
*Goose fat, duck fat, truffles, dried cèpes,
walnut oil, confit, cheeses (limited range),
walnuts, verjuice, high-quality meat,
farmed rabbit.*

WESTERN AUSTRALIA

Amano
12 Station Street, Cottesloe 6011
Tel: (08) 9384 0378
Web site: www.amano.com.au
*Walnut oil, verjuice, specialist cooking
equipment.*

Carl Torre & Sons Butchers
41–43 Lake Street, Northbridge 6003
Tel: (08) 9328 8317
High-quality meat, tripe, trotters.

Elmar's Smallgoods
493 Beaufort Street, Highgate 6003
Tel: (08) 9328 4050
Raw ham.

Food by Christopher Hiller
151a Rokeby Road, Subiaco 6008
Tel: (08) 6380 2000
Cheeses.

The Grocer
145 Stirling Highway, Nedlands 6009
Tel: (08) 9389 8144
Web site: www.thegrocer.com.au
*Goose fat, truffles, dried cèpes, foie gras,
walnut oil, confit, chestnuts (peeled and
vacuum-packed), verjuice, high-quality
poultry.*

Kailis Bros Fish Market
101 Oxford Street, Leederville 6007
Tel: (08) 9443 6300
Web site: www.kailisbros.com.au
Live yabbies.

King Street Food & Wine
Shops 2 & 3, 172 St Georges Terrace
Perth 6000
Tel: (08) 9321 9907
*Goose fat, truffles, walnut oil, confit,
verjuice.*

Rabbit Supplies WA
25 Zeta Crescent, O'Connor 6163
Tel: (08) 9314 2944
Farmed rabbit.

Re Store
231 Oxford Street, Leederville 6007
Tel: (08) 9444 9644
72 Lake Street, Northbridge 6003
Tel: (08) 9328 1032
Dried cèpes, foie gras, eau-de-vie, raw ham.

Southern Trading Co.
7 Adams Street, O'Connor 6163
Tel: (08) 9331 3199
Live eels.

Terranova Quality Butchers
113 Aberdeen Street, Perth 6000
Tel: (08) 9328 7244
High-quality meat, tripe, trotters.

NEW ZEALAND

A Cracker of a Nut
Tricketts Road, West Melton
RD6, Christchurch
Tel: (03) 347 8103
*Walnuts, walnut oil (call for
distribution outlets in New Zealand).*

Epicurean Workshop
6 Morrow Street, Newmarket, Auckland
Tel: (09) 524 0906
Web site: www.epicurean.co.nz
*Verjuice, specialist cooking equipment,
e.g. canelé moulds, muslin.*

Good Things
163 High Street, Christchurch
Tel: (03) 366 3894
*Truffles (tinned), dried cèpes, foie gras
(preserved), walnut oil, confit, cheeses,
walnuts, chestnuts, eau-de-vie, verjuice,
raw ham.*

House of Knives
24 Mt Eden Road, Mt Eden, Auckland
Tel: (09) 302 2980
Web site: www.houseofknives.co.nz
Specialist cooking equipment.

Milly's Kitchen
273 Ponsonby Road
Ponsonby, Auckland
Tel: (09) 376 1550
Web site: www.millyskitchen.co.nz
*Verjuice, specialist cooking equipment,
e.g. canelé moulds, muslin.*

Ormond Aquaculture
Wairau Valley, RD1, Blenheim
Tel: (03) 572 2770
Live koura (farmed freshwater crayfish).

The Prenzel Distilling Company
Sheffield Street, Riverlands Estate
Blenheim
Tel: (03) 578 2800
Web site: www.prenzel.com
*Fruit brandies made from locally grown
fruit. Tasting room open to the public.*

Sabato Ltd
57 Normanby Road, Mt Eden, Auckland
Tel: (09) 630 8751
Web site: www.sabato.co.nz
*Duck fat, truffles, dried cèpes, foie gras,
walnut oil, confit, cheeses, verjuice.*

South Island Gourmet Distributors
366 Cashel Street, Linwood, Christchurch
Tel: (03) 377 1030
Web site: www.sig.co.nz
Duck fat, farmed rabbit, poultry, eels.

Swiss Delicatessen & Fine Foods
68–70 Greenmount Drive
East Tamaki, Auckland
Tel: (09) 274 4455
Web site: www.swissdeli.co.nz
*High-quality meat, including raw
ham.*

Traiteur
Cnr Aikmans Road & Papanui Road
Merivale, Christchurch
Tel: (03) 355 7750
Web site: www.traiteur.co.nz
*High-quality meat and poultry, including
farmed rabbit.*

Vinotica
Unit D, 3 Henry Rose Place
Albany, Auckland
Tel: (09) 415 5942
Web site: www.vinotica.co.nz
Cheeses.

Wick's Fish
389A Worcester Street
Linwood, Christchurch
Tel: (03) 389 7675
Live eels.

UNITED KINGDOM

Bluebird Foodmarket
350 Kings Road, London SW3 5UU
Tel: (020) 7559 1153

Carluccio's
28a Neal Street
Covent Garden WC2H 9PS
Tel: (020) 7240 1487
Web site: www.carluccios.com

Comptoir Gascon
63 Charterhouse Street, London EC1M 6IIJ
Tel: (020) 7608 0851
Cheeses, foie gras, charcuterie, bread.

Fortnum & Mason
181 Piccadilly, London W1A 1ER
Tel: (020) 7734 8040
Web site: www.fortnumandmason.co.uk

Harrods
Knightsbridge, London SW1X 7XL
Tel: (020) 7235 5000
Web site: www.harrods.com

Harvey Nichols
109–125 Knightsbridge, London SW1X 7RJ
Tel: (0870) 873 3833
Web site: www.harveynichols.com

Jeroboams
96 Holland Park Avenue
London W11 3RB
Tel: (020) 7727 9359
Web site: www.jeroboams.co.uk
*Cheeses, foie gras, charcuterie, bread,
wines.*

La Fromagerie
30 Highbury Park, London N5 2AA
Tel: (020) 7359 7440
Web site: www.lafromagerie.co.uk
*Cheeses, foie gras (preserved), walnut oil,
confit, Armagnac, earthenware pots and
dishes.*

Le Tour de France
135 Sunnyhill Road, Streatham SW16 2UW
Tel: (020) 8769 3554
Web site: www.letourdefrance.co.uk
*Cheeses, truffles, dried wild mushrooms,
rillettes, Bayonne ham, Armagnac.*

Scott & Sargeant Cookshop
24–26 East Street, Horsham
West Sussex RH12 1HL
Tel: (0845) 601 2815
Web site: www.mycookshop.com
Specialist cooking equipment.

Villandry Foodstore & Restaurant
170 Great Portland Street
London W1W 5QB
Tel: (02) 7631 3131
Web site: www.villandry.co.uk
Cheeses, charcuterie, fruit, vegetables.

Contacts in France

Most towns have a *syndicat d'initiative* (tourist office) where you can get information on small producers, tourist sites and accommodation.

ACCOMMODATION
Bienvenue à la Ferme
For a booklet contact the organisation below, or any local tourist office.
Agriculture et Tourisme
Chambre d'Agriculture
4 et 6, Place Francheville
24016 Périgueux Cedex
Tel: 05 53 35 88 90
Fax: 05 53 53 43 13
Web site: www.bienvenue-a-la-ferme.com

Simply Périgord
Place de la Farge
24260 Le Bugue
Tel: 05 53 54 54 31
Fax: 05 53 54 11 01
Email: simply@simply-perigord.com
Web site: www.simply-perigord.com

La Vieille Grange
Email: info@mercadiol.com
Web site: www.mercadiol.com

RESTAURANTS
Auberge de la Truffe
24420 Sorges en Périgord
Tel: 05 53 05 02 05
Fax: 05 53 05 39 27
Web site: www.auberge-de-la-truffe.com

Auberge du Sombral
46330 Saint-Cirq Lapopie
Tel: 05 65 31 26 08
Fax: 05 65 30 26 37

La Ferme Auberge Fort de la Rhonie
(Coustaty family)
Boyer, 24220 Meyrals
Tel: 05 53 29 24 83 or 05 53 29 29 07
Fax: 05 53 29 62 58
Web site: www.coustaty.com

La Rapière
Place de la Cathédrale
24200 Sarlat
Tel: 05 53 59 03 13
Fax: 05 53 30 27 84

Le Bistrot d'en Face
24510 Trémolat
Tel: 05 53 22 80 69
Fax: 05 53 22 84 89
Email: vieuxlogis@relaischateaux.com
Web site: www.vieux-logis.com

Le Centenaire
24620 Les Eyzies de Tayac
Tel: 05 53 06 68 68
Fax: 05 53 06 92 41
Email: contact@hotelducentenaire.fr
Web site: www.hotelducentenaire.fr

Le Pont de l'Ouysse
46200 Lacave
Tel: 05 65 37 87 04
Fax: 05 65 32 77 41
Email: contact@lepontdelouysse.com
Web site: www.lepontdelouysse.fr

Le Présidial
6, rue Landry
24200 Sarlat
Tel: 05 53 28 92 47

Les Jardins de l'Opéra
1, Place du Capitole
31000 Toulouse
Tel: 05 61 23 07 76
Fax: 05 61 23 63 00

Paris
Au Trou Gascon
40, rue Taine
75012 Paris
Tel: 01 43 44 34 26

Le Carré des Feuillants
14, rue de Castiglione
75001 Paris
Tel: 01 42 86 82 82
Fax: 01 42 86 07 71
Email: carredesfeuillants@
  top-restaurants.com

Le Grand Véfour
17, rue de Beaujolais
75001 Paris
Tel: 01 42 96 56 27
Fax: 01 42 86 80 71
Email: vefour@relaischateaux.com

SIGHTS
Château de Fénelon
Sainte Mondane
Tel: 05 53 29 81 45
Fax: 05 53 29 88 99

Château de Hautefort
24390 Hautefort
Tel: 05 53 50 51 23
Fax: 05 53 51 67 37

Château de Marqueyssac
24220 Vézac
Tel: 05 53 31 36 36
Fax: 05 53 31 36 30
Web site: www.marqueyssac.com

Château de Monbazillac
24240 Monbazillac
Tel: 05 53 61 52 52
Fax: 05 53 63 65 09
Email: monbazillac@chateau-
  monbazillac.com
Web site: www.chateau-monbazillac.com

Grotte du Pech Merle
46330 Cabrerets
Tel: 05 65 31 27 05
Web site: www.quercy.net/pechmerle

Lascaux II
24290 Montignac
Tel: 05 53 51 95 03
Fax: 05 53 06 30 94

Le Moulin de Cougnaguet (flour mill)
46350 Calès
Tel: 05 65 38 73 56
Fax: 05 65 37 13 02
Web site: www.cougnaguet.com

SMALL PRODUCERS
Château Puy-Servain (Daniel Hecquet)
33220 Port Sainte Foy et Ponchapt
Tel: 05 53 24 77 27

Château Tour des Gendres (Luc de Conti)
24240 Ribagnac

Distillerie Artisanale Jean Delpont
La Cellulose Chemin du Tour de Rond
82700 Montech
Tel: 05 63 64 72 01
Fax: 05 63 64 73 43
Email: jeandelpont@yahoo.fr

Distillcric Lacheze
Ldt Le Tranchant
47200 Virazeil

Distillerie Louis Roque
41, avenue Jean-Jaurès
46200 Souillac
Tel: 05 65 32 78 16
Fax: 05 65 32 61 28
Email: info@lavieilleprune.com
Web site: www.lavieilleprune.com

Domaine de Mordesson (GAEC)
46500 Rignac
Tel: 05 65 33 17 80

Ferme Andrévias (Guy Meynard)
24420 Sorges en Périgord
Tel: 05 53 05 02 42
Fax: 05 53 35 30 26
Web site: www.sorges-perigord.com/
   fermeandrevias

La Ferme Auberge Fort de la Rhonie
See under 'Restaurants' above.

La Truffière de la Bergerie
(Hugues Martin)
Bressac, Sainte-Foy-de-Longas
Tel: 05 53 22 72 39
Fax: 05 53 23 77 80
Email: truffiere.bergerie@free.fr
Web site: truffiere.bressac.free.fr

Les Fermiers du Rocamadour
(cheese cooperative)
46500 Alvignac
Tel: 05 65 38 86 05
Fax: 05 65 33 45 85
Email: FermierDuRoca@aol.com

Moulin de la Tour (walnut-oil mill)
Sainte-Nathalène, 24200 Sarlat
Tel: 05 53 59 22 08
Fax: 05 53 31 08 33

RESIDENTIAL COOKING SCHOOL
La Combe en Périgord
24620 Les Eyzies de Tayac
Tel: 05 53 35 17 61
Fax: 05 53 35 25 64
Email: info@lacombe-pcrigord.com
Web site: www.lacombe-perigord.com

MISCELLANEOUS
L'École Hôtelière du Périgord
Avenue Henry Deluc
24750 Périgueux-Boulazac
Tel: 05 53 35 72 72
Fax: 05 53 09 73 48
Email: Gep@perigueux.cci.fr
Web site: www.perigueux.cci.fr/ehp/

Further Reading

Alexander, Stephanie, *Stephanie's Feasts and Stories*, Allen & Unwin, Sydney, 1988.

— *The Cook's Companion*, Penguin, Melbourne, 2004.

Behr, Edward, *The Art of Eating*, No. 48, 1998.

Chaloupka, George, *Burrunguy: Nourlangie Rock*, Northart, Darwin, 1982.

Colette, *Paysages et portraits*, Flammarion, Paris, 1958.

David, Elizabeth, *French Provincial Cooking*, Penguin, Harmondsworth, 1982.

Davidson, Alan, *The Oxford Companion to Food*, Oxford University Press, Oxford, 1999.

Facaros, Dana & Pauls, Michael, *Southwest France: Dordogne, Lot, Bordeaux*, Cadogan, London, 1998.

Garrouty, Gilbert, article in *Sud Ouest*, 3 Dec. 1999.

Ginor, Michael A. (ed.) et al, *Foie Gras: A Passion*, John Wiley & Sons, New York, 1999.

Koffmann, Pierre, *Memories of Gascony*, Pyramid, London, 1990.

La Mazille, *La Bonne Cuisine du Périgord*, facsimile edn, Flammarion, Paris, 1999
      (first published by Flammarion, Paris, 1929).

Moloney, Ted & Coleman, Deke, *Oh, for a French Wife!*, 2nd edn, Ure Smith, Sydney, 1964.

Oyler, Philip, *The Generous Earth*, Hodder & Stoughton, London, 1950.

— *Feeding Ourselves*, Hodder & Stoughton, London, 1951.

— *Sons of the Generous Earth*, Hodder & Stoughton, London, 1963.

Pébeyre, Pierre-Jean & Jacques, *Le Grand Livre de la truffe*, Éditions Daniel Briand/Robert Laffont, Paris, 1987.

Penton, Anne, *Customs and Cookery in the Périgord and Quercy*, David & Charles, Newton Abbot, 1973.

Périgord Magazine, 'Gastronomie' special issue, 81.

Roux, Michel, *Desserts: A Lifelong Passion*, Conran Octopus, London, 1994.

Strang, Jeanne, *Goose Fat and Garlic*, Kyle Cathie, London, 1991.

Studd, Will, *Chalk and Cheese*, Purple Egg, Melbourne, 1999.

Wolfert, Paula, *The Cooking of South-West France*, Papermac, London, 1989.

General Index

trucs 54, 58, *70*
truffle market 232, 271, *272*, 275, *275*
truffles 258, 261, *272*, 275
    see also black truffles

veal *330, 345*, 356–7
Vergt 266
verjus 243, 246, 317, *317*
Vézac 26
Vézère River 105, 111, *111*, 228
Villeneuve-sur-Lot 12
vin de pêche 363, *363*, 366

walks 102, 105–6, 111
walnut oil 12, *186*, 189, 191, *191*
    in recipes 170, 205, 206, 208
    uses 195
    see also Moulin de la Tour
walnut paste 170, 205
walnuts 12, 33, 38, 63, 106, 186,
    189
    André's liqueur 61, 197, *198*, 366
    arlequins 195
    cracking 189, 190, *191*
    drying 189
    liqueurs 196–8

recipes *206*, 213, 214
wine 39, 345, 366, 368, *369*
    appellations *96*, 369, 373, *373*
    Baumé (Brix) *374*
    for memorable dinners 378
    tasted at Lavalade 376–7, 374
winery visits 373–4
Wolfert, Paula 9, 12, 57, 62, 68, 70, 308,
    308
wood-fired oven 42, 65, 66

yabbies 47, *47*
    see also écrevisses

Recipe Index